Clinical
Art
Therapy

A COMPREHENSIVE GUIDE

Clinical
Art
Therapy

A COMPREHENSIVE GUIDE

Helen B. Landgarten, M.A., A.T.R.

Director, Graduate Department, Clinical Art Therapy
Loyola Marymount University;
Coordinator, Art Psychotherapy, Cedars-Sinai Medical Center
Thalians Community Mental Health Center,
Family and Child Department of Psychiatry,
Los Angeles

Published by
Brunner-Routledge
29 West 35th Street
New York, NY 10001

15   14   13   12

Library of Congress Cataloging-in-Publication Data

Landgarten, Helen B.
   Clinical art therapy

   Bibliography: p.
   Includes index.
   1. Art therapy I. Title. [DNLM: 1. art therapy. WM450.5.A8 L256c]
RC489.A7L36   616.89'1656   80-22564
ISBN 0-87360-237-1

Manufactured in the United States of America on acid-free paper.

To those persons who have:

Spoken with their hands
Listened with their eyes
Seen with their heads
Touched with their hearts

FOREWORD

The title of this book reveals the author's intention of providing a unified text and reference source for the field of clinical art therapy. Ms. Landgarten has been successful in providing complete and clear case studies supporting her theoretical statements in each of the 24 chapters of this book. The 148 illustrations and several tables provide visual support to the clinical descriptive material. A very substantial list of references and a bibliography of more than 300 entries complement the text of this book.

I am most impressed by the contribution of this book to the innovative use of art therapy — both in the choice of settings not generally considered conducive to the practice of art therapy and in the choice of patient categories not usually included in art therapy. For instance, samples are given of successful art therapy in a medical pediatric unit and an innovative, well documented chapter deals with methods of working with chronic pain patients.

For art therapists providing family art therapy, tables of comparative data on the involvement of several family members in art therapy should serve as a model of case recording. Convincing case vignettes are also provided on the participation of single-parent families and geriatric family members in family group art therapy.

The book contains a number of practical guidelines, as well as advice on the use of media in different settings and with different types of patients. For example, somewhat contrary to the general practice in art therapy, Landgarten gives a very good suggestion to use "clean" media, such as pencil, with patients who have problems with impulse control and change to "messy" media after impulse control has been achieved. She demonstrates the use of problem-oriented group art therapy with outpatients or day hospital patients, while suggesting that in other settings, such as schools, medical hospitals, pain centers, churches and youth centers, art therapy can be used to foster self-expression, communication and socialization.

A very commendable therapeutic approach is presented by the author in what she calls "positive lifetime review," where geriatric patients are requested to create an album of pictures, based on pleasant memories of their past. Through this method self-identification is improved and an opportunity arises for positive reinforcement by the therapist for the patients' past achievements and current creativity.

The substantial merit of this book is its clarity, the details of the case histories, always illustrated, and the systematic overview of the application of clinical art therapy in a variety of traditional and newly suggested settings. The author's experience serves as a model for students and professional art therapists. This book fulfills it aim of serving as a source of reference for art therapists. I highly recommend it to all those who want to use the art media to its fullest potential in the treatment process.

IRENE JAKAB, M.D., Ph.D.
Professor of Psychiatry
University of Pittsburgh
School of Medicine

PREFACE

For many years, psychiatric literature has acknowledged the therapeutic facets of the patient's involvement in art. The benefits cited are usually in reference to catharsis, sublimation and creativity. However, the use of art in terms of *primary treatment* is relatively new. Therefore, this book was written as a unified text and reference source for the field of *clinical art therapy* or *art psychotherapy* (used synonymously). The theory and case histories herein illustrate its use with persons of all ages in individual, family and/or group treatment. Numerous settings are also presented to clarify variations in this modality. In all cases, identifying information has been changed to protect the patients. An emphasis is placed on *why* and *how* specific themes and art media are used. The aspects of mental health treatment which are unique to clinical art therapy are delineated within a perspective which encompasses three essential elements: process, content and product. The book's major focus is on *artwork as a basic agent for change and an everlasting testimony to growth.*

HELEN LANDGARTEN

ix

ACKNOWLEDGMENTS

I extend my thanks to:

Reader for the entire book: Maxine Junge

*Children of the Holocaust: Consciousness Raising and Data Collection and
  Assessment:* Judy Flesh, Consultant, and Lee Cooper, Reader

Psychiatric Hospitals: Suzanne Silverstein, Consultant

Day Treatment: Suzanne Silverstein and Robin Toland, Consultants

Rehabilitation: Jane Bonney and Sue Thompson, Consultants

Chronic Pain: Jane Bonney

Photographers: Benyas Kaufman, Photographers, Oak Park, Michigan;
  S. M. Tapper, Photographer and Film Director, Los Angeles, California; Geoffrey Berkin, Los Angeles, California.

For support towards my developmental growth as an art psychotherapist:
  Cedars-Sinai Medical Center, Thalians Community Mental Health
  Center, Family and Child Psychiatry, Department of Psychiatry: Saul
  L. Brown, M.D., Director Department of Psychiatry; Frank S.

Williams, M.D., Associate Director, Family and Child Psychiatry; staff of psychotherapists in the various disciplines and the secretarial staff.

For support to complete this project: my husband Nate.

The following publications have granted permission to use material from articles which were originally published in their journals.

American Journal of Art Therapy, Art Therapy as a Primary Mode of Treatment for an Elective Mute. Elinor Ulman (1975), *14,* 121-125, #4.

Pergamon Press, Adult Art Psychotherapy. H.B. Landgarten. *Art Psychotherapy, an International Journal,* 1975, *2,* 65-76, #1.

Pergamon Press, Art Therapy as an Innovative Approach to Conjoint Treatment: A Case Study. H.B. Landgarten and M. Harris. *Art Psychotherapy, an International Journal.* 1973, *1,* 31-43, #3/4.

Human Sciences Press, Art Therapy as a Modality for Crisis Intervention: Children's Reaction to Violence in their Community. H.B. Landgarten, M. Junge, M. Tasem, and M. Watson. *Clinical Social Work Journal,* 1978, *6,* 221-230, #3.

CONTENTS

ILLUSTRATIONS

xv

PART I

An Overview

CHAPTER 1

Introduction to Art Psychotherapy

This book presents a working model for clinical art therapy or art psychotherapy as it is practiced by the author. Major emphasis is placed on the dynamically oriented art therapy theory which was formulated by Margaret Naumburg (1966).

Although a neo-Freudian frame of reference is at the base, the reader will find a flexible and often innovative approach is utilized to meet the needs of the client. The chapters herein display a conceptualized approach, accompanied by illustrations of its application through the case material and artwork of populations ranging from latency age through geriatrics. The focus of art therapy may vary due to the treatment setting; therefore, this text introduces methods which are pertinent to a variety of environments, including outpatient settings (clinics, schools, geriatric centers, rehabilitation programs and private practice), psychiatric day treatment and inpatient units, and medical hospitals. Examples are given for individual, conjoint, family and group work during stages of prevention, brief crisis intervention, diagnostic evaluation and treatment.

The artwork presented demonstrates the effectiveness of clinical art therapy for gaining awareness, reality-testing, problem-solving, revealing unconscious material, catharsis, working through conflicts, integration and/or individuation. During each session the clinical art therapist offers techniques, subject matter, media and/or free choices which are pertinent to the changing needs and therapeutic goals of the client. The individual may make a conscious choice of what to convey through the artwork or may begin in random fashion; he or she may work on a particular topic suggested by the clinician. Directives given may be in the realm of general or specific themes, such as emotions, wishes, dreams, fantasies, plans, self-images, family constellations, environments, situations, etc.

The nonverbal aspect of art psychotherapy holds an important and unique position in the realm of mental health work, for it gives the clients an opportunity to *listen with their eyes*. This is especially significant in our current society, where we are constantly bombarded by speech through personal contact and the communication media. The common tendency of individuals to "tune out" what they prefer not to hear makes the visual image a powerful tool for treatment.

Clients are introduced to clinical art therapy by being informed that this method is used to help them better understand themselves and how they function as individuals and/or part of a family or a group system. Participants are purposely involved with simple art media to facilitate creativity and to lessen superego demands on performance. The art psychotherapist provides materials which have a direct relationship to immediate and/or long-term treatment goals. The size and particular properties of the media are also factors which may have an effect on the patient's emotional state and adaptive mechanisms. Using the art supplies requires no technical skill. Most commonly used are oil pastels, felt markers, watercolors, tempera and acrylic paints, plasticene, clay, tissue paper and magazine images.

Art products can be interpreted from several frames of reference, such as Freudian or Jungian, according to the therapist's orientation. However, it is essential to understand the client's own interpretation. The author believes in individual symbology, which may change during various life cycle stages. For instance, a "clock" has different meanings: To a child it may represent time to go to school, eat, or go to bed; for the young adult its symbol may imply time to decide on a career, marriage, children, etc.; for the mid-life person, the clock may represent time to evaluate value systems, plan goals or make changes; the old person may see it as a symbol for completion or the end of life.

Both two- and three-dimensional art forms frequently make a tangible statement about the client's hidden emotions, thoughts, or mode of functioning. This is due to the participants' new experience in communication where they are detached from their usual defenses. Although this aspect of art therapy has a special value in treatment, precautionary measures must be taken when repressed material surfaces quickly; the therapist must evaluate which, if any, intrapsychic images the patient should work on. All too often the neophyte therapist plunges into intrapsychic evidence before having had time to pull back and decide on the "appropriate timing" for dealing with the displayed material.

A distinctive characteristic of clinical art therapy is the clients' advantage of recording their own therapeutic process, through both the image and written commentary. Art therapists educate participants to write down thoughts, emotions and free associations which relate to their artwork. In cases of younger children, statements or stories are dictated to and written down by the therapist. This commentary adds to the patients' ownership and responsibility for their own work in therapy. That the artwork can be reviewed at any time during the treatment or termination phase of therapy is a bonus. At the completion of therapy this procedure acts to reinforce gains and gives the art therapy participant a rite of passage experience.

The section on *family art therapy* illustrates the use of clinical art therapy for diagnosis and treatment. A clarification of the term "diagnosis" as it is used in this context is essential. In family treatment, diagnosis refers to the family system, that is, how the members function within their family unit, the role each person plays, methods of interaction, and family strengths and weaknesses. Family art therapy is often task-oriented; the family creates art products together, sometimes nonverbally and other times with discussion. The process is observed and explored by the family and summarized by the art psychotherapist. The mutual art forms provide a platform for understanding and strengthening communication skills. They become the microcosmic trials for improving family relations.

In the following sections of the book experiences in working with group art therapy within various age categories are presented. Regardless of the age group involved, participants work on interpersonal and intrapsychic material. Communication is encouraged through the art therapy format, with group members expressing and sharing themselves both visually and verbally. This procedure is especially helpful to persons who have difficulty in asserting themselves in a group and is effective in therapeutically limiting the overly aggressive participant.

Groups in *outpatient settings* are composed of populations which are heterosexual or the same sex, contain peers or cross-generational individulas, include specifically unrelated persons, or couples, or families. Some groups are formulated around specific issues, problems or symptoms. They may be composed of single-parent households, intact families, families with a chronically ill member, and so on. In such cases, the art is created around the issues relevant to the population. The art therapy format has also been used for consciousness raising and for data collection and assessment.

In the *day treatment* or *partial hospitalization* program, group art therapy serves a major function of resocialization. Cooperative art tasks are specifically designed to desensitize the individual to group process and serve as a nonthreatening method for decision-making and interpersonal contact.

Within the *psychiatric hospital setting,* the art therapy groups are often thematically oriented to reveal the individuals' and group's strength. Concrete tasks help patients connect to their internal problems, with a special emphasis on external realities.

There are many nonclinical settings which offer mental health services, including public schools, residential centers, medical hospitals, physical rehabilitation programs, pain centers, camps, churches, youth centers, geriatric centers, etc. In these environments art therapy is utilized with emphasis on self-expression, improvement of communication, socialization and rehabilitation skills.

The clinical art therapy approach affords a wide source of variations and goals; therefore, it is an accepted therapeutic modality wherever mental health services are offered. Several chapters in this book describe the use of art therapy within the nonclinical settings.

ILLUSTRATIONS

To briefly acquaint the reader with some of the issues which are dealt with through clinical art therapy, simplified examples from case histories are given in this introductory overview.

Diagnosis

The onset of clinical art therapy includes a diagnostic evaluation. In addition to the verbal developmental history, art tasks are an important part of the assessment. The psychotherapist's observation includes: the client's approach and process; the product in relationship to form, space, color and composition; content, attitude and physical response to the art materials. All of these aspects are essential factors in diagnosing the client and in making treatment recommendations to suit the need of the individual.

During the evaluation period, Mr. Stockton used the collage media. He selected pictures by looking them over one at a time, then neatly placed various subjects in separate piles. The choices were devoid of people; the image of a tree with dying leaves was carefully trimmed around the leaves in an attempt to "do it perfect." The other pictures included a desolate desert and a junkyard. The client placed six dots of glue on the back of each picture. He became upset when a drop of glue touched his fingers. Mr. Stockton placed the pictures very carefully on the page, trying desperately to have them pasted at equal distance from each other. When asked to write a statement under each picture, he expressed his desire for a ruler so his printing would be even in size. Mr. Stockton's low frustration tolerance was exposed when he swore as an edge of one of the pictures curled away from the paper.

One picture does not provide conclusive evidence towards any diagnosis.

However, the media and procedure lent themselves to giving clues important for the evaluation. The man's ritualistic method of dealing with the media, low frustration tolerance, extreme concern around cleanliness, refusal to touch wet glue, avoidance of human subjects (in view of the fact that these were available in the vast majority of pictures), the lifeless manner in which he selected the pictures and their placement on the page—all offered the evaluator a great deal of material in a very brief length of time. The question of an obsessive-compulsive personality was later confirmed by the manifestation of analogous rituals, attitudes, and reactions in daily life.

Assessing Family Systems

Families can improve their communication when they discover how they function as a unit. A family with a teenage son was instructed to *draw a picture together* (Figure 1). The procedure included the parents' instructing their child to start the picture by doing whatever he pleased. He immediately drew a horizon line, then took a long time to fill up the entire right side of the page. The father went next to draw a sail on the left side of the paper, leaving a void in the center of the page. The last turn was taken by the mother, who drew a very tiny house in the middle.

During the discussion, the parents expressed anger towards their son for taking up so much space and time. They had forgotten their statement to

Figure 1.   Family drawing displays dynamics

him to do as he pleased. With the psychotherapist's help they began to realize they had set no limits, yet their expectation was for him "to take up less space." Mother, feeling terribly upset, explained that there was no room left for her after her husband and son took over so completely. She said it was necessary to *squeeze* in her tiny house. When confronted with the picture itself, it was obvious there was plenty of space; she could have drawn larger. Father had also felt left out; after he examined the artwork he was utterly surprised that he had taken up much more room than his wife. The boy thought that everyone was "equal"; he had taken it for granted that his parents, like himself, "had thoroughly enjoyed" drawing the picture together. The family realized that their individual perceptions of the process differed greatly. They had projected preconceived ideas and emotions onto the artwork.

The art task orientation gave the art therapist and the family a vehicle for understanding how the family functioned as a unit.

Ongoing Diagnosis: Reflection of Family Life

In the House-Tree-Person projective test, Hammer (1971) postulates the house represents an individual's psychological response to the family situation. Ira Styne, a 10-year-old boy, performed poorly in school in spite of a high IQ. He was rejected and scapegoated by his family and peers for his provocative behavior. In clinical art therapy he created a great many clay houses which consistently reflected his self-image and family role.

Ira Styne was seen both in individual and family art psychotherapy for a year and a half. During the first four months of clinical art therapy, the houses which he attempted to make never had a foundation, pathways, steps, or supports; the roof invariably caved in. In the fifth month, as the family explored their functionary system, Mr. and Mrs. Styne began to understand their son's negative attention. It served to divert the focus from their marital conflict. As emphasis was placed upon family interaction and communication, Ira's clay sculptures began to include supports. However, they were only placed on the edge, with none at the center. The child still neglected to give the house enough substance to maintain an upright position. As Ira's self-image and family situation improved, the house became more solid. At the end of eight months of therapy, the sculpture, now more solid, included a foundation, a center, as well as corner supports and a roof which was not too heavy. However, it never had a door or windows. At that time, although Ira's family interaction had made gains, he felt the children at school had not recognized his more positive change.

By the end of a year, Ira's school performance and behavior improved, and his classmates were more accepting of him. He was sublimating through karate and guitar lessons. When family treatment was about to end, Ira's house had a small opening for the door and a few windows; this indicated his social availability and resolved confict around "family secrets." Several months later, the boy asked for poster paints to decorate his sculptures, conveying his good feelings about his home situation. After 16 months of treatment, the terminating phase took place. At that time, Ira, in contrast to his lengthy, frustrating initial struggle to build a collapsing house, was able to produce a sturdy abode in approximately 30 minutes.

It was interesting to note that during times of family stress, the child's house was less substantial and aesthetic, although it still remained upright.

During the last month of treatment cowboys and Indians were introduced. At first the Indians surrounded the house and the endangered cowboys were inside. This may have indicated the fear of family regression with the termination of therapy. However, with confidence in the family's adaptations, Ira had the cowboys and Indians unite to form a circle around the house. The repeated house sculptures served as the child's mechanism for mastery and the therapist's vehicle for ongoing diagnosis.

Expression of Immediate Emotions and Transference

A single mother, Mrs. Jones, and her two children, Frank, seven years old, and Sally, 10 years old, were seen in art therapy for several months. Since the family had made gains, Mrs. Jones, in a family art therapy session, expressed her desire to discontinue the visits. As she was explaining her reasons, Frank nervously grabbed the newsprint paper; in his agitation he attacked the paper with his colored markers. Tearing parts of the paper with the markers, he drew a house aflame, and titled it "emergency." He explained, "There is a fire and a person stuck in the house. They were on their way to the emergency station when he got stuck and had to go to another place. Something is going on. The person on the stretcher got hurt. In the house that is on fire three people live there."

The family examined the picture. The art therapist suggested that the atmosphere of the flaming house and the concern about someone being stuck and getting hurt were a reflection of Frank's feelings around the issue of terminating therapy. The boy agreed to the interpretation about his worry of how the family and he in particular would get along if art psychotherapy were discontinued.

Mrs. Jones, able to take in her child's concern, agreed to continue family treatment. While mother finalized her decision by making future weekly appointments, Frank made another picture and he declared, "It's firemen who help people stay away from the danger of the burning house." The family who had become educated to the symbolic content of their art realized the fireman in the role of rescuer stood for the therapist herself.

Marital Art Therapy: Couples in Group

Couples who were in long-term group art therapy had the opportunity to see how each partner perceived the other. Husbands and wives were asked to *make a collage which depicts facts about your spouse and a fantasy of changes which you wish to make.* One husband used a picture (Figure 2) of a man and the words, "Tell someone." He put down the hair and neck of a woman, then proceeded to add radishes for eyes, a squash for the nose, and a tomato for the mouth. For his wife's hand, he pasted on a fish, underneath he wrote, "My wife is just a bunch of vegetables." His fantasy showed a man's hand holding an electric drill pointed at his wife's chest; he wrote, "drill feeling into her." (It was interesting to discover that she suffered from ulcers.)

When this husband had made analogous statements in the past, his wife accepted them passively. However, this time, as she looked and listened to his statements, she became furious and began to draw. The therapist questioned the wife about her picture and her feelings. At first she saw only a red and black ball in full motion, but she soon sensed the nonverbal message behind it and was able to shout "angry, darn it!" After spilling out her pent up feelings, the wife no longer tolerated being the object for her husband's displeasure. Her husband began to examine his motivation for scapegoating his spouse. Together they began to redefine their goals in marital art therapy treatment.

Insight: Working Through Grief and Mourning

Jim, an 11-year-old boy, was being considered for placement by his biological father and his stepmother. Jim was incredibly dirty. He seldom washed, emphatically refused to bathe. The family considered his actions as stubborn, oppositional, and hostile. In school, the boy's unkempt demeanor became the topic of the students' jokes. His belligerent attitude triggered off a great deal of anger and discord among his stepmother, father and himself. The stepmother threatened to leave her husband if his son remained in the home.

During the art therapy sessions, Jim was engaged in drawing childhood memories. He painted and reminisced about several of his birthdays and presents which he had received. During one session, Jim became completely absorbed in a series of three drawings. He was involved in portraying the

Figure 2.   Fact and fantasy regarding spouse

pictures with a great deal of care. The first part contained a tall building; the second showed two people in the bathroom, one a boy in the shower, the other person standing near the sink; the third picture showed a coffin with pallbearers. When Jim began to talk about the content of the artwork, he broke into tears. Later he explained, "My mother went to the hospital on my birthday, she died a couple of weeks later. I was in the shower when I found out!!!" The interpretation tied his fear of water to the connection of "bad news." In the following months, Jim did a great deal of work on grief and mourning by creating scenes of his mother, her illness, and her death, and through the expression of his feelings of sadness, abandonment and loss.

Media as an Instrument for Developmental Gains

David, nine years old, was diagnosed by his school as retarded with emotional overlay. His behavior was disruptive; he lacked impulse control and had a history of enuresis. At the beginning of therapy he depicted himself through the theme of a wagon. For example, initially the child said, "This is a wagon who is out in the middle of the street and gets runned over." The content of the child's picture revealed his lack of impulse control and fear of being in an unprotected environment.

In this case, the use of the media played an important part in the treatment. At first, David was supplied with materials which helped to give him a more contained experience. For example, colored pencils were used at the beginning and then he was transferred to felt pens as he learned to stay focused. With impulse management, oil pastel and plasticene were made available. When David was able to ventilate his anger without regression, watercolors were introduced. The intermediate stages sometimes contained mixed media to aid the transition. The size of the paper was consciously selected, going from a confined area and graduating to larger space. This was due to an effort to expand David's limits within tolerable parameters. Trays and boxes were utilized to set boundaries for the child. Directives were given which encouraged an appropriate means for the expression of his emotions.

The selections of the media, space and topic were consistant in organizing a "protected environment" for the child.

David's progress included the cessation of enuresis, improvement in impulse control, sublimation, and understanding of cause and effect. As the boy's behavior became appropriate and he developed learning skills, his family became more accepting of him.

In contrast to his early artwork, David's forms became clearly defined and the pictures colorful. He created images of people, no longer using "objects" to portray his feelings. During the terminating phase of art therapy, as a diagnostic comparison, David was asked to draw a wagon, then to talk about the picture. He made a sturdy orange wagon. Pleased with the picture and himself, he looked at the therapist and said, "I have fun, I color a lot, I draw good, I color fun, I color good, the wagon is colored. I did the wheels. Aren't the wheels good? I made the stick, the top, the handle. I made everything. I have fun. I feel real and good."

Awareness of Family Dynamics

In an adolescent group, Adam, a 14-year-old youngster, constantly said

Figure 3A.   Child perceives father as the victim of marital abuse

Figure 3B.   Projection: Father's sadness over thoughts of punitive wife

his household contained "no problems." He frequently painted a singular theme of a couple who were hitting, killing, or thinking rageful, injurious thoughts about one another. These pictures were created when the direction to *draw a picture you feel strongly about; it can be a person, place or thing* was given. Examples of his art were drawings (Figures 3 A, B, C) of a man whose wife was thinking about either hitting her husband over the head, or shooting him. After several months the group pointed out the ongoing subject, stating that it must have special significance to him. As Adam listened to the group, he was saddened by his insight; he said, "I guess that is how I really feel about what goes on between my mom and dad, even though they pretend things are okay." this awareness helped Adam to openly deal with his anxiety regarding his parents' marital dissension.

Figure 3C.   Projection of parental dynamics

Body Image Perceptions

In an obese adolescents art therapy group, Elaine found "the blob" to be her favorite art form. However, when the group members were asked to create self-portraits, Elaine used the plasticene to mold herself as thin (Figure 4). The art therapist pointed out that in spite of her obesity, Elaine's self-image was actually a compensatory configuration. It showed her as she was in her childhood, using denial as a means of defense. Several group members brought up the fact that they were able to relate to the "blob" through their own shapeless figures and their difficulties in "reaching out to other people." Within the context of an empathic environment, Elaine emerged to acknowledge her obesity as a first step towards working on the problem of being overweight.

Vehicle for Revealing Emotions

In a young adult group, Jenny was graphically portrayed as "someone who is really self-assured and always at ease." When group members were asked to do a collage of *how do you feel in this group?,* Jenny was the first person to share her artwork. It contained a Band-Aid, which meant "it hurts"; a bronze death mask signified "I feel out of it"; a face with features

Figure 4.   Obese adolescent perceives a thin body image

cut out symbolized, "people don't really know me"; a clock and a pretty girl related, "In time I will emerge most beautiful."

Jenny, who was fearful of rejection, usually managed to use a confident facade as a defense. However, the collage became a means for risk-taking, and was used to convey the message of how scared she was and her inability to show her true self. The other group members, impressed with Jenny's honesty, used her as a model to share their art and themselves and to make a commitment to the group.

Observing the Subconscious

Mr. Wald was a man who denied his emotions through the defense of intellectualization and alcohol abuse. He made gains through the group art psychotherapy modality and towards the end of treatment he created a mixed media collage (Figure 5) which defined his experience. He began with the

Figure 5.   Tapping the unconscious

image of an animal, which symbolized "I started off having a difficult time here. I would make something that had nothing to do with the suggested theme, and then I would discover it was very revealing, sometimes it came from way deep in my gut. Although the animal looks benign, it is also a monster which I keep locked inside." He completed the collage as he added a clock, playing card, a door, and a person stretching. He said these objects represented "time, risks, escape, and my own growth." Mr. Wald concluded by claiming, "Many times art therapy initiated subjects that I would otherwise not have dealt with."

Life Span Review

Art products are useful in surveying a person's life span. Art offers an opportunity to express feelings and thoughts regarding an individual's present state of life, and about the past, and future. Arthur, a member of an adult group which was coming to an end, was asked to do a collage of *where I came from, where I am now, and where I am going.* This instruction was given without any further explanation.

The picture of a poor family answered the directive *where I came from;* he wrote, "I'm hungry. Where is my mommy and daddy?" Not only did he come from a poor family, but his mother and father, who worked on several jobs, were seldom home, and as a boy he felt emotionally undernourished. In response to *where I am now,* he used the picture of a man with glasses upon which colors were reflected; he wrote, "Seeking and wanting to reflect inner beauty." The statement was synonymous with Arthur's life-style change. While in group he began to write poetry and prose in connection with his artwork. He had also allowed himself more time off from work and was going to the beach to sun and swim. Arthur had discovered that people liked him for the nice person he was, rather than for his "powerful position at work."

The third part of the collage *where I am going* was displayed by an image of a man yelling, "Hey guys, life is okay." This picture was especially meaningful for Arthur when he reviewed his artwork. He saw that most of his earlier pictures contained depressed people accompanied by words lamenting the "helplessness of man."

Recall: Factor in Experiencing Joy

A geriatric group tended to ruminate around their sense of hopelessness. They were asked to *portray pets you enjoyed.* One of the apathetic members, Mr. Torin, was resistant to any type of activity. However, in an art therapy session where he watched a woman paint her old canary, Mr. Torin remembered a bird house he had built many years ago. He became animated as he drew a replica (Figure 6), recalling the image in great detail. When he shared the picture, he remembered the pleasures which accompanied the bird house. For the first time he held the group's attention. Later Mr. Torin painted an abstract design, which notified the group he felt "alive" for the first time in years. An important aspect to this incident was Mr. Torin's motivation to sculpt a series of birds when he was home.

Although Mr. Torin's experience was the most dramatic, the rest of the group members also experienced feelings of joy while pictures of dogs, cats, fish and a turtle surfaced on the page. The sharing aspect was extremely beneficial since it allowed for individual attention and empathy. An important factor in the recall was the triggering mechanism which stimulated additional memories for other members of the group.

Figure 6.   Recall of the past activates involvement

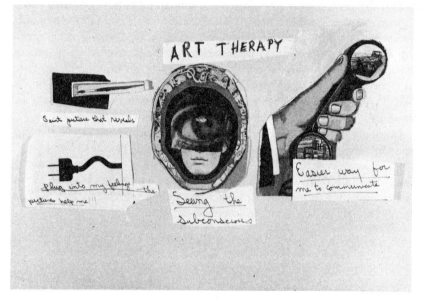

Figure 7.   Art therapy defined

Defining Art Therapy

Susan, a middle-aged widow, lived alone. She entered art therapy treatment with complaints of backaches, depression and a sense of isolation.
Her childhood history included incestual molestation and physical abuse.
Susan had no friends. She worked in a factory where she could function in
spite of her selective mutism.

Highly intelligent and deft in gaining awareness through her artwork,
Susan made impressive gains towards self-discovery. As she worked
through her childhood trauma, she made developmental gains, using the art
therapy for self-actualization. While reminiscing about her clinical art
therapy experience, she made a collage (Figure 7) defining the modality.
Susan selected a *paint brush* to explain how she had discovered her inner
self through the process of painting a picture that reveals, an *electric cord*
and *plug* images to represent "plugging into my feelings," then a *portrait
with a large superimposed eye* to symbolize "seeing the unconscious," and
lastly a *telephone* to relate how art therapy had been an important instrument which made it "easier for me to communicate."

PART II

Family Art Psychotherapy

Dynamically oriented family art psychotherapy as it is practiced by this author is based on "family systems theory," which stresses the influence family members have upon one another (Bell, 1953; Ackerman, 1958; Bowen, 1960). The family is viewed as a group functioning as a system. Rather than focusing on the designated patient, the family therapist validates the existence of each member. Within the family art therapy approach, Kwiatkowska (1978) was the first person to recognize the value of working with the entire family. Her method included instructions for the family to create both individual and group drawings.

During the family systems diagnostic evaluation and throughout treatment, this author utilizes a here-and-now family interchange approach through the art task orientation. This technique lends authenticity to the assessment of the family's mode of functioning; instead of leaning on the reporting method, credibility is based on the familys' behavior as it is observed through a problem-solving art task. The artwork is concrete evidence of the family's interactional performance. Where verbal dynamics reveal the family's manifest style of communication, nonverbal visual elements provide a dimension for displaying the subtle mechanisms which are in operation.

While the family is engaged in creating an art product, the clinician watches the *process* to gain an understanding of interpersonal dynamics. The family members' approach to the art, the level of involvement and the evaluation of the artwork give the art therapist an opportunity to observe the gestalt of the family's structure, assigned roles, alliances, behavioral patterns, communication systems, and style. The art task's process and content offer information in the realm of understanding underlying messages, family secrets, defenses and ego strengths of the individuals and the unit.

In observing the family, the clinician may look for evidence of familial dysfunctional styles. Bowen (1965) contends that the family may have established a differentiated or undifferentiated way of operating. That is, do they tend to function as a "we" unit (wherein they perceive themselves as thinking and feeling alike), or do family members function autonomously. The possibilities of marital schism versus a marital skew (Lidz et al., 1957) may exist. The skewed type of relationship exhibits overt harmony; in this marriage the roles are complementary—one spouse is a dominant central figure whose independence collaborates with a dependent partner. The schism is represented by incompatible roles, which result in overt hostility and conflict.

Some families exhibit a pseudomutuality stance which Wynne et al. (1958) define as: "A type of surface alignment that blurs and obscures from recognition and conscious experience both underlying splits and divergencies, on one hand, and deeper affection and alignment on the other. The family pushes away any threats to its unity; it maintains the homeostasis by avoiding the discomforts of intimate relations."

Patterns of communications are observed by the therapist, who sometimes perceives a pathological communication system. It may include the "double bind," a theory formulated by Bateson et al. (1956). They related that entrapment is set up through an obscure and/or contradictory instructional system. An illustration of this mixed communication is portrayed by a mother who has difficulty in tolerating her son's closeness. She repeatedly finds herself making excuses to get rid of him. For example, with a frown on her face, mother says, "I love you so much that I want you to go outside and get some fresh air so you can stay healthy." The patent's overt message denies her feelings of wanting to push her son away. If the child correctly perceives the annoyed expression and confronts his mother, he would be punished by her accusations of not being appreciated for her love and concern. Therefore, to avoid punishment the boy deceives himself into believing he needed fresh air rather than question his mother's motives. The child is placed in a situation where his own internal messages, as well as those of others, are falsely discriminated.

In working with families, the clinician often encounters "a resistance to change" (Brown, 1972) as the family may collude to maintain a "family homeostasis" (Jackson, 1959; Satir, 1967). Therefore, as an agent of change (Bell, 1964), the therapist intrudes upon the family system in an attempt to upset the homeostasis and to give support to a restructured family system. Within the art therapy approach, a large portion of the intrusion is accomplished through the dynamically oriented method of requesting families to create mutual art tasks with a variety of themes, art media, and at times role designations, which are therapeutically based.

As therapy progresses, the therapist attempts to help the family overcome rigid solutions. The art therapy approach includes asking the family to work together in new ways, to risk new patterns of communication and interaction.

Members are encouraged to become aware of their own actions and reactions, with an overall exploration of the interactional network. As one or more family members begin to change, the established family system is weakened. At that time the family art therapist acts as a facilitator to maintain a balance during the family's phase of restructuring. The family is helped to shift with the needs of the individual members and through new stages of family development.

This part presents information on diagnosis and treatment with families. Chapter 2 contains information on the author's clinical art therapy diagnostic evaluation procedure for an initial interview. The example of a single parent and her son illustrates the assessment process. Chapter 3 is a case history of Mr. and Mrs. Brown and their three children. The documentation takes the Brown family from their initial evaluation through all the stages of treatment. Dynamic formulations and work for each member within the family system is presented. Chapter 4 is the record of a six-week brief service for multiple families in art psychotherapy. All of the parents are divorced. The clinical art therapy sessions enable the adults and their children to deal with issues pertinent to life in a single-parent household. Application of art psychotherapy techniques are presented along with illustrations. Chapter 5 presents a six-week brief service for a family with a geriatric member. The case history shows clinical art therapy as a source for communication and decision-making on the part of an elderly person. Chapter 6 contains a case history wherein verbal therapy is used with the parents in combination with art therapy for the child. This unique case illustrates how the child's art work revealed emotional responses to his parents' marital conflict.

CHAPTER 2

Initial Family Interview: Diagnostic Techniques

Beginning Instructions

Following is a simple method which allows a brief period for introduction and is a way of allowing all family members to actively participate in an art therapy experience. Each member is asked to: *Draw your initials as large as you can on the page. Now, using these initials and the design they make, find suggested ideas for pictures. It can be something real or a design. When you discover the picture, feel free to stay in the lines or go out of them, using as many or as few colors as you wish. When you are finished give your picture a title.*

This exercise is similar to the Naumburg scribble. However, the initials are less threatening, since performance concerns are alleviated by producing a familiar form.

When the exercise is completed, each person shows the artwork and states the title. It has been the author's experience that this artwork often gives information concerning the individual's personality, or sometimes contains a subconscious message pertaining to one's attitude about obtaining clinical help, or the transference to the therapist. Although the subject and/or the style of the initial drawing may offer clues, they are not dealt with during the first session. This is due to a lack of validity; also, such exploration is too threatening for an initiating session. However, these drawings may be referred to at a later time.

Nonverbal Mutual Drawing

If there are more than four or five persons in the family, they are asked to divide up into two teams. The way teams are selected and which members belong to each group are noted by the therapist. Family members are requested to: *Work together on a single piece of paper, each person with a different color felt marker. Then proceed, without talking or writing words. Take turns in making your picture. When you are finished, put your marker down. There is no special way of doing this; every family does it differently.* Upon completion, a request for a title is made.

This technique is an extraordinarily quick method for aiding the family diagnostic evaluation. The information which is gathered by the therapist is once again not disclosed at this time, for two important reasons—insufficient validation, and inappropriate timing. Nonverbal drawings are especially beneficial in cases with clients who have facile verbal defenses or limited communication skills.

Example

Nonverbally, a single mother and son (an only child) began their drawing with mother taking over. Her turn took a very long time; she kept the child waiting as she continued on in a teasing manner. When her son finally had his chance, the parent became extremely competitive. Mother persisted until most of the page was covered, and the child began to worry that there would be no room left for him. When the boy did put a mark on the paper, his mother drew around it, or extended her line over or beyond it. Finally, the child became exhausted and "gave up." Even then, mother loosely continued on her own until she eventually decided to stop.

The parent's infantile competitive behavior, and the child's frustration at not being acknowledged, were seen by the therapist in only a few minutes.

Verbal Family Task-Oriented Art Product

For the task-oriented art product, directions are to: *Create a family sculpture. This time you can speak to each other. Each person selects a piece of colored plasticene. Make sure no one else has the same color; maintain your color throughout the project. When you have finished, give it a title.*

As an alternate to the plasticene, colored construction paper may be used (with this medium scissors and glue are supplied). Another choice may be the family drawing which was originated by Kwiatkowska (1978). Regardless of the media, the experience is given a time limit of approximately 15 minutes. This procedure provides a method for observing each member's role and alliances within the family system. It reveals the pattern of communication and the gestalt of the family.

Although the technique is simple, the therapist must be watchful. It is essential for the clinician to observe and remember the *evolvement* of the product. The emphasis is on the process. The nonverbal and the verbal aspects, as well as body language, are all a part of the diagnosis. The following are some of the things to look for: How does the art form get started? Who initiates it? If there is any discussion, whose suggestions are utilized, whose are ignored? Do the family members take turns, work in teams, or do they work simultaneously? Is someone left out and, if so, how did it happen? What is the geographical location of each person's work and what amount of space does each member utilize? Do they work on their own symbols, or do they add on to the art of other members? If so, does it pertain to certain members of the family etc.? How is the title decided upon? Who writes it onto the picture? The way it is written and the title itself are contributing factors to the diagnosis of family dynamics.

When the family completes the art task, questions are asked by the therapist: "Who was the leader or the most active participant?" This gives the family a way of checking out each other's perceptions. Often what is voiced are the preconceived ideas of the roles that family members play. It is essential for the therapist to help the family deal with the here-and-now family dynamics while engaged in creating a product. This discourages the reporting of historical family material. When everyone has discussed how he or she saw the procedure evolve, the therapist always shares her own observations, lending support to the reality of the process. The suggestion is made of analogous family dynamics which may exist in their home life. The pursuit of this subject lends itself to discussion about the behavior of family members and gets them to actively think and talk about themselves and each other. It is also "family therapy" in the fullest sense, removing some of the attention from the designated patient. Frequently, this will precipitate further exploration at home. Families often refer to this experience at various times during treatment.

Example

A mother working with her son (Figure 8) began by telling him to pick out the colors for them. After he made the selection, she switched colors with her child. She then proceeded to pressure the boy to begin the project; finally, the child began by making a solid ball. He stated, "It'll be a person." Mother added two wing-like structures and said it was "a bird." Her child went along with this shift in idea, and made a head and eyes—"It'll be an owl," he said. Mother replied with, "Yeah, they are smart." Then she broke away from the therapist's "one color" instructions, picked up a new

Figure 8.   Mutually created sculpture is a part of family assessment

color of clay and added legs. As the child added the feet, he notified
mother, "You left out this important part." The parent, irritated, pressed a
piece of plasticene on the head, pushing down hard enough to distort the
face. The child became upset, saying, "You always wreck everything I
make." When they decided upon the title, the boy asked his mother what to
call the piece. She replied, "You decide." The boy suggested, "A funny
bird"; mother said, "An owl." Child responded, "Yeah, an owl who got
hurt"; mother ignored his input and wrote the title "An owl." The son felt
rejected. He pushed his chair away from the table in an effort to distance
himself from his mother.

      When the author asked, "Who did the most work on the sculpture?",
each insisted it was the other person and that they themselves had done little
to create the art form. The object was observed, the procedure reviewed.

The therapist mentioned how the child did ask for directions, and at the mother's insistence the boy made the initial move, which was undermined by the mother's input. A discussion revolved around this dynamic and it was suggested by the author that this may also happen at home.

Later the mother recalled how she had distorted the face of the wise owl. During the discussion regarding the owl theme, she stated, "My son is very smart, much smarter than me." A few seconds later the association with her former husband's intelligence was made. She became aware of how her child was the recipient of the displaced anger, which rightfully belonged to her divorced husband.

A warning must be given regarding art therapy with families in general and this task in particular: *Concrete evidence of family dynamics is extremely confronting.* The therapist's style and knowledge are important in the judgment of how much exploration is beneficial to the family.

CHAPTER 3

Case History of
an Intact Family

Mrs. Brown called the art therapist to say the family needed help in dealing with their son Henry. He frequently refused to attend school, was enuretic and disrupted the family's equilibrium by his demands and negative behavior. The family consisted of Mr. Frank Brown, his wife, Celia, and their three children: 16-year-old Nancy, 12-year-old Henry, and seven-year-old Gloria. The family had previously been in therapy for the short duration of six weeks. Mrs. Brown reported that they discontinued treatment since no change took place, adding that the sessions seemed to elicit more arguments at home.

Upon consultation with the previous clinician, the family art therapist was informed that the parents used intellectualization as a defense, and that their closed family system sabotaged any penetration into their rigid mode of functioning. Both therapists agreed that art therapy might be a treatment of choice, as the art task orientation could cut through their intellectualization and help the family confront and work upon their feelings and interaction. The Brown family was in treatment for one year. They were seen twice a week for four months, then one time a week for eight months.

INITIAL INTERVIEW: DIAGNOSING THE FAMILY SYSTEM:
FIRST WEEK

Introduction: Nonverbal Task

At the first meeting, the therapist introduced herself and made contact with each individual. Each person was asked about his or her understanding of the visit. The family members agreed that they came because Henry was a problem. In response, the clinician explained the philosophy behind family therapy: An individual with a problem was believed to be a part of a greater family problem; it was not unusual for the presenting complaints to disappear after a family was in treatment.

Mr. and Mrs. Brown immediately began to rationalize about their son Henry's behavior and the chaos he stimulated. The father, in particular, began to list the problems with their son. The art therapist politely put an end to Mr. Brown's complaints by stating that the family would be given an opportunity to engage themselves in a mutual task in which they would use simple art materials. Their endeavor would serve as a vehicle for understanding how the family functioned as a unit (for further details, see Chapter 2). The therapist proceeded to have the family members select colored markers, each one a different color, and to divide up into two teams. Mr. Brown and his daughter Nancy glanced at each other; Henry mumbled his wish to be on his father's team; however, he was ignored as father and Nancy formed their team of two. Mrs. Brown, aware of her son's rejection, told Henry not to feel badly because he, Gloria and herself would form their own group.

Each team was presented with a single piece of paper. Directions for the nonverbal mutual drawing were given and the family members were instructed not to speak to each other, to write down any words, or to gesture to one another. The suggestion was made for one person to start, then the other partner to take a turn, proceeding in this fashion until each person decided to stop. The therapist encouraged the participants to feel free to put down marks, scribbles, designs, or representational symbols. The individuality of family drawings was emphasized with no expectations as to style or content.

The father and oldest daughter got started immediately. Mr. Brown, using purple, drew a house; Nancy used her pink marker to fill in curtains and flowers. They took turns; father drew a boy going through the doorway, daughter adding a girl holding his hand. The picture continued to be developed, as father maintained the lead and daughter followed with contact gestures. Later, they were instructed to break the silence and to give the drawing a title. Together, father and daughter named it "A Happy Home."

The second team started their picture, as mother designated Henry as the person to begin. Henry used a dark green to draw a circle; Mrs. Brown used a light green (similar to her son's) to make a larger circle, which encompassed her son's symbol. Gloria with her red marker quickly drew flowers on the far side of the page; she continued to draw by herself in her own space the entire time. After Henry's initial attempt, he went on to make various designs. He was always followed by his mother, who either drew inside his design or encircled it. After a while, both mother and son worked simultaneously until the entire construction was intertwined, giving the appearance of a single mass. Just before mother put down her marker, she filled in several leaves on Gloria's flowers. When it came time to title the picture, Mrs. Brown turned the decision over to her son. Henry named it "Designs and Things and Flowers."

The nonverbal pictures were not discussed at this time. The therapist went directly on to the next diagnostic technique.

Family Art Task

The five members of the Brown family were handed four sheets of colored construction paper, oil pastels, scissors, glue and a tray. They were instructed to *create a family sculpture. On this project, you may speak to each other.*

Mrs. Brown quickly turned to her son, asking him what they should make. Henry told her to ask dad. Mr. Brown resented the fact that he was not referred to initially. However, he told everyone to get started, to work on their own; later they would bring everything together (Figure 9).

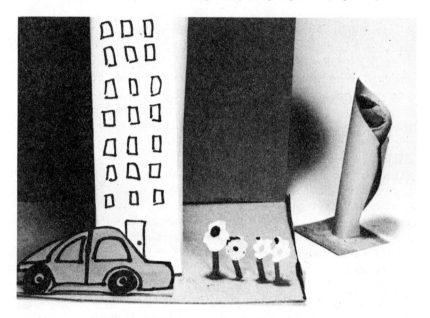

Figure 9.   Family task: father aligns himself with daughters and symbolically rejects son. A clue to mother's attachment to son is presented

The youngest child was the first person to grab a piece of paper for her flower cutouts. Father also took a sheet, which he folded into a tall apartment house. Teenage Nancy followed suit; she cut out a two-seater car. With only one piece of paper left, mother cut it, giving her son the largest portion. Henry made a cone shaped rocket, which he placed with the pointed tip touching his father's tall building. Mrs. Brown shredded her paper to stuff it into her son's rocket; she claimed it served as fuel. Father remarked he didn't understand what the rocket had to do with a building, flowers and an automobile. He asked the therapist for an additional tray, upon which he placed his son's sculpture. Mr. Brown was pleased with the way he retrieved his sculptured scene; he claimed separate themes were best served by two separate sculptures. Henry looked hurt and angry but said nothing. When the therapist asked for the project to be titled, father without consultation used his power to title both products; the one he worked on was called "High Rise," while he named Henry's piece "Outer Space Pollution."

The clinician asked the family how they felt about the experience. Mr. Brown and his daughters agreed "it was fun." They admired the artwork and pronounced their amazement at their creative ability. Nancy mentioned it was the first time the family ever attempted to make something together. The therapist asked the participants who they thought was the leader. Everyone agreed there were two leaders, father and son. Then the question was asked, "Who did the least?" Everyone decided it was mother, since her part was not visible.

The family members were encouraged to report any emotions which they had experienced. Mr. Brown and his daughters felt good about the entire encounter. Mrs. Brown related how distraught she was from the moment her son was cheated of a full sheet of paper. Her distress climaxed when her husband split up the sculpture. Henry remained in contact with his feelings of rejection, though he resisted being involved in the discussion.

The therapist without comment handed the boy a piece of plasticene. Henry fondled the medium, then he rolled out a ball and slammed his fist down on it. With encouragement, Henry related that his father never liked what he did and was convinced he was the "dummy in the family." He ventilated his anger towards his father, who repeatedly put him down and wiped him out. Henry's overwhelming sense of hopelessness left the child depleted. At first, Mr. Brown reacted with feigned innocence. He claimed he did not understand where his son had gathered "such screwy ideas." Mrs. Brown defended her son; she showed her husband his underlying message to Henry as she pointed to the separated rocket and its title—"Outer Space Pollution." Mr. Brown replied, "That didn't mean anything, it was only a fun exercise." Henry confronted his father as he said, "It could have been fun when the whole thing was on one tray but then you wrecked everything by taking my rocket off." With visual evidence to back up his son's statement, Mr. Brown began to look at his actions and his son's reaction.

The therapist left the father's introspection to shift back to the perception of other family members. Mrs. Brown's view of the family dynamics was explored. She declared that her husband took over, that he didn't take Henry or herself into account when he labeled the rocket form. She had continued to relate how she understood Henry's feelings of rejection, she tried to comfort him by showing how much she cared.

Nancy reiterated how much she had enjoyed the project and claimed her brother was overly sensitive. Gloria, the youngest child, said her brother's rocket was very nice and she wished daddy had left it on his tray. The child added, her father was always boss because he came up with the ideas. In her estimation, mother's contribution wasn't important since she could not see the fuel in the rocket.

Therapist Review of Art Task Procedure

The therapist reviewed the procedure of the art task, pointing out to the participants that they may have been unaware of some of the dynamics.

1) Mother turned over the leadership role to her son by asking him to initiate the project.
2) Henry, uncomfortable about being placed in the position of leadership, asked mother to give father the authority.
3) Father suggested initial independent artwork to be completed in a collective end product; however, he negated this plan when he separated out Henry's rocket and indirectly his wife's fuel.
4) The youngest child, Gloria, was the first person to function autonomously (similar to her nonverbal team drawing), indicating a level of independence. Her flowers give a cheery note to the paper sculpture.
5) Father quickly followed Gloria as he made a tall apartment house. It was the highest part of the scene, displaying his importance through the use of space.
6) Teenage Nancy worked quickly, along with her father and her sister. Her automobile cutout was directed away from the apartment construct. The therapist wondered aloud if this represented a need to become more independent.
7) Mother and son, who moved slower than the others, found themselves with the dilemma of a shortage of paper. When the other family members selected their paper, they were either oblivious of this fact or decided to ignore it. However, neither Henry nor his mother chose to

point this out to father or the girls. Mother chose to deal with the problem by sharing her paper, giving her son the largest piece. When the therapist questioned mother if she often played the role of the martyr, she nodded in affirmation. However, Mrs. Brown defended herself by saying there was no other choice. The therapist asked the family for possible alternatives and they made several suggestions, such as Mr. Brown might have given Henry his sheet while he shared a sheet with his wife, or everyone could have used a half sheet.

8) Henry attempted to contact father by having his rocket touch father's apartment building.

9) Mother aligned herself with her son by adding fuel to the rocket. The therapist suggested that this act seemed to indicate that perhaps Mrs. Brown expressed her anger towards her husband indirectly through Henry.

10) Father rejected his son by separating Henry's rocket. Mr. Brown objected to this interpretation. He declared the subject matter was incongruent. The therapist suggested he ask Henry what he had in mind. When Mr. Brown followed this suggestion, his son explained that the theme was a takeoff of the film "Close Encounter of the Third Kind." His rocket "was a friendly attempt" from people in outer space to communicate. After apologizing, Mr. Brown rebuked his son for not explaining the rocket's meaning. The therapist questioned if Mr. Brown maintained his blame as a defense against feelings of guilt or regret.

11) Father exerted his power by titling both paper sculptures. An additional rejection of Henry was implied through the pejorative name given to Henry's rocket, "Outer Space Pollution," which was in contrast to the positive title of his own sculpture, "High Rise." The therapist pointed out to Henry and his mother how they allowed father this move without interruption. Both Mrs. Brown and her son expressed their feelings of rage and impotence when Mr. Brown took over.

During the initial stage of therapy, the art therapist specifically avoids pointing out or interpreting the underlying symbolic messages. Bringing attention to the unconscious content is too threatening, when trust in the clinician and the process has not yet been established. Therefore, the art therapist emphasized dynamics as she suggested to the family that the manner in which they functioned during the art task might well be analogous to the way they operated as a family unit at home. She said she would make up some fantasy situations which might shed some light on their daily interaction. The art therapist suggested that perhaps mom, in front of dad, asks Henry what she should make for dinner. Maybe Henry feels odd about usurping his father's decision-making role and tells mom to ask dad. Or possibly mom asks her son to select the television shows for family viewing, or any other similar situation.

As the family nodded agreement, the clinician continued with the possibility of dad saying he wanted turkey, or maybe he wants to watch "Father Knows Best" on television. If Henry isn't in agreement with the choice, he becomes angry because father has not taken him into consideration.

The therapist addressed herself to mother's anger; perhaps it was a way for Mrs. Brown to push away her guilt for not making her own decisions about dinner or television. Was it possible that Mrs. Brown's angry feelings about herself were displaced onto her husband? Mrs. Brown replied, she needed time to think about the last suggestion. However, she admitted to "feeling my son's anger, right along with him." Perhaps she did have trouble in separating out the real reason. The therapist commented on how closely Mrs. Brown identified with her son.

The family was amazed at the accuracy of the therapist's guesses and interpretation. Gloria said, "Mom always asks Henry what he wants, not only about desserts, but even where we should go on Sundays. But daddy always knows what we should do."

Recalling the removal of the rocket, the art therapist asked Mr. Brown if it were possible that Henry's attempts to get close to him were in some ways put aside. Henry's father thought for a while. Finally he remembered an incident which happened on the weekend. Henry offered to help him fix his car, but when the boy got in the way he was told to go help his mother with the vacuum cleaning. Mr. Brown told his son that he was "useless as an auto mechanic." Although the boy looked sad at the memory of the incident, he appeared relieved to have his rejected image validated.

Once again Nancy's symbol of the car was interpreted as a desire to get away from the house in an attempt to grow up.

The youngest child was referred to as the free spirit of the family. She was capable and allowed to be on her own; Gloria didn't feel the need to align herself with any special person or team. It was pointed out how this child seemed to play the role of the "family's enhancer, she liked to make things nicer or prettier" both in her drawings and in her attempt to defend Henry's rocket.

The family members were impressed with the therapist's interpretation; the parents declared the session had been very helpful and the family had a lot to think about.

When the art therapy session came to an end, the family was instructed to continue to observe their interactions throughout the week. The therapist suggested they become more conscious of their interactions; their awareness would give them a clearer understanding of what and how changes in their family could be implemented.

TREATMENT:
SECOND WEEK

The week after the initial interview the Brown family returned to share their family interactional observations. Mr. Brown took his homework very seriously. He explained how in the past he was only aware of his son's provocative behavior. He had known that it was often necessary for him to punish Henry, but had never before realized how often his punitive gestures included "pushing my boy away from me." Mr. Brown went on to relate how the initial art psychotherapy interview had been very painful, but insightful. "It really helped our family look at ourselves," commented Mr. Brown. Mrs. Brown and Nancy added that the session had been very interesting. They, too, had given thought to the poignant way art tasks had laid out the family dynamics. Henry waited to be asked about his thoughts on the previous session. Gloria, rather than participate verbally, showed her delight in returning by asking permission to use the art materials while the family talked.

Source of Emotional Responses

It was mother who said she wanted to talk about the weekend. Both she and her husband began to report what had happened, with the children interjecting their thoughts. To limit intellectual reporting, the art therapist set out plasticene and a tray; she asked the family to *create the home scene*. The family became involved immediately. Each person was asked to tell what his or her sculptures meant. Henry showed himself in his room making a model plane, mother was seen crying in her bedroom, father presented himself fixing his car, Nancy was trying on clothes and Gloria playing with the dog.

Henry explained he was busy when his mom came into his room to give him some hugs and kisses; mother interrupted to say she was "feeling loving." Father injected Henry was getting too old for "that kind of stuff." Nancy agreed as she stated, "Mom still babies Henry." The boy went on to explain he got angry with his mom for bugging him; she was overly affectionate. Mrs. Brown told how rejected she felt. She ran into her room to cry.

Henry cited his mother's continued requests to watch television with her (on the days he skipped school), the frequent challenges to play checkers when dad worked late and her insistence that he go to the market with her.

Referring to the tray sculpture, the other family members were asked what happened to them during this episode. Everyone pointed out how they were engaged or withdrawn into their own activities, leaving Henry and mother to deal with the situation themselves.

Figure 10.   Mrs. Brown's baking reminds her of the loss of a grandmother

Mrs. Brown was asked what made her go into Henry's room to kiss him. Responding through a role-playing device, she took her crying plasticene figure and backed it out of the room, placing herself in the kitchen where she had been baking "grandma's cookies" (Figure 10). She portrayed herself baking and feeling terribly sad, remembering how she missed her dead grandmother. She explained that the family had been on vacation when her grandparent died and she had difficulty in believing the loss was forever. Through the plasticene figure, Mrs. Brown related her feelings of grief and a sudden need for body contact. It was Henry to whom she turned for emotional comfort. Nancy and Henry both told their mother she should be kissing her husband instead.

Mrs. Brown took the figure and marched it out to the plasticene Mr. Brown to give him a kiss. Mr. Brown's figure shrugged her away. He said if he hadn't heard the figures thinking out loud he would probably push his wife away because he was busy with the car. An important discussion ensued around the family's need to be more expressive of their inner feelings.

Clarifying Communication

Returning to the issue of Mrs. Brown and her relationship to her son, the therapist asked Mrs. Brown to *portray your feelings when Henry told you* to stop kissing him and for Henry to draw *what you are thinking when mother kisses you.*

Mrs. Brown picked up the plasticene figure of herself and placed a little heart on the chest. She said her feelings were hurt when her son shouted at her to "Stop." In turn, Henry's picture showed him yelling "stop" while he was thinking, "she treats me like a baby, I wish she would let me be grownup." With Henry's and Nancy's help, the therapist explained that what Mrs. Brown thought was a gesture of rejection was actually her son's age-appropriate need to distance himself from her in an attempt to individuate.

THIRD WEEK

Family Treatment Goals

In the third week of family art therapy, the participants were asked to *create your goals in therapy.* Mr. Brown began to organize a mural. Remembering how his wife and son were once caught short on paper, he marked off equal space for each person.

Mrs. Brown used fine, subtly toned oil pastels to form a unified design. She titled her portion "Blending." She said each color represented a family member; her goal was "let's get together." She hoped everyone could be comfortable and understanding of one another.

Gloria drew a campfire. She wrote, "we can go camping and not fiet" (sic).

Henry drew himself in bed. He said it meant "not going to bed mad." During the discussion, the therapist mentioned the bed may also represent his desire to stop bed-wetting.

Mr. Brown used a photo of a happy family and a telephone under which he printed "Better communication." Nancy drew her father as a king, which depicted her goal of getting father to loosen his reins for he ruled the household "with too much strictness."

Mr. Brown's method of not dealing with his daughter's complaint was to point out to Henry that his drawing was lopsided. The art therapist interpreted the timing of Mr. Brown's remark.

The gestalt of the family goals was positive. The parents and Gloria were viewing therapy goals in terms of making improvements among all the family members. Henry was interested in helping himself and, although Nancy complained about her father, the therapist wondered aloud if part of this message might bring about negotiations between Mr. Brown and his daughter.

Individual Concepts

Several family members referred back to mother's "blending" picture. They wanted mother to explain exactly what she meant by her phrase "let's get together." Rather than let mother give an immediate answer, the therapist decided it would be valuable to check out individual perceptions of this thought. She asked the participants to create their own artwork which showed *what "let's get together" means to you.* Nancy drew two pictures (Figure 11A). One was of a heart with five people joining hands;

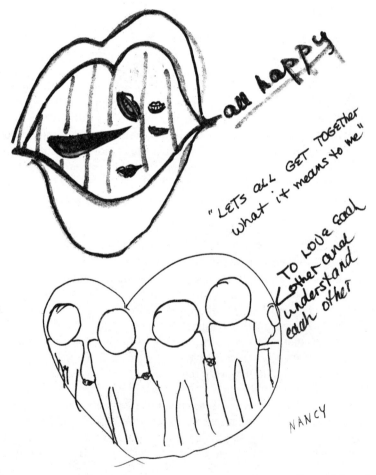

Figure 11A.   "Let's go together" means love and understanding and happiness
to older daughter

underneath she wrote "to love and understand each other." The second was a drawing of a large smile with five small photos of mouths pasted onto it, the picture meant "everyone happy."

Mother made a collage (Figure 11B) with a group of people sitting around a table; a hand was encircling them. She indicated its meaning as "touching each other—feeling our needs—expressing feelings. The hand belongs to Mrs. Landgarten."

Mr. Brown selected a picture (Figure 11C) of a tremendous stack of dirty dishes. Next to it, in bold print he wrote "why don't we wash our dirty dishes and say what we mean?" His collage included another picture of a clock being touched by a woman's hand, accompanied by the words "to be able to spend our time together without getting out of hand." When he talked about his picture he added, "let's all get together also means without blowing our minds, I'm the worst offender." Henry refused to do a picture; instead he played with the plasticene. Father was furious about Henry's lack

Figure 11B.   Touching each other and understanding needs is mother's interpretation

of participation, saying it "was costing a lot of money." Gloria selected a picture (Figure 11D) of a family at the beach.

The family at first discussed the similarity of the meaning of "Let's get together." Then they addressed themselves to the dirty dishes. Henry refused to participate; he was sure the picture referred to him.

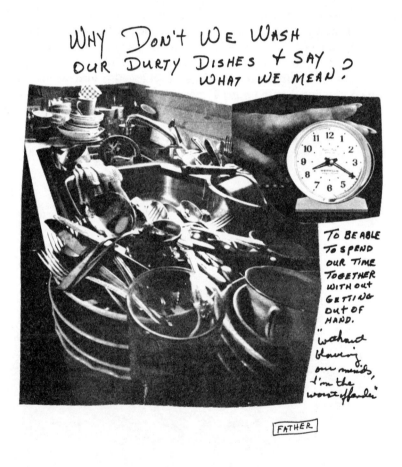

Figure 11C. Confrontation and spending quiet time together is father's version

Gloria "at the beach

Figure 11D.   Enjoying free time is Gloria's meaning

SECOND MONTH

Identification and Projection

Childhood self-perceptions, on the part of the parents, may offer information on identification and projection. To offer the family and the therapist insight on this issue, the family members were asked to *draw a scene when you were younger.* The parents were instructed to *draw yourself at an age similar to one of your children.*

Without hesitation, Mr. Brown drew himself (Figure 12A) at Henry's age, in a scene where his father was yelling at him for "doing everything wrong." He was being sent to carry out the trash and to help his mother. Mr. Brown's scene was similar to the one which he reported during the initial meeting. It became obvious that he projected his own problem child role onto his son. Mr. Brown began to realize that he placed his son in the very role which he had played and so bitterly resented.

Mrs. Brown drew herself (Figure 12B) at age 12 in a scene where she was being hugged by her mother. She explained that her father died when she was 10 years old, leaving her very close to her mother. Mrs. Brown reported that her mother had always been sensitive to her feelings, just as she was to Henry's. Upon further investigation, it became apparent that a three-

Figure 12A.   Mr. Brown remembers his father yelling at him in his youth

generational symbiosis existed. Mrs. Brown was tied to her mother as well
as to her son. Her fear of separation held her a dependent captive.

Nancy's picture showed herself at age eight, happily taking dancing
lessons. Gloria's picture also portrayed a joyful time at her sixth birthday.

Henry showed himself age 10. However, he was unable to identify the
reason for selecting that age. It was Nancy who remembered that was when
Henry's dog, Spark, was killed. Henry teared up as he recalled the death of
his dog.

Figure 12B.   Mrs. Brown remembers closeness to her mother due to father's death

Loss

Deciding to stay with the issue of loss, the art therapist asked the family to create artwork which depicted *someone or something important which is gone*. Henry drew his dog, Gloria grieved a doll that broke, Nancy represented a close friend who had moved away, Mrs. Brown mourned her grandmother, and Mr. Brown drew a co-worker who was dying of cancer. The family members realized that they all suffered from losses which were painful to them. However, they were comforted by relating their sadness.

Mourning

The following week, the mourning process was continued. The family was asked to make a mural together on *feeling sad because of people or things which we lost* (Figure 13). This was the first time that each family member drew on his/her own part of the page, then connected to the others in a complementary way. The family was profoundly affected by a mutually empathic experience.

Figure 13.   Family draws mural to express mutual feelings of sadness

THIRD MONTH

Exploration of Concerns

Children are often cognizant of their parents' worries, whether or not the parental concerns are openly discussed. Laying out the family problems gives the children a sense of relief and the parents a greater awareness of the messages which they convey to the children. In a session where Mr. and Mrs. Brown hinted that something was bothering them, the family was asked to *portray what this family worries about.*

Mr. Brown used the pasticene to model: an auto, which stood for Nancy's staying out late when she drove the car; a book, for his concern over Henry's school attendance; and a computer, as a symbol for his job which he felt was in jeopardy. Mrs. Brown formed a clock, reflecting that she, too, was concerned about Nancy's late hours, and a thermometer, showing her apprehension about her mother's ill health. Nancy made a butterfly to convey her qualms about her grades in biology. Henry (Figure 14) modeled a bed, which portrayed his concern about bed-wetting (although he reported it had decreased considerably), a dollar sign representing his worry about the family's finances, and a boxing glove indicating his concerns

Figure 14.   Henry's bedwetting portrays his worry

about his mother's and father's arguments. Gloria made a purse—she thought her parents were worried about being broke.

Mr. and Mrs. Brown couldn't understand where Henry and Gloria "got those ideas." When the entire family entered into a discussion around money matters, the children accused their father of conveying double messages on this issue, backing up their accusation with examples. For instance, Mr. Brown would claim "we haven't a cent left in the bank account," yet later he would take the family out to the theater. At times he had scolded his son for having wrecked his jeans, saying "I'm going broke clothing you kids"; however, a few days later he told Nancy to buy a pretty dress for a family affair. He often bawled his wife out for cooking an expensive type of meat, but shortly after dinner he would go to the ice cream parlor to buy a half gallon of expensive hand-packed ice cream. Mr. Brown was inundated by the examples. He admitted he had never realized how often he contradicted himself around the issue of money.

The therapist told Mr. Brown that some of his messages were guilt-provoking. The children were encouraged to tell their father how he could reprimand them without letting it become a blame game. The therapist also encouraged Mr. Brown to address himself to the difference between "feeling broke" and "being broke" to clarify the children's worry about the family financial situation.

FOURTH MONTH

Gloria: Defining Her Role

In numerous sessions Gloria played the role (as in the initial diagnostic drawing) of the "enhancer." She repeatedly snuggled close to the person who expressed sadness. The family began to notice how Gloria drew pictures for anyone whom she sensed was in pain. Nancy pointed out how her little sister acted like the "nurse" in the family. Although everyone agreed, they shifted to mention what a joy Gloria was. The art therapist brought the family's attention back to a discussion of Gloria, the "little nurse." The participants struggled with Gloria's need to fulfill this role. They knew that when alliances were formed, Gloria was seen as a free agent; perhaps she was the only one left to observe the family's dynamics and vulnerability. The family reminisced how very often Gloria's insight and sensitivity caused her to step in and comfort her parents or siblings. The family decided if they learned to pay attention, rather than talk, Gloria would be relieved of her designated role. The therapist led the family into a discussion on mutual nurturance.

FIFTH MONTH

Uncovering Misconceptions of a Family Secret

The therapist noticed a repetition of fetus images, appearing in the artwork of Mr. and Mrs. Brown and their son. At one point she mentioned her observation and asked the family if it held any special meaning. Each person claimed there was no intent other than the overt meaning which had been explained. The therapist pressed for free associations. Although the family seemed blocked at first, father finally admitted he had wanted a fourth child. Mrs. Brown broke out in a torrent of tears as she reported she had miscarried a fourth child and was no longer capable of bearing children.When the therapist asked for more specific information about the miscarriage, both parents were reluctant to talk. After a brief silence, Henry ventured to say, "It was all my fault." He explained how he had left his toys around one night when his mother was pregnant and she tripped and lost the baby.

Mr. and Mrs. Brown were amazed that Henry remembered the incident, especially since no one, including husband and wife, had ever discussed it. The therapist gave each person a piece of plasticene "to play with" and encouraged the family to talk about the aborted fetus. As the family recalled the details of the event, Mr. Brown constantly squeezed his piece of platicene, Mrs. Brown rolled out a ball shape which she repeatedly patted, Henry poked away at the plasticene with his finger, Nancy created a hot dog, and Gloria made a "jigsaw puzzle."

When the family finished talking about the miscarriage, they were asked to identify a feeling or a thought to the forms they had created in plasticene. Mr. Brown immediately said he was "still angry because his wife couldn't have any more children." Mrs. Brown revealed that she had never talked about the lost baby. She recalled that the nurse had told her she had lost "a boy." She had so much wanted another son to complete her family. Mrs. Brown went on to tell Henry that she did not miscarry because of his toys. She had a physical problem from the beginning of her pregnancy and her doctor had predicted the miscarriage; in fact, he had advised her to abort the fetus due to complications around her health. Mrs. Brown explained that she had experienced immense pain that night; in fact, she was on her way to phone the doctor to ask him to meet her at the hospital when she tripped. The fall was definitely not the cause of the miscarriage.

Mr. Brown was shocked to hear that his wife was on the way to phone the doctor that night. He had slept soundly that night and had always thought the fall had precipitated the labor pains.

Nancy remembered the miscarriage. She recalled that while her mother was in the hospital her father had taken her to Disneyland where he bought her a hot dog. The therapist asked herself if the symbol represented Nancy's oedipal conflict. Receiving a reward while mother was in the hospital may have exacerbated her fantasies.

Gloria's plasticene jigsaw puzzle seemed a message about the family secret which had never before been discussed.

The family was sad but relieved to let go of their hurt, guilt and blame around the misconceptions of the event which had happened years ago. Mrs. Brown said she realized her patting gesture on the plasticene was significant of her own mourning for the lost child and the children she would never have.

SIXTH MONTH

Nancy: Demand for Freedom

One day, as the family entered the art therapy room, Nancy announced her desire to discuss her problem around her lack of freedom. The family was asked to *create something which shows your attitude around Nancy's demand for freedom.*

Mr. Brown (Figure 15A) used a paper bag. He drew two faces, one on each side. One face looked young and pure, the other was heavily made up with a "joint in her mouth." Nancy's father said he was concerned about Nancy's new friends—the boys were older, called late at night and were probably into drugs. He was worried about his daughter's activities outside of the house. Mr. Brown claimed Nancy never called if she was not going to keep her curfew. He thought she wanted more freedom than she was ready to handle.

Mrs. Brown cut out several magazine pictures and threw them in a bag, as she said her daughter did not reveal herself. She thought Nancy kept a secret life which was not shared with the family. Mrs. Brown wondered if there would be "less fuss if we trusted Nancy a little more."

Henry (Figure 15B) drew his sister taking up a great deal of space. He said lately his parents seemed to be giving more of their attention to Nancy. He felt sorry for her.

Gloria (Figure 15C) drew her sister all dressed up with high heels. She said her sister was as big as her mother and that mommy and daddy should treat her like she was big.

Nancy drew pictures of the family. Underneath each person she wrote a message. To illustrate—mom was portrayed with her hands on her hips as she said to Nancy, "Get to school on time, and get better grades." The message to her mother was "I would probably do better if you left me alone." Father was drawn with no hands and a very large necktie. Nancy's statement to him was "Stop accusing me of things I haven't done, stop yelling at me. Instead, talk to me. Stop hurting me when we play fight." Henry was told, "Stop telling mom things that aren't true about me." Gloria was drawn as a doll.

The family was asked to respond to the artwork. Nancy told her parents that she only smoked one joint on Saturday nights. If they didn't accuse her

Figure 15A.   Mr. Brown sees Nancy as having been a good girl but is concerned about her current social life

of keeping secrets, then she wouldn't feel the need to do so. She was angry about the Saturday night 12:00 curfew, saying 12:30 was more practical. The family was encouraged to negotiate. The parents agreed to change the curfew to see if Nancy's attitude improved. They asked Nancy to bring her friends over to the house more often, saying that if they knew them better perhaps they would feel more confident when she was with them. Everyone agreed to discuss the outcome of the negotiation in the weeks to come.

As difficult as it was, Mr. Brown worked very hard on letting Nancy have more distance. He began to see how hanging on was antagonizing his daughter. In one session he drew lemons and peaches to depict how their "sour" relationship was beginning to improve.

Figure 15B.   Henry sees Nancy as taking up all the family space

Figure 15C.   Gloria perceives Nancy as grown-up

SEVENTH MONTH

Reassessing Treatment Goals

The Brown family members became more direct in their communication. They seemed determined to change their mode of interaction. As insights were gained, it was beneficial for the family to redefine their goals in therapy.

Family members were asked to *paint abstract symbols which represent what family and self changes you want to make, and good things about your family.*

Table 1 compares the response of family members.

A discussion revolved around the similarities in the responses. The therapist helped the family members accept one another's statements without becoming defensive. She reminded the family of the original goals

TABLE 1

Member	Family Changes	Self Changes	Good Things About Family
Father	1) Henry stop starting trouble. 2) My wife not to baby my son. 3) Get along better as a family.	1) Be more patient.	1) We like going to the ballgames.
Mother	1) Husband stop harassing Henry. 2) "Let's get together." 3) Get Henry back to school. 4) Nancy to settle down.	1) Tell husband when I'm angry. 2) Have more fun out of life.	1) We are intelligent. 2) We care about each other. 3) We are here in art therapy.
Henry	1) Father stop picking on me.	1) Stop wetting the bed. 2) I'm mad all the time.	1) My sisters are nice.
Nancy	1) Want my father to stop being so strict. 2) Better communication.	1) Do better at school. 2) Get a job.	1) People are here to change.
Gloria	1) Want do do more things together.	1) Not to eat so much.	1) We have fun when we make things.

in the therapy artwork and noted how each person now took more self-responsibility and was more direct in communicating feelings and needs.

EIGHTH TO TENTH MONTHS

At the beginning of treatment, hostility was frequently displayed; much of it was displaced and never discussed. Family members would poke away at each other with snide remarks, which were left hanging, with no verbal response. To clarify the source of anger and to objectify its displacement, the art therapist asked the family members to *draw your anger*. When they finished, they were instructed to *give it to someone in your family*. This technique was offered in the beginning and again in the final stages of treatment as a tool for assessing possible gains. By coincidence, in both sessions Mr. Brown was held up at work and arrived late, lending greater validity to the comparative pictures.

The pictures were discussed by the participants with the art therapist making therapeutic interventions to facilitate exploration and insight in each session. Table 2 gives information on the "anger symbol," to whom the anger was given, and comments made by the family member.

ELEVENTH MONTH

Comparative Perceptions of the Family

Towards the end of therapy, a second *draw your family* request was made. This was used with the family as comparative data pertaining to change in perceptions and attitudes (see Table 3).

The pictures show a general shift toward equality. The sizes and the alignment are more similar. The second drawings reveal the feeling of greater competency through more complete figures. The issue of identification as seen in similar ways of dressing has shifted more towards the father/son and mother/daughter.

The comments on the first drawings were made mostly by father. He negated his son and self and complimented Nancy. In the second drawing, the family's positive comments were made by various members. There was an air of joviality. The family's interaction and their family drawing style verified gains which were being integrated towards a productive, functioning system.

TABLE 2

ANGER

Picture One in First
Month of Treatment:

Picture Two in Tenth
Month of Treatment:

HENRY					
Symbol	Given To	Comments	Symbol	Given To	Comments
0	0	0	Stop sign	mother	She bothers me about homework.

Remarks: Henry refused to participate. He was sure he would get everyone's angry picture.

Remarks: Henry began to understand cause and effect. He learned to separate out his anger. Instead of feeling hopeless, he would check out and respond to negative remarks.

FATHER					
zero	wife	none-laughed	clock	self	Got caught on the phone at work, arrived late to therapy session.

Remarks: Father was angry with therapist for insisting upon seeing the entire family when Henry was the designated patient.

Remarks: Father accepted responsibility for his own shortcomings. He was consistent in placing it on the appropriate source and dealing with it.

MOTHER					
scribble	torn in half: Nancy and Henry	remarked on their disheveled appearance	pointed fore finger	husband	Being late to therapy session.

Remarks: Mother was angry with her husband for his negative attitude about family therapy and for being late. Also, she was angry at Henry for failing to participate in this exercise.

Remarks: Mother learned to confront her husband directly, instead of displacing her anger on her children or using Henry as her vehicle for angry communication.

TABLE 2 (continued)

ANGER

Picture One in First
Month of Treatment:

Picture Two in Tenth
Month of Treatment:

Symbol	Given To	Comments	Symbol	Given To	Comments
		NANCY			
red and blue arrows	Henry	gave the anger to Henry as they were there to help him, yet he refused to participate	purple graph	Henry	She began to give it to father for screaming at home so much. However, she remembered he was changing. She was miffed by Henry's insistence to be driven to Scouts.

Remarks: Nancy was also angry with father for coming late.

Remarks: Nancy almost used old perceptions for anger. However, she could retrieve her emotions to place them in perspective.

		GLORIA			
lips	Nancy	Nancy would not let her play with her makeup	automobile	father	Angry with daddy for getting to the therapy session late.

Remarks: Gloria's symbol was not directly related to angry feelings. This may be due to Gloria being too young to understand what is expected in the way of symbols, or possibly a denial of anger.

Remarks: Gloria had learned to draw symbols directly related to her feelings. The issue of Gloria's denial as a defense was substantiated throughout the therapy and again through this technique.

TABLE 3

FIRST DRAWING	SECOND DRAWING

Henry's Pictures

FIGURE PLACEMENT · FIGURE PLACEMENT

Gloria	Mother		Father	Nancy	Gloria	Mother	Nancy	Father	Self
		Self							

Style: Everyone except himself has facial features and appendages. Mother, father and Gloria have their hands in their pockets.

Self: No facial features. Entire figure colored in yellow. Has an appearance of an effigy.

Comments: When father saw his son's picture he said, "Gosh! You draw as rotten as I do!"

Style: Everyone drawn appropriately including himself. Father and himself are drawn with their hands in their pockets.

Comments: *Nancy said it was a "pretty good drawing."

*Therapist pointed out the comparison. First picture showed him as different from the rest of the family. Second picture has him similar to the rest of the family.

Nancy's Pictures

FIGURE PLACEMENT · FIGURE PLACEMENT

Father	Self		Henry	Mother	Father	Self	Mother	Henry	Gloria
		Gloria							

Style: Well drawn. She and father are the same color, self facial features reveal narcissism.

Comments: Father complimented Nancy on her drawing talent.

Style: Similar to the first, except Nancy and father are different colors.

Comments: Several members noted Nancy was more colorful than the rest of the family.

TABLE 3 (continued)

FIRST DRAWING	SECOND DRAWING

Gloria's Pictures

FIGURE PLACEMENT   FIGURE PLACEMENT

Father	Mother	Nancy	Henry	Self			Self	Nancy
						Father	Henry	Mother

Style: Father, no feet. Mother, no hands. Henry, no hands or feet.

Comments: Family members were pleased with Gloria's participation. Mr. and Mrs. Brown had their doubts about the necessity for Gloria to attend the family art therapy sessions.

Style: The family was presented in a scene where father and Henry were gardening, mother barbecuing, Nancy sunning herself and herself playing with the dog.

Comments: Henry said he liked Gloria's originality.

Father's Pictures

FIGURE PLACEMENT   FIGURE PLACEMENT

Nancy	Self	Wife	Gloria		Nancy	Self	Wife	Gloria	Henry
				Henry					

Style: Family members drawn as stick figures, no hands, feet or facial features. No color.

Comments: Father apologized for his drawing. Gloria told her father it was "really good."

Style: Stick figures. Included facial features, hands and feet. Henry and himself wore ties. Females wore skirts. Curly hairdo.

Comments: Family jokingly supported father's improvement in drawing.

TABLE 3 (continued)

FIRST DRAWING	SECOND DRAWING

Mother's Pictures

FIGURE PLACEMENT   FIGURE PLACEMENT

Nancy	Husband	Self	Henry	Gloria	Nancy	Husband	Self	Henry	Gloria

Style: Sketch quality. Included all appropriate features. Emphasis on the male's crotch. Everyone has on jeans and belts. Gloria and her own breasts are emphasized. *Comments:* Mrs. Brown said she purposely oversized Nancy and Henry because the took up so much family space. Henry and Nancy were disgruntled by her remarks.	*Style:* Firmer line quality. Women are wearing dresses. Men have on suits and ties. Father's pants have a delineated fly. *Comments:* Mother said she "dressed up the whole family" with a fantasy of going out somewhere nice.

TWELFTH MONTH

Family's Summation of Treatment

During the terminating phase of treatment, the family members were asked to use the media of their choice to convey *what family art therapy meant to you.*

It was interesting to note that the males responded to one medium, the females to another. The gesture was indicative of the shifting alliances within the family structure. As mother loosened her symbiotic tie to her son, she became more open to a relationship with Nancy, while father, giving his eldest daughter more autonomy, found himself more available to Henry.

Mr. Brown combined drawing with magazine photos. His picture (Figure 16A) showed the Brown family all holding hands as they were walking away from the art therapist's office. The artwork was titled, "Let's Go Together and Do Together." He explained that it was in contrast to his first picture showing his perception of "Let's Get Together;" at that time he portrayed a pile of dirty dishes with the message that the family must expose themselves in order to go through a cleansing process. Mr. Brown proudly proclaimed, "Coming to art therapy had a real payoff." Henry laughed and teased his

Figure 16A.   Mr. Brown pleased with art psychotherapy treatment

father as he reminded him that references to money matters were no longer supposed to be a part of dad's style.

Mrs. Brown used two plasticene scenes to create "before and after therapy." The first scene was of a house collapsing. She said the roof was falling in, due to troubles with Henry, Nancy, her husband and herself; everyone was angry all of the time. The "after" scene (Figure 16B) showed all the children and herself going off to school and Mr. Brown heading for work.

Mrs. Brown explained that Henry was attending school, Nancy's grades were better, the family was treating Gloria more like a little girl than a mother, and she herself had been motivated to do more for herself. She had enrolled herself in a real estate course. Mrs. Brown said her husband had worries about his job, but at least they could talk about it. She was pleased with their communication. "Of course," she said, "life still isn't a bowl of cherries, but at least we aren't upset all the time."

Figure 16B.   Mrs. Brown pleased with her own involvement and a return to school

Nancy (Figure 16C) made a plasticene head with very large eyes and ears. In the hair she stuck a felt marker, oil pastel, paint brush and scissors. She titled it "Let Your Hair Down in Heart Therapy." Nancy felt her parents were doing better in paying attention to their children's needs, rather than their own. However, she wondered if their improved interactions would continue after treatment ended.

Gloria (Figure 16D) created a plasticene art therapy office. She showed the family sitting around the table with Mrs. Landgarten. Each person had a small piece of paper in front of them. She said they were drawing their problems. She titled the scene "A Good Place."

Henry (Figure 16E) used the picture of a surgeon. On the door of the operating room he printed "Mrs. Landgarten, M.A. A.T.R." Next to it he drew a boy lifting weights and another of his father and himself playing ball. Across the top he wrote "Mrs. Landgarten Helped Dad and I Get Along." Picturing the therapist as an omnipotent surgeon who cut away the family's difficulties, Henry revealed his transference to the therapist. He attributed the family's growth to be as a result of her magical influence on his parents. The therapist placed the credit for the family's growth back onto them, where it belonged. Her reply was a reminder of their commitment and dedication to change. The next week she had the family look over their art-

Figure 16C.   Nancy states, "let your hair down in heart therapy"

Figure 16D.   Gloria finds drawing problems beneficial

Figure 16E.   Henry is grateful to therapist for improving family relations

work to review the highlights of their gains. It is important for the therapist to reinforce the family's effort as its own agent for change and the artwork is presented as evidence of this statement.

CHAPTER 4

Single-Parent Families in Multiple Family Art Therapy

INTRODUCTION

Due to the large increase in divorce rates, the need for treatment services to newly structured families has been recognized. The brief service art psychotherapy approach places a major focus on the issues of separation and loss and on developing communication skills for the changed family unit.

The ideal group is large enough for interaction to take place among several families. A workable size consists of three single parents, either mother or father, and their children. Initially, the parent is seen in a classical verbal interview, then each family is seen separately for an art therapy diagnostic interview. This is followed by six multifamily art therapy group sessions, which meet for an hour and a half. When the group terminates, a final session is held with each family separately.

In some cases the nine-week course of art therapy is a crisis intervention, which functions as a complete form of service. At other times it serves as an extended diagnostic procedure with recommendations for further treatment.

Group art psychotherapy provides a variety of communication experiences where group members can relate and explore their dynamics in relationship to their parent or child, and/or siblings. Parents also benefit from observing their child interacting with peers and other parents. In addition, the total group experience is valuable due to the problems which the single-parent households have in common.

Within the art psychotherapy approach, both structured and spontaneous artwork is created. The participants work on individual and joint projects. Joint projects may involve single families, the peer group and/or the total group.

In working with members of single-parent family households, specific themes are introduced: loss, separation, as well as guilt and anger regarding the separated parent or spouse. The group also deals with the parent members' frequent sense of helplessness and frustration over their lack of freedom. However, the manifest problems which the designated patient displays may shift the issues which are worked upon in various groups. Therefore, the techniques which are offered *do not proceed in a consistent order, nor are the presented directives always used. Creative variations are essential to treat the needs of each group.*

Methodology for diagnosing family systems has been previous described; the total six-week treatment plan is discussed here. The group described consisted of four single parents and their children. Illustrations of each art psychotherapy session are presented, along with objectives for each step of the procedure and working suggestions.

FIRST WEEK

Group Warm-up

Refer to Chapter 2, pp. 25-26 for detailed *warm-up* instructions. This technique is a simple method for everyone in the group to learn each other's names and to break through some of the anxiety connected to an initiating session. All the group members participate in drawing, then share their pictures. This procedure facilitates a commitment to group work.

Reason for Treatment

The warm-up is followed by a directive to create a collage which displays *why are you here for therapy?*

The collage medium is particularly useful while initiating group art therapy, for it tends to lessen the anxiety level related to artistic performance. The directive itself encourages each person to objectify and to share the reasons for seeking treatment.

This procedure is usually followed up with an abstract drawing depicting the feelings which were evoked during the personal information-sharing process. In a six-week group, it has proven valuable to immediately lay out the participants' reasons for seeking professional help. The therapeutic

Figure 17.   Mother reveals her own needs to the group

brief service pace is both rapid and structured, in order to cover the important issues which single-parent families have in common.

Example

Judy Tillson, an 11-year-old girl, was a withholding child. She refused to express her emotions or thoughts and was generally described as "standoffish." In response to the question regarding therapy, Judy ignored the collage instructions and drew a picture which totally ignored the issue. In contrast, her mother, aware of her own problems (Figure 17), displayed an image of "scissors" to depict her wish "to cut out the lack of understanding" between herself and her daughter. Another picture showed an ostrich with its head in the sand, which illustrated her tendency to avoid painful situations. Also included was a photograph of an obese woman, which represented Mrs. Tillson's "desire to lose weight."

The collage gave Judy a chance to realize that her mother saw art therapy as a place to get help for their relationship as well as her own personal problems. This acknowledgement alleviated Judy's fears of being *the* family member who had *all* of the problems.

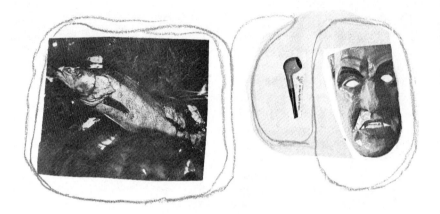

Figure 18.   Lack of contact results in child's emptiness

SECOND WEEK

Advantages and Disadvantages

It is profitable for family members to confront and declare the benefits and detriments of having a one-parent household. Therefore, the author requested the children to *draw and use collage materials to show the good and bad parts about having only one parent at home.* The parents were asked to use the same media to display the *good and bad aspects of being a single parent.*

Example

Judy Tillson's five-year-old brother, Shawn, used a picture of a woman hugging someone to reveal "It's *good* to have my mommy to myself." For the *bad part* (Figure 18), the boy pasted a pipe and a mask to represent his father and a "dead fish," which related how empty and devastated he was on Sunday when he didn't hear from his dad. After Shawn explained the collage, his mother, unable to tolerate the child's pain, made numerous attempts to deny his feelings of rejection on Sunday by reminding him of the fun he, Judy and herself had together on weekends. However, the therapist and the group used the "dead fish" picture as a focal point to help mother acknowledge her son's overwhelming feeling of abandonment.

The picture which Mrs. Tillson created was of a woman with a wedding ring on her finger, which revealed the *bad part* of being primarily financially responsible for the family. The *good part* displayed a mother and her two children hugging; this symbolized the loving closeness between herself and her children. This portrayal precipitated Shawn's admission of guilt feelings over his parents' separation. The boy believed he had caused the marital separation. This issue was dealt with by his sister and several other children in the group who were similarly affected by their parents' divorce. It is essential for parents to clarify their reasons for divorce in an attempt to alleviate the child's unjustified feelings of guilt.

THIRD WEEK

Separation Fantasies

"Free choice" artworks often display the unspoken concerns of group members. The participants were given plasticene and asked to *make whatever you want. It can be created in an abstract or realistic manner.*

Example

Buddy Rodriquez, a nine-year-old boy, formed a "snowflake" out of construction paper (Figure 19). During the discussion period, the child explained that this symbol conveyed his concern about a family who was absent from the art therapy group. The snowflake represented some catastrophic event which prevented the family's appearance. The child reported his worries, "maybe an accident or they went back East and got caught in a snowstorm—it must be something bad or they would be here."

In this instance, the initial "free choice" revealed the child's worry about the missing group family member. However, in each art therapy session where some member or family of the group is absent, there is a request to *create something which shows where you think the person or family is and what they are doing.* The discussion provides additional working-through in reference to the separation theme pertinent to one-parent families.

Example

In response to the "free choice" sculpture, Mr. Rodriquez, Buddy's father, elected to mold three chairs (Figure 20). Two were occupied; the third was vacant. When questioned about its meaning, Mr. Rodriquez said

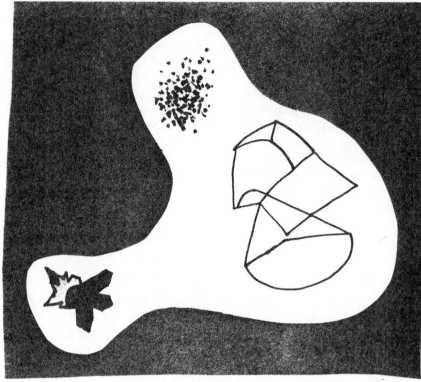

Figure 19.   Snowflake symbolizes boy's concern about absent family

Figure 20.   Empty chair conjured up feelings of isolation

he was not aware of any conscious message. However, the empty seat conjured up numerous free associations by other participants. The majority of group members, parents and children alike, ventilated their emotions around the issue of divorce. The empty chair evoked feelings of: emptiness, rejection, loneliness, being forgotten, anger and hate. The children expressed their desire to have both mother and father in their home. A few youngsters blamed the parent participant for denying them a complete household. The adults presented their wish to have a significant other for companionship and to share in family responsibilities. For several members, this was the first time their thoughts and emotions were openly discussed.

Cross-generational and peer understanding engendered a cohesive group spirit and granted most of the participants a measure of relief and comfort.

FOURTH WEEK

Phenomena of Giving and Receiving

This particular session pertains to important issues which evolve out of the group. For instance, one group had several members who were withholding and unresponsive emotionally, while other participants had difficulty in accepting any positive feedback. In this situation, the following instructions were given to each person: *Make any kind of object out of plasticene.* Upon completion the directions stated: *Give the piece you made to someone in the group.* After this procedure, participants explored their feelings around the theme of "giving" and how they felt about parting with the object which they had made. Then emotions which were evoked through the "receiving" process were examined. Questions which stimulated self-exploration were asked, such as, "Did you like what you got?" "Were you surprised?" If you received several objects or possibly none, "How did you feel?"

Example

Mrs. Tillson made a face mask and handed it to her daughter, Judy. The parent said it symbolized how she hides her own feelings. Then, speaking to Judy, she added, "You mask your feelings too; you must have learned it from me. The mask belongs to both of us." By coincidence her daughter made "two snow people" (Figure 21). In agreement with the symbols of mother and child, the rest of the members voiced the difficulty they had in getting close to this pair. They pointed out how their friendly overtures had received little or no response.

Figure 21.   Mother and daughter have difficulty in showing feelings

FIFTH WEEK

Dealing with Termination

Although the number of remaining art therapy sessions is mentioned at each meeting, the emphasis in the fifth week is on preparing to end the group experience. A directive is given to *express your feelings about this being the next to the last session.* The drawings or collages are made individually. As each person shares his or her picture, it is pasted onto a large sheet of paper and becomes a group project.

Example

Highly motivated, Mr. Rodriquez and his son, Buddy, had made positive changes. In response to the subject of termination, Mr. Rodriquez declared his anger because the group experience was ending. He related, "I feel as though I'm losing some of the tools I had to work with; it's a helpless feeling." This father used the image of a monkey in the snow to represent, "it's cold outside and I want to insulate my problems again." Mr. Rodriquez ventilated his sense of isolation as he expressed his loss and fear of regression for himself and his son.

Buddy, an extremely infantilized nine-year-old, had made remarkable progress in six weeks. After declaring his problem in the group he had stopped drinking from a baby bottle—with the help of peer suggestion, he substituted his oral needs with Pepsi Cola. The child proudly reported that he was dressing himself (a new accomplishment) and had improved in school. A collage drawing (Figure 22) expressed his sadness and the fact that he "doesn't fel (sic) too good." Although very fond of the therapist, he expressed ambivalent feelings as he showed a boy fist-fighting. Similar to his father, he showed his anger toward the therapist for ending the group. Nevertheless, with a great deal of pride, he explained the drawing of a zig-zag line which meant, "I've unzipped my feelings here in art therapy."

SIXTH WEEK

Initial Step for Closure

The creation of an *individual,* then a *group, sculpture of plasticene* is a technique for giving closure to the group. Therefore, each person is instructed to *make something out of the clay which expresses your feelings*

Figure 22.   Boy unzipped feelings in art therapy group, is sad and angry about termination

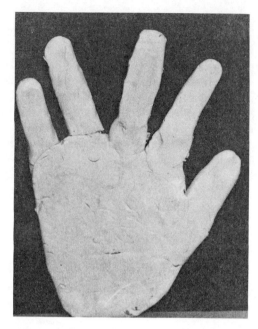

Figure 23.   Last session—woman creates hand to represent final contact

about the art therapy group ending today. The form can be an abstract shape or one which can be recognized. When everyone is finished, individuals randomly volunteer to place their artwork on an extra-large single piece of paper, it becomes part of a group sculpture.

Whether or not people speak during this process depends on the therapist's sensitivity to the mood of the group and the type of closure which seems most appropriate. Discussion revolves around each individual's feelings about the group ending.

Example

Mrs. Stefano made a clay hand and said, "I would like to do 12 hands together to represent the group (Figure 23). The group has been helpful. I'm sorry to see it ending."

In the Tillson family, the mother made an intermeshing abstract form, which meant "Our family is more together in the last month." Judy, her 11-year-old daughter, made a braid which exemplified, "The three lines, like our family, show we are closer now." Five-year-old Shawn shared a sun with a down-turned mouth; he said, "I'm sad we are going to stop. I like to come here."

Figure 24.   Boy thinks attending group therapy was "a bunch of crap"

The resistant group member, Martin Simpson, an 11-year-old boy, made (Figure 24) a toilet filled with feces which he declared showed his pleasure about discontinuing therapy because as far as he was concerned, "It was a bunch of crap."

Sustaining Closure

To sustain the work on termination and separation, felt pens or crayons are chosen to draw on the large paper upon which the plasticene figures have been placed. An important factor is that the participants have the opportunity to correct or make some changes, giving them a dimension of control. This exercise also sustains the acknowledgment toward separation. Many times it has a cathartic effect and prepares group members for the next step in their termination or further work in individual or family treatment.

FINAL INDIVIDUAL FAMILY EVALUATION

The last individual family session is a review of what the family members experienced in the art therapy group. They are also asked to assess, their future treatment needs. After this discussion, the therapist offers a directive which is therapeutically appropriate for each individual family.

Example 1

The Simpson family's last interview sounded much like the first with a great deal of chaos and bickering. It is interesting to note that Darren, the designated patient, had subdued his acting-out behavior in school since the beginning of art therapy. The final family session was not devoted to Darren. It dealt with the problem of family members' invading one another's personal space, and the recurring pattern of the children's teasing, fighting and being physically harmed, while their mother passively withdrew.

The Simpsons were given a plastic tray, felt markers and clay (Figure 25). They were instructed to *show on the tray what space you want; then your mother will help make decisions which are fair. She will designate each family member's space with the felt markers.* All of the children wanted

Figure 25.   Marked tray is example of limit setting

more than an equal share of the tray. However, Mrs. Simpson, contrary to her usual position of withdrawal, was encouraged to negotiate her sons' and daughter's space by being an active decision-maker. This was followed by the therapist's request for family members to *make something out of clay or other available materials and place it in the space sectioned off for you by your mother.* A discussion regarding feelings about the experience took place. Its purpose was to bring to consciousness the needed change in communication and decision-making. The clinician gave positive actions reinforcement and pointed out negative, nonproductive or destructive acts. This technique helped Mrs. Simpson understand how she could appropriately set limits and give structure to her family.

Example 2

The Stefano family had worked very hard on improving interactional skills. They had never forgotten their initial family interview, when all of them made isolated cylinders which they titled, "Each person by themselves." Although the paper sculpture was indicative of family dynamics, seven-year-old Gordon had fond memories of the time when his sister, mother, and himself all worked simultaneously to make their constructions. It had left a marked impression on the child, and he asked the art therapist if they could build something together once again.

The contrast in process between the first and the last project displayed the changes which the family had made. In the final session Gordon acted differently. He was able to cooperate and take in suggestions. The Stefano family combined their ideas to create a single paper sculpture (Figure 26) titled "A Vase of Flowers." The family members made their own interpretation. They explained how the flowers stood for their "more pleasant home life" and the vase symbolized the safety of feeling contained, protected and involved with one another.

SUMMARY

Task-oriented art forms serve as a vehicle for observation and change. Families are given the opportunity to gain insight into their mode of communication. Individual feelings and family dynamics are explored through the various art products.

In the six weeks of group art psychotherapy for one-parent families, major themes which have been experienced by all the participants are worked upon. Separation and the difficulties which it encompasses are dealt with through the concrete art form and discussion. Art psychotherapy provides a safe place for participants to openly explore their loss and problems in dealing with a single-parent household.

Figure 26.   Family art task shows greater cooperation and unity between mother
and children

CHAPTER 5

Involvement of Geriatric Family Member

The Stone family case history is an example of how family art therapy was used to focus on a specific problem. It will review this approach as a catalyst for exploring the elderly mother's needs, the reasons for the children's resistance and the problem-solving process.

Mrs. Stone was an 86-year-old woman who found living alone increasingly difficult. She sought advice from a personal friend, who suggested she join her in moving to a retirement apartment. Mrs. Stone seriously considered this change. In spite of her cheerful attitude, her children and grandchildren strongly objected.

Mrs. Stone had formerly attended a number of clinical art therapy sessions at a Center for the Elderly. She contacted the art therapist requesting a limited number of family art therapy sessions to help her with a problem. She attended four sessions, accompanied by her son and daughter.

In the first session, Mrs. Stone's children said they objected to their mother's move because she would be "unhappy." The daughter suggested that her mother move into her home, and the son offered to get his mother a daily househelper. When the family members were asked to draw their feelings, Mrs. Stone expressed herself very easily, but her children were hesitant to get involved with the art media. To lessen their self-consciousness, the art therapist asked the family to make a picture collage which would be titled *"Momma."* Everyone joined in as they quickly put together their artwork; it showed a woman cooking, gardening, driving, hugging children; included, for no apparent reason, was a picture which was identified as "mother in a crowd." The therapist asked the family what "a crowd" meant to them. The daughter said it referred to "strangers."

Mrs. Stone's son and daughter were asked to amplify the meaning of "strangers." To the daughter it meant "people knowing your business"; to her brother it portrayed "what the community thinks about you," whereas to their mother it was "only a group of men and women."

When the therapist asked the family to tie the "stranger" associations up to the picture of *"Momma,"* in a short time the son and daughter confronted themselves with the issue beneath their facade of "mother would be unhappy." They admitted being embarrassed that their friends would perceive them as "uncaring children."

In the second session, the family was asked to produce a picture which showed *Momma's needs on one side of the page* and *children's feelings on the other side.* The product showed a contrast in the two parts as it poignantly revealed Mrs. Stone's son's and daughter's conflict. The children openly explored the difficulties around taking care of their mother, as well as their own emotions.

An important aspect of the third session was revealed through a collage where Mrs. Stone asked her family to create a picture together about her "new place." When her children resisted, she continued on her own (Figure 27). Among other images was a nurse and next to it a drawing of an old bent tree. Although Mrs. Stone claimed she consciously put in the nurse to define the "nurse's office" at the facility, the tree was innocently drawn to create an "outdoor environment." The therapist interpreted the tree as some part of Mrs. Stone herself and asked the elderly woman to elaborate on its placement next to the nurse. The Stone children tried to sabotage their mother's answers, but the therapist held steadfast to the question. Finally, Mrs. Stone shared her worry about accidentally overdosing due to her absentmindedness. She was relieved to know medication would be handed to her in the retirement facility. The family admitted this had also been a concern to them. This led into further discussion of Mrs. Stone's forgetfulness and her difficulties in caring for herself. As the session ended, the Stone children reluctantly agreed to look over the retirement apartment.

Mrs. Stone finalized her decision to enter her new home with her daughter's support. In the last art therapy session she created a scene of herself in her future environment. She made a plasticene afghan draped over a small chair prop (Figure 28). Mrs. Stone said it was "something old on top of something new." She went on to mold herself relaxing in the lounge "where there would always be company."

The Stone children were touched by their mother's artwork. They realized how creative she was and how much she still sought life with zest. Her son mentioned he was ashamed of his minimal involvement in the art media; he

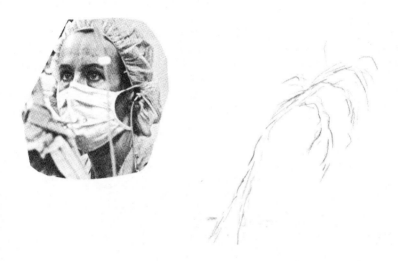

Figure 27. Concern about self-care is communicated by aged mother

Figure 28. Afghan is something old in new environment

saw his resistance as a way of "acting like a stubborn kid." Mr. Stone left the meeting with a promise to give his mother's decision more thought. As the family was ready to depart, Mrs. Stone's daughtter remembered it had been many years since the family "had made something together." She said the art part of the experience had stirred up old memories. Somehow it made her feel closer to her mother and brother. Mrs. Stone felt good about her children's responses and her determination to maintain her decision.

CHAPTER 6

A Child's Symbolic Expression of His Parents' Marital Conflict

INTRODUCTION

The Barnes family case history is an example of combining two modalities—the conventional verbal family treatment and individual art therapy. These approaches were utilized simultaneously by the two clinicians, an art psychotherapist and a psychologist. The co-therapists worked as a family therapy team, encouraging the child to express his feelings through the art in order to supplement his verbal comments.

THE BARNES FAMILY

Seven-year-old Alfred Barnes was born in Canada. He was an only child. He was enuretic and exhibited bizarre facial gestures and infantile and hyperactive behavior both at home and at school. His school performance was poor. Alfred's classmates scapegoated him for being "cuckoo." His provocative manner was expressive of Alfred's barely disguised anxiety.

The family history indicated a great deal of marital conflict. The parents were divided into two enemy camps, each vying for the child's allegiance. Mr. and Mrs. Barnes claimed their marriage was maintained for "the sake of our child."

PREVIOUS ART THERAPY

Alfred made many developmental gains during six months in a latency-age art therapy group. The media and the artwork focus served as an excellent means for self-expression and containment. Alfred was able to tolerate peer feedback when the artwork acted as an intermediary, for it appeared less harsh and more acceptable to him. While in group, the bizarre facial gestures stopped. The boy's actions became more appropriate and the group members began to accept him. When the group ended, the child began individual art therapy treatment. At the same time, Mr. and Mrs. Barnes attended conventional marital therapy with a psychologist.

Alfred was highly motivated towards self-improvement. Within a few months of individual treatment, the enuresis ceased and school reports indicated gains in performance and peer relationships. Alfred's transference to the art therapist was an essential feature in his developmental growth. However, the child's fondness and trust in the therapist elicited competitive feelings on the part of his parents. They refused to understand the relationship in terms of a therapeutic alliance. When Mr. and Mrs. Barnes found this factor intolerable, they sabotaged their son's treatment. Although Alfred's improvement was not fully integrated, his mother and father decided he was "just fine" and no longer had a need for therapy, contrary to the therapist's recommendation. Rather than discontinue therapy altogether, the therapist bargained to keep the family in treatment. She suggested individual treatment for Alfred be terminated in lieu of conventional family therapy with the child "free to draw." The rationale for this recommendation was the parents could expand their conjoint treatment into family therapy. At Mr. and Mrs. Barnes' insistence, they used verbal therapy, whereas their son would continue to draw as an added dimension for communication. Both the art therapist and the psychologist worked with the family.

PARENTAL DISSENSION ELICITS REGRESSION

At the beginning of each session, the art therapist selected the art media and placed it in front of Alfred. The only instructions to him were to create whenever and whatever he wished. The therapist started the initial meeting by asking the Barnes about the week's events. They began by talking about an argument they had over their pet. Alfred drew throughout the session. His first picture was a landscape, and the second was a dog. However, as his parents began to quarrel he began to draw abstract designs. As the argument became heated, Alfred's drawing pace increased until he frantically drew one quick picture after another. Each successive image became more vague than the previous one. The final works were merely smears of color. The therapist interpreted the boy's regression as an anxious response to his parents' arguments.

LOYALTIES: CAUGHT IN THE MIDDLE

In the next meeting, when Mr. and Mrs. Barnes began to fight about their expectations and disappointments, their child drew mother and father fighting. At one point, the couple asked Alfred for his opinion on a household matter. Rather than respond verbally, their son drew himself (Figure 29) between his mother and father and wrote " The answer" on the picture. Again, the art therapist interpreted how the child found himself caught in-between his parents. The gesture was so obvious that Mr. and Mrs. Barnes could not deny the meaning of their child's picture.

Alfred continued to express his response to his parents' marital difficulties. For example, one time when his parents refused to negotiate on a point in question, he portrayed a person with a head so swollen it seemed about to burst. The picture indicated Alfred's psychosomatic reaction. When the parents were confronted with the drawing, the boy verbally validated his headache by saying, "You fight so much my head hurts."

FEAR OF ABANDONMENT

Mrs. Barnes reported a quarrel between herself and her husband in the

Figure 29.   Child feels responsible for interventions

session; she described how he ran out of the house "In a mad." Alfred made a picture of a "Man slamming the front door shut." When the child was asked about the meaning of the drawing, he related his fear of being abandoned by his father. Mr. Barnes was appalled to hear his child's perceptions. He soon agreed to communicate his feelings and gestures more explicitly to prevent his child's fear of abandonment.

PARENTS INTERPRET CHILD'S WISHES

Mr. and Mrs. Barnes were constantly quarreling. During one such performance, Alfred drew a person carrying a stop sign (Figure 30) while people were locked up in jail. This time the art therapist asked the parents how they would interpret their child's picture. They understood the "stop sign" as a message to them to "Stop quarreling." Several guesses were made about the jailed persons—perhaps the child felt trapped in a bad family situation, or maybe he wanted them to be locked up to be rid of their arguments. These suggestions were certainly insightful. Alfred, fearful of having his subconscious seen by his parents, denied the interpretations and said it was "just a robber." The art therapist interjected with "sometimes children feel robbed during their daily life—it could be of their parents'

Figure 30.   A wish for parents to cease quarreling

time, a television show they didn't get to see, a toy they might want, etc.'' Alfred felt relieved by the interpretation and his parents could understand how frequently Alfred and they themselves felt cheated. When the parents were about to leave, they mentioned how meaningful that particular meeting had been for them.

FIGURE SIZE—A GAUGE FOR EMOTIONS

On close observations, it was seen how Alfred drew his parents in different sizes. This factor depended upon his parents' discussion or the mood which they conveyed. When the child was in individual treatment, he could lean on the therapist's ego strength more heavily. However, with the diluted transference, Alfred merged into the emotional environment set up by his mother and father. When the family managed to be amiable, everyone was an appropriate size. However, when mother and father fought, they loomed large on the page while his own size was reduced. Omnipotent fantasies were evidenced by his increased self-size.

For example, when Mr. and Mrs. Barnes were discussing money matters, he drew a man and a woman. As their discussion increased in intensity, a series of pictures showed a couple getting larger. Sometimes a small animal was included. At one point, when Mrs. Barnes stomped out of the room in anger, Alfred ran after his mother, then they both returned dismayed. The family was encouraged to talk about their feelings instead of running away. Alfred anxiously joined into the discussion; however, he squeezed a piece of plasticene to release some of his rage. When the parents calmed down, he went back to drawing a man and woman who were average size. In this picture Alfred made himself very large.

OEDIPAL FANTASIES

The family's sleeping arrangements were inadvertently brought up. It seemed when either parent was uncomfortable with the other's snoring, restlessness or illness, he or she would leave the conjugal bed and sleep with Alfred. Unknown to Mr. and Mrs. Barnes, Alfred wrote "fuck" across his paper, then scribbled over it. The child may have responded to his parents' sex life. His oedipal conflict was blatantly revealed in Alfred's next picture, when he described the drawing: "This little boy is a king. His mommy is the queen. Daddy is outside—he is the gardener.''

TERMINATION

The family met for several months. Alfred had the opportunity to put out material which otherwise would have been submerged. Mr. and Mrs. Barnes gained awareness about their son's emotional responses to their interaction. Nevertheless, they terminated, saying they had gained a great deal from therapy and could manage their lives on their own. Although the child pleaded for continued help from the therapist, therapy was discontinued. The therapist felt the gains in therapy had been minimal; Mr. and Mrs. Barnes' decision was contraindicated. The parents' pathology maintained their homeostasis with their resistance to change impenetrable.

FOLLOW-UP

A two-year follow-up was made. Alfred's bizarre gestures had not recurred; however, the rest of his developmental advances had regressed.

PART III

Latency-Age Children

Boys and girls in middle years of childhood—ages six to twelve—are "ready to begin the quest for independent identity and existence" (Stone and Church, 1957). They state latency represents a time when the child is essentially moving away from parents "towards a genuine sense of self," for it is during this stage that the capacity to view themselves with a certain detachment and objectivity becomes possible. The clinical art therapy approach for latency-age children places major emphasis on helping the child meet the developmental tasks necessary for a sense of self.

The author finds the theories of "play" or "play therapy" as appropriate to clinical art therapy with children. Erikson (1959, p.85) postulates child's play as an "infantile way of thinking over difficult experiences and restoring a sense of mastery." Axline (1947, p.16) proclaimed play as a natural medium of expression where the child can play out his "accumulated feelings of tension, frustration, insecurity, aggression, fear, bewilderment and confusion." She also stated, "by playing out those feelings he brings them to the surface, gets them out in the open, faces them, learns to control them, or abandons them. When he has achieved emotional relaxation, he begins to realize the power within himself to be an individual in his own right, to think for himself, to make his own decisions, to become psychologically more mature, and by so doing, to realize selfhood." Kramer (1971) claims the child's involvement in art can serve similar psychological functions, while Betensky (1973) stresses the phenomenological, dynamically-oriented art therapy approach as the method for facilitating growth.

Art psychotherapy for latency-age children is presented in Chapters 7 through 11. Chapter 7 contains the case history of "Cora," a seven-year-old elective mute, in individual treatment. It portrays the role which art therapy played in helping the child take communication and socialization risks. Although Cora had an observable impairment, the reader may bear in mind how the approach would be applicable to children with different symptoms and problems. Chapter 8 places the emphasis on group art psychotherapy. It presents a variety of cases collected from diverse groups. The selection offers the reader a collective glimpse into the numerous issues and techniques involved in exploring intrapsychic material and interpersonal peer relationships. Chapter 9 shows the use of individual art therapy on a pediatric unit in a medical hospital. Vignettes of individual cases display the benefits of this approach as patients reveal fearful areas and work upon the trauma of hospitalization. Chapter 10, also related to the medical hospital setting, offers a five-step procedure for group art therapy with children. The patients are provided with a prophylactic experience by expressing and sharing their mutual concerns and fantasies. In Chapter 11 the focus is placed on a single session for crisis intervention as a preventative measure. The intervention is related to a situational crisis. Three examples are demonstrated: 1) a child suffering from an earthquake trauma; 2) group art therapy in a public school for latency-age children who experienced violence in their community between the Los Angeles Police and a group of terrorists; 3) an adolescent admitted to a medical hospital.

CHAPTER 7

Individual Treatment: Case History of an Elective Mute

Due to the nonverbal aspect of clinical art therapy, it is especially successful in treating persons where speech is electively withheld.

The author has treated numerous children and adults who exhibited elective or selective mutism. Although the art therapy modality was always utilized, the approach and techniques have varied to meet the unique needs of the patient. Both the source and symptom have been treated. All of these elective mutes, except for one, ended up speaking to the therapist and in the community. Some clients still appeared "shy," although their verbal communication had markedly increased.

In many cases the author offered interpretations. Initially she entered into drawing with the patient for symbolic contact, took an active part in portraying protective imagery, led patients to reveal and deal with intrapsychic and family trauma, and sometimes worked conjointly with the mother, parents or family. These techniques contrast with the method which was utilized with Cora. Common approaches during treatment included free expression, story-telling about the artwork, role-playing, and an emphasis on learning to make, and voice, choices. Cora was the first elective mute whom the author treated, many years ago. This case history presents the progress of a child in treatment over a period of seven months.

CASE HISTORY

Cora, a seven-year-old black girl, was referred for therapy by her school because she refused to talk. She was set apart from the other children due to her mutism, which was accompanied behaviorally by extreme physical rigidity. The child did not function in school, although she managed to keep up with the class by doing her work at home. When at school, Cora sat the whole day without eating or going to the bathroom. Recess was the only time she moved; when it was time to go on the playground, a ritual was attached to Cora's leaving the classroom—someone touched her to indicate that it was time to leave, another child would shove her sweater on, then she would be tapped on the back to move in the outdoor direction. During the entire play period, Cora would stand frozen and expressionless on the playground. The severity of her stiff body movements made the teacher and the school nurse erroneously suppose that Cora had some physical disability.

The child's teacher suspected her to be of gifted intelligence, but due to her mutism she attended a special class. Cora was found to be organically healthy, including her hearing ability. The child was electively mute; she spoke only to her family (when no other persons were present) and a few quiet words to her dedicated teacher when school was over.

Cora's problem seemed to be a symptom of a larger family pathology, which involved marital discord between the parents and excessive restrictiveness and protectiveness on the part of the mother (Morris, 1953; Browne, Wilson and Laybourne, 1963; Putstrom and Speers, 1964). As often appears in elective mutes, the parents, particularly the mother, were resistant to therapy. The latter denied the importance of the problem, insisting that Cora would "get over it." (Interesting similarities can be noted here to a case of electively mute identical twins described by Mora, DeVault and Schopler, 1962.) It was, in fact, at the mother's instigation that therapy was prematurely terminated after seven months. Fortunately, significant progress was made during this relatively short period of treatment.

Therapeutic Approaches

Because Cora's case appeared immediately as an expression of larger family problems, the treatment of choice would have included family therapy. However, the parents were uncooperative and, therefore, Cora was originally seen with her siblings, then in individual treatment. Towards the end of therapy, the mother did join Cora in a conjoint art therapy session. Art therapy offered the child a means for exposing the source of her problems. At the same time, the format provided a distancing factor for threatening material. It was particularly beneficial in this case where communication was the crucial issue.

The value of this technique will show itself more clearly in the discussion of Cora's therapy, but it is important to note that the patient's drawing developed from paint dabs and ambiguous collages, to direct representations and messages. As therapy progressed, Cora began to correlate her drawing with her real-life experience.

A flexible approach to the art tasks was essential. It included: 1) repeated themes pertaining to the enhancement of Cora's self-image; 2) drawing and discussing emotions evoked during the session; 3) depicting in artwork and discussing significant current developments; 4) modeling and rehearsing the alternate choice of verbal communication; and 5) reinforcement of artwork which showed emotions or elicited speech.

As in play therapy (Axline, 1947; Peller, 1971), artwork was encouraged as a form of self-expression. In addition, the creative and sublimating aspects were attended to (Moustakas, 1966; Kramer, 1971). In this particular case, the author rendered very few interpretations. The issue of central importance was that Cora had things *she needed and wanted to say.*

Description

Cora, age seven, was the youngest child of a large family. She had recently moved from Detroit, Michigan to Los Angeles. When the therapist first met the child, she exhibited a robot-like, extremely stiff gait. She showed no affect, her mouth was tightly puckered, and she repeatedly blinked her eyes very hard. Cora was very thin; her skin was dry with patches of eczema behind her knees. The child was neatly dressed, and her hair was beautifully done in a charming style. Cora's behavior outside of her home was bizarrely tense and withholding.

Initial Treatment

During the first art therapy session, Cora was seen along with two of her siblings. This was an attempt to lower her anxiety around a new experience. She did throw out a few words, then a sentence which titled her art product. However, most of the time she would stand frozen in the corner, with her hands in front of her face. She refused to communicate.

It seemed profitable to continue art therapy for Cora with her siblings present. Their pictures and discussion stimulated the patient to follow their model. It also allowed the therapist to view the sibling dynamics. It was the eighth art therapy session in which Cora began individual treatment. Although her siblings worked with her intermittently, their visits diminished until Cora was seen twice a week alone, until treatment was terminated at the end of seven months.

In the beginning, the children were given cookies and candy freely. They quickly stuffed large amounts into their mouths; their appetites were insatiable. It was soon evident that this pattern of endless feeding would have to be changed. Therefore, a reward system was instituted. If the children were cooperative in creating artwork, they received a limited number of cookies as a recompense. This was consistent with the idea which had been presented to them that art therapy was work—a way of working to help Cora talk.

Content of Artwork

In Cora's drawings and collages, three salient and consistent themes were present—sometimes interwoven, sometimes distinct from each other: 1) oral needs; 2) conflict and anxiety about the family and her role in it; 3) "the little girl theme," which related to a growing consciousness of her ability to communicate fears, desires and fantasies.

Orality

Cora's ravenous attitude toward the food which the therapist offered her at a nearby coffee-shop had a counterpart in the oral theme of her drawings and collages. In one of her first products (Figure 31) she pasted together pictures of a man and woman (titled "Kissing"), an apple, (labeled "Eat"), and a surgeon with pursed lips (titled "Listen man"). The kissing and the apple represented her desire for nourishment, and the doctor was associated with someone who could hear her. Since patients often use a surgeon picture to symbolize the healing power of the therapist, it is assumed the message was directed towards the author.

Thus, very early in treatment, Cora related her oral needs with her wish to have them heard. Over and over again the artwork conveyed a stress on hunger. For example, under pictures of people she would say, "They are starving." Although the nourishment theme continued throughout therapy, it was most prevalent during the first few months of treatment.

Self-Perception Within the Family Unit

The second theme was related to Cora and her place in the family. The therapist assigned drawings related to the family. Some were drawn by the

Figure 31.   Oral needs expressed

child alone, while others were cooperatively created along with her siblings. While Cora could draw and express ideas about a family member (particularly her mother), when it came to seeing herself within the family unit, or relating to it, she became hostile, anxious and withdrawn. Her first picture of the family began with a large drawing of herself, and ended in a mass of jagged lines as her anxiety rendered her near helplessness. She was tremendously motivated by the cookie reward to finish her drawing, but it was obviously a great effort for her.

During a similar session (in the fourth month of therapy) when the patient and her siblings were asked to draw members of their family, Cora immediately went about her task by drawing a picture of herself. However, when the art therapist discussed her siblings' pictures, which displayed the parents punishing the children, Cora's anxiety rose to such a point that she ripped her picture in half (Figure 32).

The following week, when the siblings were again present, a large sheet of wrapping paper was placed on the floor and the only instructions given were *all of you work on a picture together.* Each member drew a separate picture

Figure 32.   Anxiety evoked by thoughts of punishment

on the same piece of paper. Cora, once again, found herself overcome by the possibility of conveying family material and barely managed to place a line in red crayon which resembled a question mark. Immediately after this effort, she ran into the corner where she tried to hide. She refused to utter another sound.

During one of the last sessions in the art therapy treatment, Cora and her mother were present. They were asked to *draw a picture together*. Cora promptly regressed to some of her earlier mannerisms (mouth puckered along with a facial tic) in response to the mother's demanding and critical attitude. The parent scolded Cora, "Hurry and get started. Don't use the new felt pens, use the old ones. Turn the chair around so it's straighter." The child cupped her hand about her drawing to protect it from her mother and colored a little girl with a purple face. The picture conveyed Cora's bottled-up anger. It was most impressive that Cora was able to express her

Figure 33.   Little girl pictures serve as a surrogate self

frustration in this drawing; especially gratifying was the fact that she had
the capacity to exercise her creativity in face of the negative and an-
tagonistic attitude of her mother.

Because of the mother's overtly hostile attitude towards the Clinic (which
seemed to be aggravated, rather than diminished by Cora's improvement),
it was decided that there was little which could be done to improve family
relationships. Therefore, for the remaining sessions the focus was on the patient herself and on termination.

Metaphor: "The Little Girl"

The third major theme was "the little girl." One of the constant subjects
of Cora's drawings, assigned or unassigned, was the figure of a little girl
(Figure 33). Cora named this little girl figure, which served as an obvious
surrogate, for herself. At first, her little girls were only outlines, always

without hands, and sometimes without feet. Early in the fourth month of therapy, with increased self-esteem and a greater involvement in the art, the patient displayed a greater ability to concentrate and sustain her interest and focus. She also began to express a clearer and more fully developed self-image. She drew in hands, feet, fingers and eyebrows, and began to color her little girls black, like herself. Cora gave more attention to these drawings, and willingly dictated stories about them. Utilizing role-playing techniques, Cora began to express her fantasies, fears and desires through her "little girl" pictures.

At times her ventilation and self-expression served as a creative trial for something that Cora would later attempt outside of therapy; for example, during the fourth month of treatment she drew a girl and then said, "This is a girl whose mama won't let her go out and play. She has a girl friend. Her name is Bubbie. Her mother won't let her go to Bubbie's house. She feels sad because her mama won't let her go anywhere but to school." In the story Cora revealed a very real desire for a friend and a fear that her mother would cut her off from any personal contacts. Shortly after this picture was produced, Cora's teacher had the opportunity to see it. Her immediate response was that the girl in the drawing was strikingly similar to a new pupil with whom Cora had become friendly. Several weeks later, Cora drew a picture of a little black girl; she was deeply involved and pleased with her drawing (Figure 34). This is the story she composed: "She is poor. She goes home. She was playing with her friend and then she feel down. They play handball." (At this point Cora says, "I do too.") "They say 'hi' to each other. They would like to call on the phone. She, Susan, is a sad girl, because she fell down and went home. She told her mother. Her mother said, 'Who pushed you down?' She said, 'Nobody.'" This tale is significant for several reasons: Once again Cora stated the wish for a friend; she identified with the child in the story; she thought her mother's response would be negative; she ventured to stand up to her mother by making a definitive statement.

Cora's repetition of her fears and wishes in the artwork, as well as in the verbal story-telling, played a large part in her progress. On one occasion Cora pasted several pictures of people with phones calling up their friends (Figure 35). This material was utilized by the art therapist and the child as they role-played with disconnected toy phones. Over and over Cora painted pictures titled "Calling a Friend." This was followed by the "calling a friend" game. It was gratifying to discover that one day Cora had actualized this role in the everyday world. She made a friend with whom she talked in school and later played.

As time went on, Cora connected her drawn desires with concrete actions.

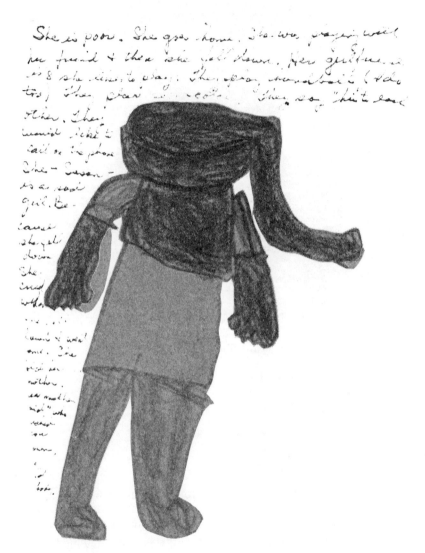

Figure 34.   Drawing serves as a model for role-playing

He is happy because
she has a phone. He
is calling his friend.
It is is saying
"hello"

Figure 35.   Phone is a symbol for speech

One important example of this was when Cora spoke into a tape recorder. In her story she stated, "I drew a cake. Then I went home and made a cake. Then I ate a cake." Therapy was allowing her to connect and integrate her hopes with reality; it was in this area that Cora made her most clear-cut and tangible progress.

Widening the Verbal Community

Cora's verbal community was widened by putting her in a situation where a few spoken words were a natural expectation. The therapist introduced her to a secretary who was instructed to give her candy if she *asked* for it. Although quiet and timid at first, she became willing to participate in this experience. Later, the art therapist also took Cora to a nearby shop where the waitresses served her food only if she ordered it directly from them.

As part of the communication effort, arrangements were made whereby the art therapist's next patient, nine-year-old John, arrived fifteen minutes early, overlapping his time with Cora's. Cora agreed to be together with John for a short time. For their first meeting, the children were taken to a playground, where Cora played alone in John's presence. The next time they worked with the art media. Cora quickly adjusted to being with another child. If she wanted to be with John again, she was instructed to ask him to join her the following week. Although she was hesitant the first time, she spoke more freely during the following dyad art therapy sessions (they worked together four times).

As Cora's circle widened, and her therapy progressed, she began to do little tasks on her own and to deal more adequately with strangers. For example, she was sometimes brought to her therapy by various volunteers. On one occasion, when a strange transportation volunteer came to take Cora home, the therapist did not notify him about the child's mutism. When the therapist spoke to him later, he reported that Cora didn't speak much; *she only answered his first three questions,* then remained silent. This little incident supported the theory of Cora being trapped into a role of the "no-talker."

The teacher at school was encouraged to positively reinforce Cora's speech and movements, so that instead of tacitly accepting her silence, there would be an expectation for her to talk. Instead of acquiescing to the children's surprise at Cora's newly developed willingness to move, jump and play, the teacher began to say, "Of course, Cora can run, jump and play." In this way the child was freed from some of the external pressure to perpetuate the role she had fallen into.

Collages Display Family Secrets

In reviewing Cora's art therapy, it was observed how at the beginning of treatment the child usually whispered words. Though she sometimes spoke in a louder tone, she was generally withholding and withdrawn. By the third month, she had begun to express herself more freely in relation to her drawings, and by the fourth month she had initiated and carried on conversations with the art therapist.

An interesting footnote to this is the particular role that the collages played in Cora's therapy. It became apparent that whenever "family secrets" or new, surprising material came out, it was triggered by her free associations to the pictures. For example, a series of pictures of men boxing (Figure 36) not only expressed Cora's aggressive feelings, but was ambiguously related to the issue of her parents' possible infidelity. She related, "Once upon a time there was a man who was thinking about a lady, a mean lady." In reference to another picture, she claimed, "He thinks about the other man, he says to himself, 'I am going to kill that man because he will think about a lady.'"

Another collage, which included a picture of a glove, triggered off a long conversation about the family's sleeping arrangements: The father slept with one of his daughters, brother with a sister, mother on the couch, etc.

Figure 36.   Collage reveals family secrets

In contrast to her occasional regressions to stubborn withdrawal and silence, Cora showed a new ability to vent her rage at the art therapist by threatening to destroy herself. When the clinician refused to give in to her endless demands for food, the child declared she would throw herself down the stairs with accusations of being "pushed" down. The therapist was stripped of her role as the "good" mother, since to Cora the refusal for ongoing nourishment transformed the clinician into a destructive person. It was only after the therapist repeatedly used physical force, holding her tightly, carrying her down the stairs, while assuring her that she would not permit Cora to hurt herself, that the patient stopped splitting the art therapist into the good mother and the bad one. Cora also ceased the threat to destroy herself.

During the fourth month of treatment, the school teacher reported that Cora led the class out to the playground. The same day, also at school, Cora punched her brother and sister. The next month, she attended a school picnic at the beach and astonished her classmates by her ability to perform and play games just as they did. Cora's progress was now evident to her family and the community.

During the fifth and sixth months of treatment, Cora was reported to have gone to the neighborhood grocery store. At her mother's request, Cora ordered a few items. At this time she played outside with a friend, and also talked to children on the block who played in her front yard. Cora began to keep up with the schoolwork in class, although she kept her speech to a minimum.

In the seventh and last month of therapy, Cora began to work on watercolor paintings. Initially, she was easily frustrated by the difficulties presented by the new medium. If the paint dripped, Cora would lose her temper, crumple her picture, then throw it into the trashcan. At one such juncture, the art therapist intervened by painting with Cora, making her "mistake" into a flower. The patient and the therapist painted together for several sessions. Afterwards Cora's response to the uncontrolability of the medium had changed radically. Accidents that formerly led to frustration now became a creative challenge; entirely on her own Cora was able to integrate unpredictable happenings into a unified picture. The child felt rewarded when her painting was placed on the wall of the art therapy room. This final painting (Figure 37) was viewed in contrast with her first "House" picture as evidence of improvement in frustration tolerance and painting skills.

Follow-up

Nine years later the author inadvertently obtained some follow-up infor-

Figure 37.   Previous frustration becomes creative challenge

mation. Cora, an adolescent, performed extremely well in school and was well liked by her classmates. There were no obvious problems. The only hint of her former mutism was the remark that Cora was "rather shy."

Cora's experiences after art therapy are unknown. Whatever happened in her life to aid her ego development is currently a mystery. However, it is the author's guess that the treatment during Cora's latency period had a profound effect on her life, for it served as her initial liberator from the bonds of elective mutism.

SUMMARY AND CONCLUSIONS

In this case, art therapy was used as a mode of self-expression and communication, rather than a vehicle for interpretation. The therapy was presented as a method of working towards the goal of helping Cora talk. Although treatment was incomplete, Cora had made significant progress in her attitude towards giving and risking, both essential elements in talking to people. Expressive art gave this elective mute a chance to reveal aspects of herself, her fears, her desires, and her fantasies. Art therapy paved the road to a destination of speech and communication.

CHAPTER 8

Clinical Art
Therapy for a
Latency-Age Group

INTRODUCTION

The latency-age or middle years of childhood have often been referred to as the "gang age"; this phrase is descriptive of the child's peer affiliations. It is during this period that the discovery of a same-age society takes place and the developmental task of learning to relate and work with peers lays the foundation for social interaction. This phenomenon points out the importance, for mental health workers, of providing latency-age children with a group where a corrective therapeutic experience can take place.

Historically, latency-age groups have been play or activity oriented. Successes were reported with children who could enhance their self-esteen through games and other activities and who had sufficient ego strength to improve their peer relationships. Then, during the popularity of the "rap" session, latency-age groups were constituted more frequently on a strictly talk level; often the therapist reported the need for intermittent activities or a snack to help contain the acting-out members of the group. On a spectrum of children's behavior, from acting-out to withdrawn, it is the children in the center of the continuum who respond most frequently to the purely verbal form of treatment. This modality is most productive for boys and girls who respond to hearing and being heard in a therapeutic environment.

Many therapists are seeking new methods for reaching latency-age children who lack impulse control, are self-destructive in relationships, have difficulty in staying focused during the group process, and/or display withdrawn behavior. The seclusive child is especially threatened by both the activity and verbal format, thus adding resistance to group therapy. In helping children with these problems, the art therapy approach has proven to be the treatment of choice for latency-age children in outpatient clinical facilities and therapeutic and public school settings.

The art therapy groups are task-oriented. This mode provides a method for each child to express herself or himself, first by creating simple art, then through sharing its contents visually and verbally. The product becomes the platform for each child to reveal ideas, feelings, and perceptions about the self and significant others. Also portrayed are past memories, hurts or joys of the present, fantasies of the future and illustrations of alternate choices of behavior. With such personal and meaningful communication, the art itself serves as a major means of maintaining the group's focus.

Theme-oriented directives are frequently utilized, providing the means for children to explore material which they have in common. This technique facilitates empathy and relatedness. The mutual themes tend to accelerate the group's progress. This is of particular importance for time-limited treatment, which requires the therapist to work at a rapid pace.

The structure of the art therapy session lends itself to equal time for each child. This is helpful in keeping the strongly verbal or acting-out members from taking the power positions, and gives the quiet child an opportunity to work, other than on a vicarious level. For children, it is especially satisfying to be in a group situation where all members are expressing themselves simultaneously, with the knowledge that each child will have a chance to be the center of attention when the open discussion takes place.

One of the major motivations for group artwork is the area of peer relations. Cooperative art projects are an ideal model for dealing with the interpersonal aspects of group therapy. Task orientation may be structured to arrange for work in dyads, triads, small groups and/or the total group.

Art forms are viewed in relation to content, process, and feelings involved in the act of creation. Many of the illustrations which follow have printing or writing directly upon them. Children have the option of doing their own recording or dictating the information to be written by the therapist. The latency-age child in particular is duly impressed when the psychotherapist values his or her thoughts enough to write them down. The artwork remains in the office. Since the boys and girls clearly identify themselves with their creations, they see the therapist as a person who knows their worth and keeps their personal art in a safe place.

In an attempt to give a brief and simplified understanding of how the latency-age art therapy group functions, the following will be reviewed: objectives, methodology, and examples of therapeutic issues.

ILLUSTRATIONS: GROUP ART THERAPY
WITH LATENCY-AGE CHILDREN

Clarification for Treatment

It has been found that early clarification regarding treatment brings a sense of relief to the children and establishes an understanding of group objectives. During a first group session, after several warm-up exercises, the children were asked to make a collage showing *why are you here in therapy?*

Philip, an eight-year-old boy, drew his family fighting (Figure 38) and titled his picture, "I'm going to tell my trables (sic)." Other group members agreed with Philip; they, too, would talk about issues which were troubling them.

Empathy

Presenting problems early in group development provides an atmosphere for openness and develops empathy. It accelerates the commitment to work in group. In answer to the directive *what are your problems?*, Jane drew her mother. She complained about this parent's lack of communication. Jane went on to explain how it provoked a great deal of anger and resentment within her. Presenting this problem enabled other group members to share similar feelings toward their own parents. A general discussion around the

Figure 38. Reason for therapy clarified

issue of lack of communication ensued. The follow-up directive dealt with *persons with whom I would like to improve my communication.*

Eliciting Verbalization

During the first art therapy group session for latency-age children, Carl, a 10-year-old elective mute, fulfilled the request to do a collage telling *why am I here in this group?* He pasted a picture of a head of a statue (Figure 39) and wrote "I can't communicate." As he shared the picture, Carl voiced his reason for being in the group. The child's surprising verbal experience negated his self-fulfilling prophecy of being unable to communicate.

Figure 39.   Collage facilitates speech

Collages as a Distancing Factor to Aid Self-expression

Group members were asked to *select and paste pictures of people, then write down what they are thinking and saying.* On construction paper an 11-year-old boy, Ephrim, glued down a photograph of a doctor examining a young child (Figure 40). He wrote that the child said, "I know you are just doing your job, but aren't you getting a little personal?" Ephrim then added, "The doc thinks 'This kid's going places.' When the child is leaving, the doctor thinks 'going places like the hospital.'" Based on the fact that doctor pictures usually symbolize the therapist, two interpretations were made: One, Ephrim had concerns around exposing personal information;

Figure 40.   Fears of treatment are safely expressed

two, he was worried that the therapist might see him as a child who was crazy and needed hospitalization. Ephrim acknowledged both interpretations. Other group members also discussed their worries around being placed in a group with "crazies." Additional directives led the children into drawing how they had fantasized the group, as well as the reality of their group experience.

Metaphors: A Catalyst for Exploring Feelings

A group composed of boys and girls, seven to eight years of age, was told *on one part of the paper, purposely draw a picture in a way which you consider looks "bad" and on the other part, something which looks "good."* When the children finished their pictures, the therapist encouraged the boys and girls to describe their feelings which went along with each picture (Figure 41). Cynthia said how "icky" it felt when she drew and looked at the messed-up scribble. Then the child went on to talk about the pleasurable feelings connected to the good picture. Most of the children related similar thoughts and emotions. During the discussion, analogous situations were

Figure 41.   Good and bad drawings a distancing device for self-expression

brought up—the good and bad at school, home, etc. The boys and girls began relating what conditions at home evoked each feeling, how it affected them "inside" and how their parents reacted to their good and bad behavior.

The children with behavior problems who were most resistant to talking about their home situations responded very positively to drawing the "goods and bads." This preliminary step eased the group members into explaining personal material regarding self-esteem and family interactions.

Insight as a Vehicle for Parental Confrontation

In a group of 11- to 12-year-old boys and girls, children painted *free choice pictures*. Jonas made a watercolor picture (Figure 42) of two persons with smeared and blurred faces and titled it, "The perfect couple." They were saying "jurgle gurgle" and other nonsense words. At first the child said he had nothing in mind when he drew the two people; later, he decided it was of "a man and woman who had smeared faces because they never

Figure 42.   Double talk insight

showed what they were really feeling." As Jonas finished talking about the picture, he realized the underlying meaning; it portrayed the double talk which he received from his mother and father. The child was able to clarify that he never understood what messages his parents were giving him. The boy was asked if the picture could be brought into his family session. With his consent the painting was shared with his parents to point out their confusing form of communication. References to this illustration were made in several family art psychotherapy sessions, since it vividly demonstrated the double messages.

Art as a Basis for Interpretation

In a group of children who had difficulty with peer relationships, nine-year-old Randy drew a picture of a boy cutting off his nose (Figure 43). The therapist was able to use the picture to point out how the child often "cuts off his nose to spite his face." Group members, agreeing with the interpretation, gave examples of how Randy provoked them into rejecting him. When the discussion ended, the therapist also interpreted the yell for "help" as Randy's way of asking for assistance with his problems. The child looked relieved to have his veiled message understood.

Concretizing a Desire and Making a Commitment to Change

In a long-term art therapy group, composed of eight-year-old girls, the children were asked to *make something which shows what you wish you could change.* Rene, an enuretic child, made a plasticene figure which she placed on a toy toilet (Figure 44). During discussion rounds, she emphatically stated that it was of "a little girl who goes on the toilet, not in her pants." One month after this episode, her mother reported that Rene had been dry for four weeks. Evidently, the concrete aspect of the art and the accompanying verbal commitment made to the group motivated this child to change her behavior.

Art as a Tool for Revealing Secrets or Scary Feelings

In an open-ended group for seven- to nine-year-old girls, a request was made to *create a sculpture or an assemblage which shows "something you feel strongly about."* One little girl, Gerry, made an assemblage inside a closed container and on the lid she wrote, "Do not open." The therapist and group members respected her desire not to share her artwork. The piece

Figure 43.   Provocative boy yells for help

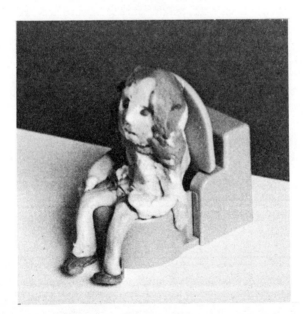

Figure 44.   Child makes commitment to stop wetting her pants

was left on the counter of the room for several weeks. One day the child decided she was ready to display the contents of her box. She lifted the lid for the girls to peek in. They saw figures closely huddled together surrounded by a fence. Gerry explained that a day before she made the assemblage she had been in an automobile accident. An interpretation was given as to how the artwork displayed the child's need for a protective environment. The therapist led the children into helping Gerry ventilate her fears around the trauma of her accident. Additional artwork was created as other group members worked towards mastery over their own traumas of "getting hurt" and fear of the "unknown."

Increased Self-esteem

The following five illustrations are an individual case history taken from a six-week brief service art therapy group. The group was composed of five acting-out youngsters and Jimmy, an 11-year-old adopted boy who was being physically abused by his parents. He was extremely passive, school phobic, fearful of being abandoned and withdrawn both in school and at home.

At the first meeting, the children were asked to *make a scribble, discover suggested figures or forms and then develop them more fully.* Jimmy stayed within the lines of his scribble, making sure to be very neat. His picture, like his personality, was contained. In this beginning session the other boys drew dirty pictures, made sarcastic remarks, and threatened to control the meeting. Jimmy was obviously frightened by the lack of control which the other participants displayed.

In the second session, a *free drawing* showed a person hanging from a cliff, yelling "Help!" (Figure 45A). Below him is a fish swimming in the ocean waiting to eat him up. The picture revealed Jimmy's fears and insecurity. The painting was well developed, showing a good deal of investment in its portrayal and the subject. The group responded with admiration for the boy's talent. The theme of the painting caught their attention and facilitated a discussion around their own frightening experiences with police authorities, teachers, and parents. As Jimmy listened to the group, he worked on a vicarious level around the problem of insecurity and the threat of authority figures who lacked empathy.

Later, the other children drew toilet scenes and wrote "dirty" words on their pictures. Jimmy appraised the therapist as a person who could accept all kinds of pictures, exhibiting various thoughts and emotions. Jimmy participated only briefly in the discussion around ground rules.

When the group met for the third time, an argument broke out between

Figure 45A.   A cry for therapeutic help

two members. Jimmy drew an arrow on the paper in front of him. In explaining its meaning, he made a fist with his right hand and slapped it into his left hand. He then turned to the two boisterous members, complaining that "rules should be made" in order to "keep our group from getting wrecked." The boys were surprised to hear him speak up so clearly for what he wanted.

In the fourth session, all the group members were encouraged to get their aggression out in the art where it could be accepted and tolerated. At a moment when the boys were arguing and provoking one another, they were

asked to *draw what you want the group to hear.* Jimmy drew the various
members of the group (Figure 45B). His picture showed him putting a
firecracker and dynamite onto the boy who was "messing up the group,"
labeling him an "ass." Somehow, Jimmy himself looked bigger and braver
when he shared this picture. He sat up straight and his voice was forceful.

Figure 45B.   A show of anger

Unaware of the big change, he acted as though this had always been his usual manner. On the way out of the room, Jimmy literally had a fight in the hall with the disruptive member.

In the fifth session the boys were asked to do a picture about *the feelings you had when you left group last week and how you feel now.* Jimmy used a picture of the magician Houdini. He placed a gag on his mouth and crossed out the tied hands, showing they were about ready to be freed; underneath he wrote "I did it" (Figure 45C). He explained that the picture was connected to the fight the previous week, reporting it was the first one he had ever provoked. He claimed that his motivation was to "protect the group." Jimmy was proud of himself; the rest of the group, including the boy he beat in the fight, shared his pride.

In the sixth and final session a group sculpture was created. Jimmy made a large brave man whom he placed in a central position, revealing his improved self-image. Then, in drawings, he and the other participants were able to express their ambivalent feelings of anger towards the therapist for ending the group and the sad feelings which termination provoked.

Figure 45C.   Breaking the chains of fear

Symbolic Agent for Setting Limits

In a group for young girls, two eight-year-olds literally grabbed the leadership role by doing the most and largest pieces of art. Although the verbal aspect was controlled through the "taking turns" format, a great deal of resentment was still felt on the part of the quieter girls. To create more equality, the therapist used a plastic tray as a means for regulating territorial rights. She helped the children mark off a fair amount of space with felt markers onto the tray. Then each child made a clay sculpture which she placed in her own space. Limiting some children while allowing more room for others was an experience the children welcomed. When the individual families were seen, most of the girls talked about the tray experience. The child's need for structure, or more freedom, became the theme of the family session.

Relationship of Space in Cooperative Art and Its Unifying Function

Six lively 12-year-old boys formed a long-term art therapy group. They were unable to work cooperatively. Interaction merely provoked great stimulation and chaos. Therefore, emphasis was placed on individual work for several months. The boys began to calm down after each of them had created artwork which repeatedly ventilated their feelings around the reputation of "being bad." This common theme among group members had a sobering effect; appropriate cooperative projects were then introduced. In the beginning, sheets of butcher paper long enough to cover the width of the room were placed on the floor for the group drawing project. Each child worked on his own picture within his designated area. The next step was to unify the individual parts to give the artwork an image of totality. As time went on, the allotted space was purposely reduced in order to bring the boys physically closer together. This method allowed the boys to be eased into physical proximity which was at first tolerable, then comfortable. Toward the group's end, only one cardboard tray was utilized as the total space.

During the last session, a cardboard tray was used as a canvas with the raised edge as the frame. Each boy made colored construction paper cutouts which were pasted down to the tray (Figure 46). The collage contained a house, an auto, a road, a tree, a cloud and a sun. A discussion took place around the look of the artwork. They all agreed it was "really nice." However, they felt it needed to stand out more, and people were missing. The boys moved on to a problem-solving discussion. Again they cooperated—tissue paper was crumpled and glued down to give the three-

Figure 46.   Final project displays unified approach

dimensional quality to a full branched tree, then a red flower was added to it to make it "extra nice." Magazine photos of small boys with smiling faces were placed in the windows and door of the house.

In this final construct, it was difficult to recognize individual contributions; the piece portrayed a totally cohesive work of art. The boys voiced their sense of pride; this was justified, not only by what they had created, but by the way they had learned to respect one another and the group spirit which they had formed.

SUMMARY

Art psychotherapy for latency-age children can be utilized as a method for dealing with the following therapeutic issues and objectives: 1) to clarify the basis for treatment; 2) to present problem areas in a way which provides an atmosphere for openness and develops empathy; 3) to create collages as a distancing factor to help the child reveal his/herself; 4) to introduce important themes which serve to portray analogous material; 5) to help the children gain insight; 6) to provide a means for appropriate parental confrontation; 7) to create artwork which can be used as a basis for interpretation; 8) to concretize a desire through the art which lends itself to making a commitment to change; 9) to reveal unconscious secrets and frightening feelings which can be pointed out and dealt with; 10) to provide tangible evidence for a child's needs; 11) to integrate through the creative process developmental gains; 12) to express aggression and anger in a socially acceptable way; 13) to provide a symbolic agent for setting limits; and 14) to foster peer relationships through cooperative art projects.

CHAPTER 9

Individual Clinical Art Therapy on a Medical Pediatric Unit

INTRODUCTION

In a Public Health Service publication, *Red is the Color of Hurting,* Milton Shore (1971) states that fear of punishment in children ages four through six is related to their developing capacity for fantasy with limited reality-testing. This factor "leads to the beginning of 'mutilation anxiety' based on fears of bodily harm of a more subjective nature." He claims that diagnostic or treatment procedures are perceived as punitive measures as a result of the child's "guilt over previous aggression. Therefore, for medically hospitalized children, it is essential that they receive an educational and mastery experience." Studies which were conducted by Jessner (1959) and her colleagues indicated that children ages six through eight years were intensely fearful of loss of control of body mastery and impulse. This was particularly significant for boys and girls who had an anesthesia administered before surgery. However, adolescents, whose developmental task is to gain a sense of identity, are threatened by the hospital environment and the need to be dependent at that time. Shore says abnormalities in the adolescents' "bodily functioning and the way in which they are dealt with by the hospital staff pose questions to the patient about his or her newly changed body image; it may also arouse anxieties about adequacy as a potential adult in relation to the opposite sex."

The necessity to treat the patient psychologically as well as physically is a recognized fact. The art therapy approach is a tool for working through the hospital trauma. For the young child it is a way to reverse the passive, receptive patient role to that of the active, perpetrating doctor. Anna Freud (1936) claimed that it is a therapeutic experience for a child to imitiate the person he fears and to play out the infliction of pain upon the powerful adult. She says this impersonation loosens the bonds of the fearful emotions towards the enacted person or what he represents. The imitation mitigates the trauma and aids the child in similar future experiences.

Art therapy in a medical institution is naturally rooted in minimizing the patient's hospitalization trauma (Gondor, 1954; Plank, 1971). The art therapist's function is to provide a prophylactic service through education and psychotherapy. The goals include: explaining hospital procedures, clarifying possible misperceptions, and providing the patients with a means for relating conscious and unconscious concerns about their illness, the hospital experience and separation from home.

Group art therapy serves a unique function in the general hospital since it provides a place for the patients to talk about and compare issues, such as hospital routines, worries elicited by indirect and/or vague references to the patients' illness or prognosis, feelings aroused through the bodily assault of surgery or tests, and the fear of being forgotten by family, friends and community.

Subjects which are explored in individual or group art therapy are sometimes brought back to the patient's family or doctor or other staff members in an attempt to bring greater understanding and relief to the patient.

Art Therapist as a Procedural Educator

It is essential for the patient to understand hospital procedures which appear to them as harmful or life-threatening. In the role of an educator, the art therapist points out to the individual appropriate expectations regarding the hospital experience. The patient and the art therapist begin the process by making plasticene figures of the patient, doctors, nurses, lab technicians, the family, and hospital props. The patient is then engaged in a psychodrama technique which was originated by J. L. Moreno. It is a method which encourages children to spontaneously act out their concerns and fears. However, during the educational process the psychodrama method is utilized to explore the procedures of hospital entry, laboratory tests, X-rays, surgery and so forth. In this manner, the patient is given the opportunity to rehearse the forthcoming experience.

In cases where surgery is scheduled, plasticene figures of family members are placed on a separate tray. The therapist creates a scene showing where the family will be while the patient is undergoing surgery. For instance, the scene might show the placement of the patient's room and the visitors' waiting room. Eliminating surprises and mystery is a major factor in diminishing psychic trauma. Therefore, important steps in the hospitalization are created and played out by the patient with the help of the therapist. It is absolutely essential for the therapist to use caution in giving "sufficent information" without "overdoing it."

Revealing Areas of Concern

Artwork often reveals areas of concern which have not been verbalized. As in dreams, fears are sometimes masked and the situations are symbolized through condensation. However, the art therapist, trained and sensitive to the subtleties of the underlying messages in the artwork, can often recognize the hidden meaning which is communicated. Cautious interpretations are made only if it is therapeutic for the individual.

Example

Robert, a 12-year-old boy, was being prepared to have cyst removed from his groin. He drew hockey players (Figure 47), emphasizing the padding around the genital area. Although he presented himself as brave and unworried, his drawings revealed his fear. The art therapist mentioned that athletes use padding to protect and prevent injury to their male organs. She added that it was not unusual for boys to worry about their penises being damaged when they had any kind of problem in the groin area. The child quickly shook his head in agreement. The art therapist contacted the doctor to notify him about the boy's fears. The surgeon gave the child full details of the operation, emphasizing the fact that his penis was in absolutely no danger of being damaged. The alleviation of the castration anxiety was apparent in a follow-up art therapy session, when Robert drew "a bunch of boys having fun skinnydipping."

Metaphoric Art: A Working-through Process

The latency-age child uses metaphoric art as a part of the mastery process. The comic strip type of format, where drawings are done in sequence and words written in balloons, is best suited for the metaphoric pictorial story. Most children find this style a natural way of becoming involved. They are asked to make up picture stories about people or animals who

Figure 47.   Castration anxiety revealed

undergo situations which are analogous to their own experience and/or emotions, such as fear, pain, isolation, etc. The pictorial story is continued by the art therapist, who uses a technique parallel to the *therapeutic story-telling* by Richard Gardner (1971) in order to give the tale some therapeutic content and end.

Example

Eight-year-old Betty was hospitalized with a bone infection in her wrist. She was scheduled for surgery. To help Betty deal with her sense of isolation and fear, the clinician asked the child to *make up a picture story of a little dog who got lost*. The patient drew and dictated the following story: "There was a little dog named Cindy who went for a run in the woods. She feels (sic) down and had hurt her paw. Cindy got scared. The little dog was all alone. She had to sleep in the woods. The doggie was worried. Her paw hurt. Maybe her paw would never get better. Cindy didn't know if anyone would ever find her.''

The art therapist picked up the picture story where Betty left off. She drew a veterinarian who knew that Cindy was lost and hurt. He took a few helpers along with him to bandage up Cindy's paw. He found Cindy and, although he knew the poor little dog was hurting badly, he knew he could fix up her paw, and that it would be just fine in the future. Cindy's owners were waiting for the vet to bring the puppy out of the woods. They loved her very much. The owners made sure Cindy would get the best of care. They couldn't wait for the puppy to come home, but they knew the vet and his helpers would fix the puppy's paw so she could roll over, make tricks and run and play with the other dogs on the block.

Example

Seven-year-old Tommy was fearful of staying in the hospital. He was awakened by monster nightmares. To help Tommy deal with his fears, the art therapist handed him plasticene to *create a monster*. Tommy molded (Figure 48) a form which he described as a "monster with teeth and claws." He said, "the bad ugly monster liked to scare kids." The art therapist requested that the child form the figure of a sheriff. Then she moved the

Figure 48.   Patient creates sheriff to confront nightmare monster

figure in front of the monster, and speaking for the sheriff, she said, "Hey, I think you are just a bully. Go ahead and show your teeth and claws; you can't scare me. Show me how tough you are." Tommy had the monster advance towards the sheriff. The therapist suggested that Tommy take over both figures. He grabbed the sheriff, who knocked the monster over. Tommy laughed with glee as he declared, "That's the end of the bad monster." This theme was repeated at numerous times; it became Tommy's favorite. Even when the nightmares stopped, he continued to sculpt or draw "the monster who got scared."

Re-enactment

The art therapist activates a prophylactic process by giving the patient a chance to deal directly with the trauma of hospitalization. This is done through the patient's pictures and/or sculptures, which recreate the traumatic experiences. The patient is helped to play out these scenes in an attempt to get rid of rageful emotions.

Example

Nine-year-old Jeffrey was in an automobile accident. He suffered from broken bones in his legs and ribs and internal injuries. The art therapist invited Jeffrey to join her in creating a plasticene hospital scene. She explained it would be used for play-acting. It was suggested to Jeffrey that he use his own experiences. The patient began to form a little boy and a gigantic doctor. The therapist also made several figures which she encouraged Jeffrey to identify. He turned one into an X-ray technician and the other into a nurse. In the role of director, the patient developed the following scene:

Nurse: (Jeffrey's voice) Çome on, Jeffrey, we are late for your appointment. (*She puts him into a wheelchair.*)
Jeffrey: (therapist gives him a voice) I wonder where I'm going now. I wish I knew what is going to happen.
Situation: Jeffrey is taken into a dark scary room. The nurse leaves and a strange man is in charge.
Man (X-ray technician): (Jeffrey's voice) Now, drink this malted milk, lay still, now take a deep breath, hold your breath, don't breathe, don't breathe, okay—you did real good Jeffrey.
Jeffrey: (therapist's voice) This room is scary. I wonder what that other space machine is. I never saw this man before, I wonder where my nurse is. A malted milk, it's the pits. That stuff is awful, it makes me feel like vomiting. Hold my breath, why? I think I'm going to bust. Oh, I don't like it here. When can I start to breathe again? This is lasting forever!! I

wish my mommy or daddy was here. I must be very, very sick. I'm finished now, but I'm so cold, no one cares about me. I'm scared. I'm mad. *(At this time Jeffrey looked up at the therapist and grinned. She encouraged him to take over the scene, informing him he needn't stick to the truth, and to do whatever he wished in the play.)*
Jeffrey: *(child's voice)* I'm so mad I'm going to kick everyone around here. *(He approaches the X-ray technician, the nurse and the doctor.)* Pow, pow, pow, I'm going to kick you and beat you up. *(The child knocked the figures down. He turned to the therapist, pleased at having inflicted pain upon his tormentors).*

A Mastery Tool

It is therapeutic for a child patient to be given the opportunity to be in control. In the art, the child can create situations where he or she gives the shots, performs the surgery, and injects the pain (often gleefully).

Example

Five-year-old Angie was hospitalized for a tonsillectomy. The art therapist entered her room with a tray, plasticene, toothpicks, pipe cleaners, a few furniture props, pieces of wood, and felt pens. She explained how she and Angie would be making art and playing together.

The tray was used as a base. Upon it the therapist suggested the child set up a hospital room (Figure 49) with the toy sink, toilet, bed, and nightstand.

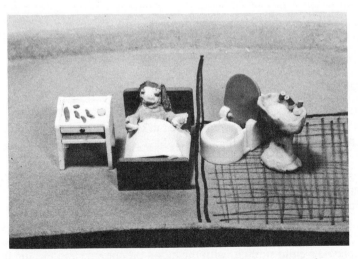

Figure 49.   Hospital scene set up to institute role-playing

The therapist proceeded to sculpt a patient, which was placed in the hospital bed.

The child was invited to take over the scene. At first Angie was hesitant. The therapist continued to make a doctor, which was placed next to the bed. Angie complained that the scene was incomplete; with encouragement she took the plasticene to form hyperdermic needles, vials of blood, pieces of cotton, and a cup for medicine. As she took over, decorating the nightstand with the proper accoutrements, she got in the spirit of the play. Within a short time Angie took over completely. She chose to give the doctor figure a voice and he said, "Now, little girl, I've got to get some blood; you are going to feel a prick, it won't hurt." All of a sudden Angie put the figure down; reaching for a toothpick, she stuck it into the plasticene patient's arm. She said, "See it hurts, see it hurts." Several toothpicks were jabbed or placed into the patient. Angie looked relieved when she completed this part of her act. She then picked up the pipe cleaners, which she placed around the figure's arm in order to take the blood pressure count, "Ah ha," she said, "That's just fine, see you are okay, you can go home tomorrow." She then gave the plasticene patient a pat, stating, "That's enough, you are finished now."

Language Barriers

Communication difficulties arise for hospitalized persons who suffer from temporary or permanent speech defects. This may be due to an impairment or the effect of recent surgery. Communication is also a problem for foreign-language-speaking persons, since an interpreter is not always available to them. Although the example describes a child, the nonverbal drawings are equally as effective with adults.

Example

Maria, a non-English-speaking Mexican child, was unable to make herself understood. The art therapist was asked to see the little girl in an attempt to gain an understanding of what she was trying to communicate. The art therapist drew a simple picture of a clock and a hand waving goodbye to indicate she would have to leave in one hour. Charades were used as an accompanying tool for understanding. Maria seemed pleased to have the art materials available to her. She drew a picture of the window with the drapes closed and the room all black. Then, on the next page, she drew the drapes open, with a smiling face. Maria proceeded with yet another picture where she displayed a child smiling, with the moon on one side and the sun on the other. The therapist wondered if the little girl was frightened by the darkened room, for she evidently expressed her desire to have the drapes open both day and night. The drawings were shared with the staff nurses and the suggestion was made to leave the drapes continually opened. The child, motivated to have more of her needs known, decided to draw both for communication as well as pleasure.

Drawings and magazine pictures and collages are simple ways for nonverbal persons to communicate messages as well as express their emotions. Art can facilitate the patients' hospitalization by eliminating the frustration of not being able to make their needs known. The hospital staff also benefits from the nonverbal communication in their desire to best serve their patients.

SUMMARY

Clinical art therapy is an important part of treatment for medically hospitalized children on a pediatric unit. The art tasks for individual treatment include: 1) education on hospital procedures; 2) ventilation of areas of concern; 3) metaphoric art as an aspect in the working-through process; 4) reenactment of the hospitalization trauma; 5) impersonation of hospital authorities as a means for retaliation and a divergent of fearful repression; and 6) communication mechanism for patients with a language barrier.

CHAPTER 10

Group Clinical Art Therapy on a Medical Pediatric Unit

INTRODUCTION

The following demonstration of group clinical art therapy is with a preadolescent group of boys and girls who were hospitalized for surgery, diagnosis or recuperative care. The procedure and therapeutic benefits, described herein, would apply to latency-age children as well as adults.

The ideal group consists of six children. The session takes approximately one hour. It is held in a room which has a large table, around which seats or wheelchairs, portable stands containing bottles of medication etc. can be gathered. Oil pastels or felt markers and five or more pieces of newsprint paper are placed in front of each child. If the group members' disabilities do not interfere with the use of more sophisticated materials, then they can be introduced at a later time.

When the group members are gathered together, the art therapist introduces him/herself to the group as a person who is there to help the participants share their hospital experiences by drawing and talking about them with other children who are undergoing a similar hard time. The artwork is explained as a vehicle for self-expression, and it is emphasized that the quality of their drawings need not be a concern.

The clinician proceeds to inform the group members that the art therapy experience will begin with a relaxation exercise to help them become comfortable.

Step 1—Warm-up

Children were instructed to relax their muscles. The therapist guided the group into relaxing face, neck, shoulders, arms, hands, fingers, chest, stomach, thighs, calves, feet and toes. This was done slowly in a tempo appropriate for the group members. Some children were not able to participate fully due to medical disabilities or to accouterments; they were given assurance that physical limitations would not interfere with the process.

Step 2

Once the children had achieved bodily relaxation, they were requested to close their eyes. The art therapist explained this was done to help them feel less self-conscious. The participants were asked to "pay attention to how you are feeling after relaxing." Then the therapist instructed them to keep their eyes closed and proceed to *draw a pattern in the air with your hand.* They were encouraged to repeat this a number of times until a rhythm was established. Then instructions were given to *open your eyes, then transfer the air rhythm onto the page in front of you* (with oil pastels). When they finished, the boys and girls were asked to write a title under the picture.

Usually, this exercise had a calming effect. Titles included: "Pleasant Feelings," "Feeling Good," "Nice," "Quiet Fun." The children were asked to share their pictures and the titles. The therapist commented on the interesting similarities and differences among the designs and colors. She complimented the group members for participating in an unknown experience.

The patients were eased into the next experience: *Draw a picture which explains how you felt about these exercises.* The pictures symbolically portrayed the pleasurable and relaxed feelings. One child conjured up an unpleasant image; this was accepted with the therapist pointing out to the patient that "this is not unusual for hospitalized persons."

Step 3

Children were led through another relaxation exercise with the suggestion that this time they imagine a good feeling permeating the room. The boys and girls were instructed to *illustrate your feeling rhythm* (as in the previous exercise), *first in the air, then on paper.* It was further explained that they could draw any kind of design which would stand for their emotions. The therapist encouraged the patients to speak about the pictures and their meanings.

Step 4

Three different pictures were drawn. Instructions were given one at a time. Discussion took place after all the pictures were finished. Instructions were:

a) *Make a picture of you in the hospital.*
b) *Make another picture showing your feelings about the hospital experience.*
c) *Draw the good or bad things about the hospital.*

The pictures of the children *in the hospital,* for the most part, showed them all alone in a large room, although many children shared their room. Where intravenous equipment appeared, it was blown up out of proportion (Figure 50). One child drew transfusion equipment so large it needed several

Figure 50.   Intravenous occupies a large space

sheets of paper. Each patient showed his/her picture while exploring his/her scary and lonely feelings.

The *feelings about the hospital* pictures revealed several different emotions. Most children used red and black, saying they didn't like being there. However, the child with leukemia, who had had numerous blood transfusions, drew a smiling face, acknowledging the importance of the hospital for life maintenance.

Example

Arnie was a withdrawn child, who was not responding to medical treatment.

As a member of the art therapy group, he, in response to the themes of "hospitalization," drew smudged designs; during the discussion period, other participants questioned if these designs held any special meaning. Arnie hesitatingly explained they represented his fears because he didn't understand the nature of his illness. No one had discussed with him his illness, the length of his hospitalization, or any possible future plans.

Arnie admitted he had not asked any questions because of his fear of the answers he might receive. The patient's unexpressed concern kept him withdrawn and in a constant state of anxiety.

The group members could relate to Arnie's feelings; several children admitted they too were worried. The children shared their own difficulties in asking the doctors questions. Some children said they could confront their parents, but sometimes felt the answers were more protective than truthful. The therapist encouraged the children to be more assertive in seeking answers about their concerns.

All the children seemed pleased with the opportunity to draw the *good and bad things about the hospital*. For this directive they were given 10 to 15 sheets of newsprint with instructions to draw each thought on a separate page. The good pictures showed ice cream, candy, nice nurses, games and television. The "bad parts" images (Figure 51) were drawn with greater force and conviction, as seen by the size, strength of lines, bolder colors and general involvement. All the children drew shots; some added vials of blood; others depicted various types of testing equipment; bad nurses, or doctors were drawn; bedpans, cold stethoscopes, intravenous equipment and several drawings of question marks were presented.

The therapist asked children with similar images to share their works as a set. Then the varied types of symbolism were examined. In this way, the children could see, then hear, mutually shared concerns and feelings.

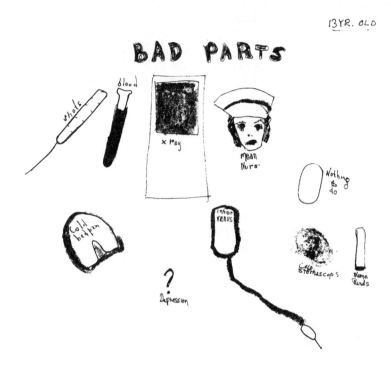

Figure 51.   Children share dissatisfaction with hospital

Step 5—Closure

For closure, the patients were asked to *draw how you felt about the art therapy session.*

The children drew colorful pictures of flowers, waves, suns and smiling faces. The ensuing discussion revolved around their positive art therapy experience. As the group ended, the participants appeared relieved of their depression and tenseness. A friendlier frame of mind was apparent. The boys and girls thanked the therapist for providing an experience where their fears could be shown and shared, and for a few, alleviated.

ADDITIONAL SESSIONS

In following art therapy sessions, warm-up techniques were used, similar to the ones already described. However, the next four steps included picture collages with the following requests:

a) *If you have some worries, draw them.*
b) In the event some children were going home, the directive was, *How does it feel to go home, and for those of you who remain, how does it feel to see these children go home?*
c) *What you would like to say to your: 1) doctor, 2) nurse, 3) parents?*
d) Closure revolved around individual pictures of the theme *group art therapy.* These were then pasted together by the therapist. Discussion followed around the meaning of their individual and collective art therapy experiences.

FOLLOW-UP

Follow-up includes reports from nurses about the children's attitude after the art therapy experience.

Positive results were reported. There was an improvement in communication and a generally more agreeable attitude. Several children were reported to be more relaxed, and one child, "a perfect patient," made a therapeutic gain by becoming "imperfect" when she began to voice discomfort to the staff and her parents. In the case of Arnie, "a change towards a motivation to recover" was cited.

SUMMARY

Group art therapy provides the patient with an empathic community where mutual concerns, fantasies and needs are explored. The support system encourages communication with the hospital staff. Clinical art therapy techniques explore: 1) emotional awareness; 2) fantasy of "positive" feelings; 3) feelings about the hospital experience; 4) negative and positive aspects of hospitalization; 5) additional issues regarding hospitalization.

CHAPTER 11

Crisis Intervention
as a Preventative Measure

INTRODUCTION

In the book *Principles of Preventative Psychiatry,* Caplan (1964) points out that emotional crisis or "upset" is "usually associated with subjective feelings of displeasure such as anxiety, fear, guilt, or shame, according to the nature of the situation." Caplan says that the individual in crisis has "a feeling of helplessness and ineffectuality in the face of the insoluble problem and this is associated with some disorganization of functioning, so that the person appears less effective than he usually is."

Crisis resolution is of considerable significance for the future mental health of the individual, for in resolving the crisis he or she may have utilized reality-oriented adaptive coping mechanisms and developed new, socially acceptable techniques for problem-solving. In this event, the experience becomes an asset, for it is available in the future as a model for coping with crisis. On the other hand, if the individual employed responses such as denial, repression and/or alienation, the possibility is greater that he will continue to deal with problems maladaptively.

Interpersonal action on the part of mental health workers promotes healthy crisis-coping. As a specialist, the clinical art therapist brings a unique dimension to crisis intervention, for the art task serves as a simple means to aid the individual in productively ventilating crisis-related affects of anger, guilt and loss. In addition, this modality provides a concrete statement which is helpful in pointing out areas for useful exploration.

The crisis event may apply to an individual, a small group, the community, or a large segment of the population. Although the literature on crisis intervention includes primary, secondary and tertiary prevention in various settings, and in reference to brief and extended treatment, there appears to be scant, or perhaps no, literature on *single-session intervention*. However, the author has found clinical art therapy to be extremely valuable in aiding the prevention of repression and other malfunctioning coping skills in a single session. The focus is placed on a *prophylactic orientation with children who have undergone a situational crisis*. The trauma which had been recently experienced was dealt with during one art therapy meeting. The approach included art tasks which explored the event, expressed concerns and emotions and clarified perceptions regarding the crisis.

This chapter includes three prevention examples: 1) an earthquake victim; 2) a latency-age group whose community was exposed to a shoot-out between the police and the Symbionese Liberation Army; and 3) an adolescent's medical hospitalization.

While reading these examples, bear in mind that *numerous other crises take place which are unlike these illustrations. However, the basic goal of therapy is the same—the review, clarification and exploration of emotions to prevent repression and/or distortion of the experience.*

LATENCY-AGE CHILD: EARTHQUAKE TRAUMA, A CASE HISTORY

The earthquake hit at 6:00 in the morning. Prior to the upheaval, Johnny White got up and went to the bathroom. As he was urinating, the floor and toilet began to shake. He saw bottles fly out of the medicine chest and could hear his sister and brother scramble out of their rooms. Johnny stood frozen for a few seconds before he could activate himself to find his parents' bedroom. The quake was over quickly. He reported trying to vomit out of fear. Upon inspection, the only major damage was to the fireplace, which shifted away from the rest of the living room. In addition, the electrical power was cut off. Johnny reported that his father had left for work at 7 o'clock, but he had wished his parent had remained at home.

Trauma: Vulnerability and Rage

Johnny, an art psychotherapy participant, happened to have an appointment with the author the day of the quake. She asked him to *draw a picture of your family during and after the earthquake*. For "during the quake" he showed himself alone in the bathroom as his sister, brother and mother cuddled together in bed; his father was alone, close to the bathroom door.

Johnny drew the bathroom on a separate page; it showed his psychological distance from the rest of the family and his feelings of abandonment. The "after picture" (Figure 52) showed the child alone by the fireplace, with bricks falling down around him; the rest of the family was in the kitchen getting breakfast; his father was outside. When Johnny was asked about the drawing in which he had placed himself near the dangerous and shaky fireplace (instead of in the bathroom), the child said he had put himself in a dangerous position "because if I was hurt my dad would be sorry."

Expression of Anger

Johnny expressed his anger towards his father through a plasticene sculpture of a man and a dog (Figure 53). He dictated the following story: "This is a man who didn't take good care of his dog; he'd go to work and the dog was alone. The dog was sad and mad when he was alone. When the man came home from work the dog bit him." The author interpreted the scene and asked Johnny to create another scene, which would show an appropriate way of showing his anger towards father. Johnny molded a piece which represented himself; then he placed it face to face with father as he

Figure 52.   Distorted perceptions of earthquake situation

Figure 53.   Child's rage with father displayed by dog biting a man

accusingly said, "You should have stayed home because I was scared that maybe another earthquake would start." The therapist pointed out the importance of communication. It would have been helpful to father had Johnny voiced his thoughts.

Mastery

In an attempt to master the trauma of fear and separation, Johnny spontaneously created a series of sculptures. The first plasticene figure was of a boy with boxing gloves; the second was of a shaky house; the third was a phallic structure which appeared similar to the fireplace; the fourth was a dog wagging his tail; the last was a house which was solid and stable. Johnny's body began to relax when he was halfway through. He hummed as he formed the dog and the stable house. When Johnny left the session he was obviously feeling more comfortable.

Follow-up

Two years later, Johnny was asked to draw his earthquake experience.

The picture showed Johnny in the bathroom when the quake started, his joining his family in his parents' bedroom, and his father going to work after he had asked Johnny if he was okay. Johnny's drawing validated his ability to work through the trauma of the earthquake during the crisis intervention session.

GROUP ART THERAPY IN A PUBLIC SCHOOL:
CHILDREN'S REACTION TO VIOLENCE IN THEIR COMMUNITY

One evening in May 1974, a shoot-out between law officers and the Symbionese Liberation Army terrorists took place in South Central Los Angeles. Many people in that community were within shooting range as they watched the gun battle. Tear-gas and thousands of rounds of ammunition were fired by the police during the two hours of violence. Patty Hearst was in the hide-out house, which was destroyed by fire. Five persons died in the shoot-out.

Two weeks after the shoot-out, a three-person mental health crisis team used the art therapy modality to work with a classroom of nine- and 10-year-old black children. The school was in the neighborhood where the event took place. Prevention of maladaptive coping skills was the team's motivating force, and efforts were made to relieve the children's anxiety around the issue of the violent aggression which took place in their community. The dangerous act had been witnessed either in person or on television in their homes at the very moment it was happening. Although "cops and robbers" killings are not uncommon on the television screen, the shock of it being "real" and not being "pretend" gave a horrendous and vulnerable feeling to the children in the community.

This example of crisis intervention will give the methodology and findings of the experience, including introduction, warm-up, recall of the event, emotional expressions and issues, reconstitution, process of closure and termination.

Procedure

The therapists introduced themselves as persons who help children and adults with "their troubles." The students were told that they could offer the therapists a chance to better understand other children who would be helped with their worries, scares, or other problems.

The classroom was divided into groups of seven children. Each group was seated at a table. Crayons, felt markers and newsprint were placed in front of each child.

Introduction and Warm-up

The author told the students that, although they would be making art-work, the way in which they drew was not important. The stress was placed on using the art as a way of expressing their feelings. She proceeded to demonstrate how different lines and colors can portray various feelings. In order to engage the children, the art therapist asked them to print their initials as large as possible on a piece of paper. She then instructed them to look at the spaces that the letters created and to make discoveries. They might find the shape or design of an animal, a person, objects, or whatever. The children were encouraged to use their imaginations. After finding these images, they were told to proceed to draw their discoveries on the page.

The boys and girls quickly made their initials. However, they hesitated to proceed to the next step. The reluctance may have been due to their concerns around expectations, self-consciousness and/or distrust of strangers. Nevertheless, after a while all the children became involved, exploring their creativity. Upon completion, they were asked to give the drawing a title. Rounds were made; each child had a turn to hold up his/her picture and to share its contents and title. The students were delighted with this exercise.

Recalling the Event

The next procedure was the presentation of the topic of the Symbionese Liberation Army shoot-out. A therapist began to mention that something unusual had happened "two weeks ago on 54th Street" and before the sentence could be completed, most of the children in the room were inflamed with anxiety. Many of them spoke at once, completing the therapist's thought, "yeah, and Compton Avenue." Then they spewed out the details of the shoot-out.

Immediately, the therapists encouraged the students to *draw your feelings regarding the incident.* As they drew and spoke, their vivid memories elicited a tremendous amount of stressful emotions. Between tightly held fingers, crayons pounced on the paper; a staccato noise was evident everywhere as a tempo which produced the bullets on the page. In a short time, flaming images emerged throughout the room. Pictures were filled with people who were bewildered, scared, angry and sad; chidren and adults were screaming, a great many yelling for HELP! There was a multitude of dead bodies.

Castration Anxiety

The children's rage, fears, sadness, and vulnerability were poignantly portrayed through their drawings, coupled with words and body language. One boy, exhibiting castration anxiety, reached and held his penis with one hand and drew with the other hand as he nervously explained his picture (Figure 54). It contained a tall, phallic-looking house, riddled with bullet holes. He drew himself in front of a police car, which he declared he wanted to blow up. He said, "There were people there and Patricia Hearst has a child." He further explained, "Patty's father went on television and talked about the child. Somebody either was kidnapped or might be kidnapped and then a man came out of the house during the shoot-out that was pregnant." He denied the therapist's attempt for clarification, stating, "Yes, the man had a big belly." The child fused the concepts of sex, violence, and aggression. On the page he wrote, "I'm mad, I was there."

Figure 54.   S.L.A.: Child expresses aggression and confusion

Separation and Loss

Loss and fear of separation were obvious themes. Some children dealt with their anxiety about loss directly. For instance, one boy used his red crayon to jab bullet holes and he added a dead man—a policeman with his car. He proclaimed, "There's the shot-up house; I saw it; I was there; they shot the house!! The policemen were behind the house; guys in the house were shooting the policemen. I don't care about the policemen." Then the child looked up at the therapist as he questioned, "Is my father going to get shot?"

Substitute Gratification

Denial as a defense mechanism was commonly used. Emotions which parents and siblings were unable to display at the time of the shoot-out were drawn by the students as a compensatory attempt towards substitute gratification. This is clearly depicted by a little girl who drew a house being destroyed by fire. On the picture she wrote, "Help me please, think (sic) you." She had nervously explained, "The house was on fire, the police came and the firemen came to put out the fire so all the people wouldn't die. The people said 'thank you' and they got out. That's it; they didn't die." The child created her own ending to the event; confronting herself with the actual deaths was evidently too emotionally overloading. She went on to voice her concern about relatives who lived in the neighborhood where the gun battle took place. She projected her feelings onto a picture through an oversized drawing of a girl crying and saying, "Too bad it was sad." When the therapist asked for more information on the little girl in the picture, she explained "She has sad feelings. She started to cry; she didn't know what to do. Her mother and brother did the same thing; they were sad." In reality, she reported her own mother and sister showed no affect.

Identification

Although children were not a part of the terrorists' hide-out, or the shooting, numerous graphics contained children, which were identified as being the same sex and age as the students. The children's identification as victims being violated was vividly seen. For example, a little girl described her picture: "The house was burning and the police were shooting. The people inside were crying and yelling. The lady said 'Help.' There was a little girl inside and she climbed out of the window. Half the people were in the basement. There were lots of cars and furniture burning up."

Figure 55.   S.L.A.: Burnt tree symbolizes innocent victim

Innocent Victim

The identification of the innocent victim was often displayed through emphasis on "the house next door" or on the nearby trees; Figure 55 is only one such example. A little boy nervously drew a bullet-riddled house aflame, police car, bullets shooting in the air, and a palm tree. In a loud and rapid voice, he ventilated his great concern over a palm tree which he believed was demolished by the fire.

Kidnap Fears

Before the SLA shoot-out, there was a vast amount of publicity regarding Patty Hearst's kidnapping. When the shoot-out occurred, it activated a great deal of confusion, personal fantasies and fears of "being kidnapped." For instance, a nine-year-old girl drew a tremendous house filled with a large number of bullet holes, with a burning house next door to it. She proclaimed her anger with the police, adding "I didn't know what was happening. I was worried; the helicopters were over us. It was scary. Maybe I could be kidnapped." At this point, several children reported they also shared this worry. The little girl then proceeded to draw a very large policeman on the side. This appeared to be an unconscious attempt to defend herself against the unsafe world.

Restitution Discussion

The noise and anxiety level in the classroom remained high. The therapists felt that it was essential to introduce a feeling of protectiveness for the children. With this in mind, they were asked to leave the tables and to seat themselves, along with the therapist, on the floor. They were asked to form a small, closed circle, holding their neighbors' hands.

Restitution talk was introduced by asking the boys and girls for ideas on alternate choices which might have been available to the police, the terrorists and the people of the South East Los Angeles community. At first, the children seemed impotent; then several students came up with ideas which they had seen on television programs regarding police work. Non-violent methods were suggested, such as starving the terrorists; it was suggested that loudspeakers could have been used to tell onlookers to go home so they wouldn't get hurt. Some of the ideas were their own fantasies, such as asking the terrorists to throw away their weapons and so would the police—one child suggested that the police bring the terrorists candy as a way of seducing them from the house. This discussion gave some children a measure of relief. Several cathartic signs were made; more relaxed body positions were observed; facial features showing terror and anger disappeared. Recounting the shoot-out and probing for alternate choices helped the children deal with this frightening experience in their community.

Preparing for Closure

In preparation for closure, the boys and girls were brought back to their drawing table. To give them a sense of empathic unity, the author laid out one large piece of newsprint paper. The request was to *draw a picture together*. The project became an extraordinarily cooperative effort (Figure 56). Sometimes, the children drew their own symbols; at other moments they would add on and enhance the drawing of another person. The mutually created picture gave the children a sense of closeness and calmness. When the picture was almost complete, one of the boys who had been most angry printed some Chinese-looking characters; when the therapist questioned their meaning, he commanded her to "write down what it is. Write 'you and me and them and us.'" The author commented, "I think you are angry with me because I'm white." The child stopped as though he had to remind

Figure 56.   S.L.A.: Satisfaction expressed during closure

himself that this Caucasian stranger was someone whom he had learned to trust, and nodded his head in assent. The group members decided to title their artwork "The Best Pitchere (sic) in the World." Although the title writer spelled extremely well, "picture" is spelled "Pitchere." The art therapist responded to the title as she said, "It certainly is the best picture in the world since there has been a pitch here and you were able to talk about worries and scaries and sad feelings and angry feelings."

Closure

The children pleaded with the therapists to stay. They were delighted with the fact that someone not only paid attention to their feelings, but also gave additional validation by writing their statements down on the drawings.

Boys and girls wrote down their names and phone numbers or addresses and passed the slips to the clinicians. One little boy wrote after his name that he was a movie star, showing his feelings of being important. The boys and girls wrote little messages, such as "I like you" or "I love you," on their hands and showed them to the therapists to indicate their positive transference.

The three therapists expressed their gratitude, thanking the children for their help. The boys and girls were surprised and pleased that they could have been of help to the helpers.

Termination

In the final phase of closure, the boys and girls in a relieved and reflective silence motivated themselves to put the supplies in order and to straighten up the room. It indicated a resigned readiness for termination.

Comments

In the author's opinion, the children with the stronger egos utilized the art therapy crisis intervention as a way of working on the trauma of violence in their community. For all the children, the single art therapy experience provided an opportunity to explore their thoughts and emotions around a threatening event. This, in itself, is therapeutic.

Although follow-up in "prevention" is not always measurable, mental health workers agree that more work in this direction is essential.

CRISIS INTERVENTION WITH AN ADOLESCENT IN A MEDICAL HOSPITAL

In a medical hospital setting where the patient may be seen for a single time, the major focus is placed on therapeutic self-expression. Patients also benefit from their favorable response to the art therapist who is a nonmedical, empathic person, and whose main interest is in the individual's emotional state rather than his/her physical condition.

In the following example, the author had no knowledge of the patient's medical history. Her visit required no time from the medical staff, yet she was acknowledged to have a psychiatric "preventative" function.

Ben, a 15-year-old boy, had been admitted to a medical hospital the day before the session. The art therapist, bringing in newsprint and oil pastels, introduced herself. She explained to the patient that he was being given an opportunity to draw something about his experience and that this was often helpful in managing the hospitalization. The quiet, friendly, adolescent agreed, telling the therapist of his interest in art. Ben proceeded to report that his doctor had requested hospitalization in order to perform a number of tests. He did not offer information on the nature of his problem.

Upward Displacement

Ben, upon request, did the standard "initial" warm-up. He was instructed to discover a form within his initials, then to elaborate on the basic design. When he was asked to tell about the picture (Figure 57) he said, "It's a man with a scarf around his head. Then there is a hat attached, a hat attached above the head." The picture contained a nose, eyes which reveal

Figure 57.   Symbol for upward displacement

hurting or sadness, an elaborate scarf tied over the head, and above this is a stovepipe hat. Although the therapist wondered if this drawing displayed upward displacement, she offered no interpretation.

Fear of Death

The next directions were to *draw something sad*. Using his brown crayon, Ben pressed heavily on the paper. The picture (Figure 58) looked like a gurney; however, when asked to title it, Ben said it was a "coffin." If the boy were in art therapy treatment, the therapist would have dealt with the imagery; she would have explored the boy's fear of death, or the possibility that he had witnessed a dead child being wheeled out. However, in this single session, the clinician merely acknowledged the fact that being in the hospital was often frightening.

Figure 58.   Fear of death

Nurturance

The third directive was *draw a glad picture*. With spontaneity and freedom, Ben drew a picture (Figure 59) of a large bird feeding two young ones in their nest. He said, "It's a baby bird being born, there are two other birds in the nest. Mother is feeding the new bird." The therapist wondered if Ben was responding to the therapist, who is often depicted in connection with food or feeding; however, again, no interpretations were offered.

Punishment Fantasies

The next directive was *draw something you feel strongly about—a person, place or thing*. Ben hesitated for a minute; then, with strong strokes, he dashed off the drawing (Figure 60) of a hand clutching a knife which was dripping with blood. He wrote the title, "Murder." When asked to give word associations, his face showed anger as he stated "hate and punishment." Considering the phallic symbols involved in the picture, the therapist wondered if Ben's physical problem was related to his genitals. He was obviously ventilating his fear, anger and rage. Fantasies of retaliation or the issues surrounding masturbation were also possibilities underlying the pictorial messages.

Future Unknown

Then a *free choice picture* was offered. Ben explained his picture (Figure 61) as a "fishing boat with the net in the water." The picture had a lonely tone, the sky was faintly scribbled in with black crayon. The largest object in the picture was the setting sun. The therapist's conjecture revolved around the "current warmth" and the possible "dark future." Immediately after the picture was titled, Ben opened a drawer and pulled out a pad of paper; he shared with the therapist drawings he had previously created. The gesture was one of pride, as well as an attempt to make a deeper connection with the therapist.

Isolation

The last directive was *draw what it feels like to be in the hospital*. Ben was lost in thought for a while; as he looked outside, he began to draw the scene he observed from the window (Figure 62). Using a black crayon he drew a lonely picture of buildings with little substance, a scattered blue sky and a

Figure 59.   Nurturance

Figure 60.   Rage

Figure 61.   Future unknown

Figure 62.   Isolation

skeletal brown steel structure. When Ben completed his picture, he sighed with relief. With little prompting he talked about his sense of isolation and the "cooped-in" feelings which were elicited by the hospitalization. Isolation is often overwhelming for the adolescent. Fear of abandonment by friends and the outside world is a major concern. With Ben's approval, his last picture was shown to other hospitalized teenagers. It gave them a frame of reference for projecting and discussing their own concerns.

Comments

It is important to note that, in spite of the art therapist's lack of knowledge regarding the patient and the nature of his hospitalization and without any interpretations, a single art therapy session offered Ben a psychologically prophylactic experience.

PART IV

Adolescents
and Adults

ADOLESCENCE

Children ages 13 to 18 are in the stage of adolescence, a period which is often described as a time of "storm and stress." Stone and Church (1957, p. 270) state, "the central theme of adolescence is finding of oneself. The adolescent must learn to know a whole new body and its potentials for feeling and behavior, and to fit it into his picture of himself." There are several preconditions which are necessary for the adolescent character formation to proceed; according to Blos (1962), these include: a phase of second individuation, handling residual traumas, sexual identity and the maintenance of ego continuity.

As a preparation for adulthood, the adolescent stage involves numerous developmental tasks; these are defined by Havighurst (1952) in terms of ten categories: 1) new and mature relations with heterosexual and unisexual peers; 2) gender identity social role; 3) acceptance of one's own body and using it affectively; 4) emotional independence of parents and authority figures; 5) assurances of economic independence; 6) preparation for an occupation; 7) preparation for family and marriage; 8) development of intellectual skills and concepts necessary for civic competence; 9) desiring and attaining socially responsible behavior; 10) establishing values and ethics as a guide to behavior.

Both the preconditions essential to adolescent character formation and the developmental tasks of adolescence may be worked upon through the art psychotherapy modality. The author's belief is in accord with Blos' statement (1962) that the process of creating during the adolescent stage "enhances infatuation of the self; it is often accompanied by excitement and carries the conviction of being a chosen and special person, the sublimated activity can be described in these essential terms: 1) it is highly self-centered, that is, narcissistic; 2) it is subordinated to the limitation of an artistic medium, and consequently is partially reality originated; 3) it operates within the modality of 'giving life to a new existence,' the self; 4) it constitutes a communication with the environment, and is therefore partially object related" (p.126).

EARLY ADULTHOOD AND THE MIDDLE AGE

Early adulthood includes the ages of 18 to 30. Erikson (1959, p.95) refers to this stage as one of *intimacy and distantiation versus self absorption*. He states it is a time which is designated for "Work or study towards a specified career, sociability with the other sex, and in time, marriage and family of one's own." Erikson relates, "true intimacy is possible after there is an established sense of indentity. The counterpart of intimacy is distantiation: the readiness to repudiate, to isolate, and, if necessary, to destroy those forces and people whose essence seems dangerous to one's own." Havighurst (1952, p.72) claims early adulthood is "the most individualistic period of life and the loneliest one, in the sense that the individual, or at most, two individuals, must proceed with a minimum of social attention and assistance to tackle the most important tasks of life." Havighurst lists the following developmental tasks of early adulthood: 1) selecting a mate, 2) learning to live with a married partner, 3) starting a family, 4) rearing children, 5) managing a home, 6) getting started in an occupation, 7) taking on civic responsibility, 8) finding a congenial social group.

Later in the life-cycle, when the individual reaches ages 30 to 55, he/she is in the stage of *middle age*. During that time societal influence reaches its peak while simultaneously civic and social responsibilities are at a maximum. Erikson (1959) defines this period of adulthood as *generativity versus stagnation*. It is concerned with the establishment of the next generation. He claims that it is essential for "growth of the healthy personality and that where such enrichment fails altogether, regression and generativity to an obsessive need for pseudo intimacy takes place, often with a pervading sense of stagnation and interpersonal impoverishment" (p.97) Havighurst (1952) says the developmental tasks of middle age come from: changes in the organism, pressures from the environment and self-demands as a result of aspirations and one's own value system. He delineates the developmental tasks as follows: 1) achieving adult civic and social responsibility; 2) establishing and maintaining an economic standard of living; 3) assisting teenage children to become responsible and happy adults; 4) developing adult leisure-time activities; 5) relating oneself to one's spouse as a person; 6) to accept and adjust to the physiological change of middle age; 7) adjustment to aging parents.

*****

Part IV covers clinical art therapy for adolescents and adults. Chapter 12 portrays a documented case history of "Lori," an adolescent in long-term treatment. In the beginning, art psychotherapy techniques were offered to the client as a means for dealing with reality and as a method for experiencing and understanding her repressed emotions. Later in treatment, Lori learned to create art and analyze her own symbolism for purposes of insight and direction. Chapter 13 focuses on the significant role of the art media in the long-term treatment of an adult named "Iris." The art materials and style were correlated with the goals of loosening up rigid defenses and working upon individuation. Chapter 14 deals with brief individual treatment for an artist with a creative block. The abstract images which she portrayed led to self-awareness and the ability to go beyond the painter's impasse. Chapter 15 demonstrates the use of art therapy for consciousness-raising and for data collection and assessment. It is a pilot exploratory research project, regarding children of Holocaust survivors. The art therapy techniques provided the means for gathering information on the effect which the middle- and upper-class survivor parents have upon their children. The techniques involved in the study are applicable for a variety of research products where simulated situations are useful. The art products conveyed collectable conscious responses as well as unconscious clues which enriched the data.

CHAPTER 12

Lori: Long-Term Treatment of an Adolescent

The course of Lori's art therapy is divided into two parts. The first part presents the initial 26 months of treatment, during which Lori gains a sense of self and an awareness of family dynamics. The second part, the last eight months of treatment, reveals the girl's rapid evolution through the stages of adolescence and the tasks necessary for a healthy adjustment.

DESCRIPTION

Lori's mother, Mrs. Walters, was a chronic schizophrenic who had a history of numerous hospitalizations. Her father, Mr. Walters, worked in a store. He was a quiet man who showed little affect. Mr. and Mrs. Walters were born and raised in Mexico; they moved to the United States after their marriage. Frances, Lori's 17-year-old sister, was a beautiful, gregarious, outgoing adolescent. Lori herself was 14 when treatment began. She was a heavy "dumpy-looking" youngster whose hair hung limply, covering part of her face. Her clothes were clean, but she appeared slovenly. Her facial expression was usually blank; if she did smile, her blank expression quickly returned. The initial evaluator stated that Lori was "withdrawn and

---

This case has been documented in the film "Lori: Art Therapy and Self Discovery." Half-hour running time, color, sound, 16 mm. Directed and produced by Tapper/Dempwolf Productions. Distributed by Art Therapy Film Distributors, P.O. Box 1289, Pacific Palisades, California 90272.

isolated, chronically depressed and indifferent to people and events. The loss of adequate mothering has also contributed to her sense of being depleted."

In the initial art psychotherapy session, Lori stated, "I'm so happy to have a place to show all my problems and to be able to talk about them." However, in the following few months she was unable to be specific regarding her problems. Shy, isolated and emotionally constricted, her constant complaint was one of being "tired." She showed little concern for her appearance. She had no friends or interests and conveyed no desire to pursue any kind of involvement, nor did she engage in any kind of physical or passive activity, such as sports, reading, listening to music or any type of creativity. Lori maintained passing grades in school, but her studying was erratic due to difficulties in concentration and a lack of motivation. In the first several months of treatment, she spoke very little, frequently said, "Nothing is happening."

The art seemed especially important to this adolescent, since her silence seemed to fill the room. Communicating in a nonverbal mode was a relief to the withdrawn girl, whose feelings were diffuse and undifferentiated. The need for some kind of expression was obviously felt by her.

TREATMENT

Lori was seen in art psychotherapy for a period of 34 months. Sessions were held one to three times a week, depending upon the stage of treatment.

SECTION I: ONE TO TWENTY-FIVE MONTHS

First Six Months

In the beginning, Lori found it difficult to engage in the process of free expression. Therefore, collages were used to relieve her anxiety and resistance, as well as to facilitate communication of conscious and unconscious material. Initially, her *free choice* pictures were filled with animals, fantasies of going somewhere, wishes for a peaceful society, and surgeons; however, most frequently selected were photos of cash registers (Figure 63). The cash register was the most important object in her life, since her school cafeteria job gave her some self-esteem.

While in the second month of art therapy, Lori and the art therapist had a coke at a coffee shop. On that occasion she witnessed the clinician's friendship with a black waitress. After returning to the art therapy room, she made a collage (Figure 64). Lori used a picture which contained both a black and a caucasian person. She wrote, "A unity between

Figure 63.   Cafeteria job the single symbol of self-esteem

Figure 64.   Transference

race—understanding between them." Then she pasted a photo of an older
woman and children. Underneath she stated, "Shows two different generations—they have an understanding (to be physically close to the young
boy)." Since Lori and the therapist were of different ethnic backgrounds
and a generation removed, the pictures revealed her positive transference
and fantasies regarding the clinician.

"Tree" pictures which were given a "voice" were periodically requested;
these served to record Lori's self-image. In the third month of treatment

(Figure 65) she stated, "I am a tree. I am lonely. I am located on a hill and I like it. I am a big tree, a sick looking tree. The climate is cold. I lose my leaves. I am a strong man tree. The lady trees are tall and pretty but weaker—not strong as me." The drawing and the free association to it revealed the identity confusion and validated the dynamic formulation regarding Lori's lack of adequate parental models. She sought to identify herself with her father, *since the possibility of being like her mother was a serious threat to her.* The picture poignantly portrayed the adolescent's sense of vulnerability and isolation.

Figure 65.   Tree image portrays confusion and low self-esteem

The client often referred to her sister Frances, who not only provided a vicarious life, but also literally served as Lori's voice, frequently speaking for her. It appeared that Frances played the role of Lori's surrogate id, while Lori served as a superego for her sister. The pathological complementary needs resulted in a symbiosis, which was illustrated in a drawing identified by the client as "two trees and a hammock. They are tied together." It was later in therapy, after similar clues were pictorially recorded, that an interpretation to this picture was offered by the therapist.

To help focus on problem areas in the early stages of therapy, Lori was asked to *create a fantasy about yourself.* She made a collage (Figure 66) which showed herself as being "Happy—taller—smart." To deal with reality, the therapist gently told the girl, "We know you can't be taller—now show the practical changes you *can* make." In response, Lori drew a chart which showed, "I can be 1) slimmer, 2) happier, 3) do better in school."

Lori's depression created difficulty in concentration and kept her depleted much of the time. She denied this emotion; for example, when Lori made mistakes as a cashier in school, she would blame the errors as the reason for her "feeling bad." The first insight was in the fourth month of therapy. On a drawing entitled "Depression," Lori wrote, "Town is a symbolism of

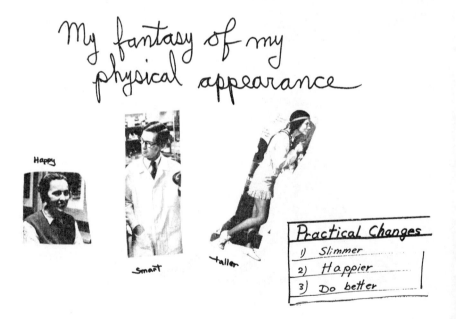

Figure 66.   A focus for change

depression to me. People don't know one another. To walk through a city gives the feeling of nobody.'' As Lori talked about this, she asked the author, "If no one talks to me, how do I know I exist?'' Before this picture, all of Lori's statements revealed only pleasantries and boredom. Her awareness of the existential question of her existence was a significant step towards growth and development.

Because Lori had so much difficulty with getting in touch with her emotions, collage as a distancing device was used in an attempt to aid her in the expression of anger. A request was made to *pick out six pictures of angry people. What are they saying and what do they wish they could say?* Included in the composite (Figure 67) is the image of a man who is saying nothing and wishes he could say, "What are your feelings?" In the second picture, also of a man, Lori stated "He is bewildered. He said, 'How's your work doing with you?' but he wishes he could say nothing.'' The third male picture provoked such a high level of anxiety that Lori was unable to write

Figure 67.   Difficulty in expressing anger

anything. The fourth photo revealed a woman, "Saying nothing and wishing she could say nothing." When questioned about what the lady was thinking, Lori replied, "I'm in pain." The fifth, a male figure, was thinking, "I'm caught in traffic," but said nothing. When asked what he wished he could say, Lori wrote in a question mark. For a considerable period of time, Lori blocked any angry emotions as a defense against her repressed rage.

Lori acknowledged only feelings of love towards her sister; any negative responses were too threatening. During the fifth month of therapy, the cafeteria manager at school asked Lori to tell her sister that she, too, could have a job working the cash register. At first, Lori denied any emotional response to the manager's request. The art therapist asked Lori to *select some words from the collage box. After pasting them down, find pictures which can be identified with the words.* This procedure was followed by a written dialogue. The finished product contained two powerful executive type male figures. They displayed strong, aggressive and decisive personalities. The words Lori used were, "Don't start." Underneath she explained that, in spite of the manager's request, she would like to tell her sister Frances to stay away and not take the limelight away from her. The other word on the collage was "Decision." The picture deals with her wish that she could make one decision and stick to it. Lori was encouraged to express her fantasies of how she might handle the situation. Drawing her sister and herself, she stated, "Well, the lady told me to ask you, and since I didn't want you to work there, don't!! Don't ever work where I am working. I really would feel there would be too much competition." A role-playing technique ensued as a rehearsal for self-assertion. The method did give Lori the courage to confront Frances, although the actual words were said in a softer and quieter fashion.

Seven through Fifteen Months

In the seventh month of therapy, one of the pictures in a *nondirected collage* elicited material which, for the first time, dealt with some of Lori's negative feelings toward Frances. A photograph of cookies evoked the following memory: "Reminds me of when my sister and her friend made a batch of cookies and ate it all. This made me mad for they didn't even share any." The remembrance of angry feelings was a breakthrough of Lori's defense of denial. It was of particular importance due to the symbiosis and the confrontative fear of rejection, abandonment and total isolation which separation represented.

In keeping with Lori's history of repressing emotion-laden content, the references to her family were always "nice." The insight due to the "cookie picture" was followed up the next week by a distancing device of metaphoric family portraits. The adolescent was instructed to *draw pictures of animals to symbolize each member of your family.* The graphics (Figure 68) were explained by Lori as follows, "The *cat* is a symbol of my *father;* he's independent and doesn't go along with what the crowd says; he's quiet and not very affectionate, only once in a while. The *mule* is a symbol of my *mother;* my mother is very stubborn and when she gets angry she really gets angry. At times when she gets lazy she would not do much work." The *lion* was reported to represent her *sister* who "Always stands up for her rights, and has the temper." She added, "it's not very peaceful when moved to

Figure 68.   Animal pictures symbolize family members

hurt." The last animal, separated from the rest, was Lori herself as a *tiger*, which she identified as having a "bad temper" and "kind of lazy."

The animal technique allowed Lori the freedom to be honest with herself and the therapist. for the first time she expressed her father's reserve, her mother's lack of household involvement, her sister's struggle to individuate, and her poor self-esteem.

Work around the family issues continued in the next session, when the art therapist instructed Lori to *pick out pictures which remind you of the members of your family.* Underneath the picture identified as her mother she wrote, "She is always grouchy and miserable. She's a lousy mother because she doesn't know how to discipline her own children and she acts childish." This insight provided the opportunity to deal with the reality of her mother's deficits, as well as the rage which was connected to Lori's feelings of deprivation. In the following few months she was helped to lower her unrealistic expectations regarding her mother as she realized they could never be fulfilled.

During the initial eight months of art psychotherapy, there were gradual and difficult efforts to make connections with life in the community. With a great deal of support in treatment, Lori volunteered to do clerical work at the Red Cross, she started guitar lessons, and, as hard as it was, she looked into several school clubs. Lori joined two of these clubs and became involved in a few of the YWCA activities. She also began to study for the driver's test, symbolizing her attempt to become independent. With her low self-esteem, she failed to pass the driver's test, but felt proud of taking the risk.

After treatment had continued for one year, Lori's sister left home. Regarding the move, Lori created a collage in two parts titled, "Changes in Me due to My Sister's Leaving" and "The Changes in My Parents." The first part of the collage (Figure 69) contained a bear, which meant "In a sense, I would become more independent and feel freer without my sister to rely on." An elephant with rope around the trunk "symbolized the bond with which I will be tied to my parents."

In the second part of the collage (Figure 70) which was titled "Changes in My Parents," lightning with a superimposed eye was displayed to indicate "the watchful eye they will keep on me." Certainly her evaluations were realistic and thus Lori prepared herself for her sister's separation. She realized the advantage of functioning independently and disadvantage of being overly protected by her family.

The following month, Lori reported an incident in school where the teacher complained about her work, but the class supported Lori. Her

In a sense I would be more Independent & feel more free without my sister to rely upon.

Figure 69.   Evaluating separation from sister

Figure 70.   Assessing parents' reaction

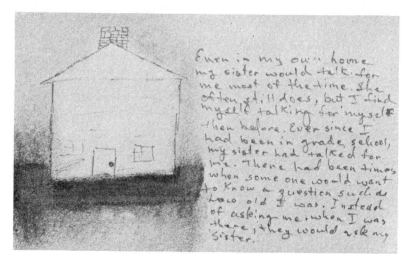

Figure 71.   Elective mutism revealed

association to this event was a drawing of a house (Figure 71) titled, "People Always Talked for Me." She elaborated, "Even in my own home, my sister would talk for me most of the time. She often still does, but I find myself talking for myself more than before. Ever since I had been in grade school, my sister had talked for me. There have been times someone would want to know a question, such as my age; instead of asking *me*, although I was right there, they would ask my sister." Lori continued to relate that, away from her family, she had been an elective mute. She never spoke during the entire time she attended elementary and junior high school. One teacher after another was informed that Lori did not speak; neither the instructors nor students directed any communication to her.

In the following art therapy session, Lori reviewed her artwork. As she looked at the pictures of the "Town Symbolizing Depression," in which she had questioned her very existence, the "House" which evoked memories of her selective mutism, and the images in which she confronted her mother's incapacity for adequate parenting, Lori gained insight into her schizoid reaction of isolation and depersonalization.

Sixteen Through Twenty-Five Months

A great deal of emphasis was placed on Lori's getting in touch with her current feelings. Since her emotions were often only fleetingly experiences, drawings and paintings helped Lori to tap into momentary emotions. They

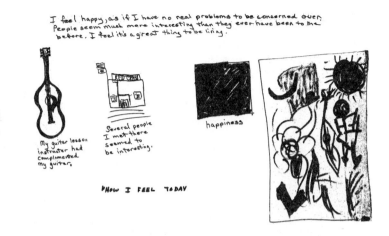

Figure 72.   Reasons for feeling good

also served to maintain that awareness. The artwork was analogous to a "freeze frame" which provided a halt to her state of flux. In this way, Lori could examine her feelings, sense her existence, and use the graphics to contact and experience her sense of self.

At the end of 16 months of treatment, Lori drew "How I Feel Today" (Figure 72). She wrote, "I feel happy, as if I have no real problems to be concerned over. People seem much more interesting than they ever have been to me before. I feel it's a great thing to be living." Included in the drawing was a picture of a boy, which depicted a story she had recently heard about a young man who was shy. It made her feel comfortable to realize that other people also suffered from problems similar to her own. Then, as Lori made a picture of a guitar, she reported to her art therapist that her music instructor complimented her and it made her happy. A Red Cross building stood for the opportunity to meet several interesting people, and an abstract painting portrayed her current "happiness."

Between the eighteenth and twentieth months of art psychotherapy, Lori's pictures and collages conveyed people making firm statements. They asserted themselves and expressed a wide range of emotions. Those images were a way for the adolescent girl to understand and allow her needs to be known to herself and her therapist. It was a rehearsal for what was barely being acted out beyond the boundaries of art therapy.

Several students and family members told Lori she was beginning to stick up for herself, was less shy and much friendlier. The positive feedback was gratifying, since it validated Lori's changing self-image.

During the second summer of treatment, Lori began to seriously diet, losing 15 pounds over a matter of months. She got her hair cut in a fashionable style. She began to use makeup lightly and started to dress with youthful good taste. In the fall, for the first time in her life, she selected and bought her own clothes without help from anyone. Surprised and delighted by the compliments she had received, Lori told her therapist, "Now I know, I, myself, have good taste. I don't have to go with someone else to pick out a dress for me. I know what I like and what looks good on me."

In the twenty-fourth month of treatment, Lori found a part-time job in a dress shop. She started out in the office and progressed to doing numerous jobs, such as office work, selling, etc. Her employer thought highly of Lori and she became friends with one of the other young employees. A few out-of-town weekend trips were made by a girlfriend and herself. Lori took a second driver's test. This time she passed the exam. She discussed the difference in her attitude toward the actual driver's test, declaring that failure versus success depended on one's self-esteem. The ability to drive on her own was a symbolic milestone towards her goal of autonomy.

SECTION II: TWENTY-SIX THROUGH THIRTY-FOUR MONTHS

Up to this point the patient had made gradual gains. The therapist, serving the role of the "good mother," was providing the child with the nurturance necessary for developmental growth. In addition, the therapist functioned as a model whose healthy ego was being creatively integrated into the patient's self.

During the first 26 months of therapy, Lori accumulated healthy adaptive skills which readied her for a gigantic growth spurt during the next eight months of her life. Many issues indigenous to the stages of adolescence, ordinarily dealt with over a period of several years, were worked through in a matter of eight months.

To give the reader a greater sense of Lori and her amazing insights, this part of the case history focuses mainly on process, rather than methodology. The emphasis is on *Lori's story*.

After 25 months of treatment, just before Christmas, Lori was very depressed. Her sister was no longer at home and Lori's mother had recently been psychiatrically hospitalized; although Mrs. Walters was now at home, she was completely withdrawn and hallucinating much of the time. School was going badly for Lori. Two days before Christmas, she painted a picture which declared, "Our house is dark; there is color everywhere else."

The therapist, who was going out of town between Christmas and New Year's, realized the importance of maintaining a connection with Lori and believed in the transmission of passive depressive energies into a creative force. Therefore, she handed Lori a paintbox and a pad of paper. She was instructed to paint daily; the length of time for her creative involvement could be anywhere from a few minutes to several hours. Lori was encouraged to record her thoughts through poetry or prose (on the back of the artwork, in a manner similar to the therapy work). The therapist caringly, but firmly, again reiterated the importance of setting time aside each day for the art form of self-expression.

After New Year's, Lori returned to her art therapy session. She brought in a large number of paintings, along with the interpretations of her imagery. Some pictures were consciously painted to convey how she felt; others were first produced, then followed up by free associations. Lori found this experience to be profoundly productive; she explained, "When I drew and then started writing down what I felt, things began clearing up for me. I couldn't believe how much the art and writing every day helped me see how things really were. It began with Christmas—I painted several Christmas pictures. Those paintings are really merry and happy. I was so surprised at how very good Christmas turned out. As I thought and painted, I realized that it was because Frances wasn't there. In the past she would tell us all when to open the presents, when to eat and what to do. She was like a general and all of us were puppets. This year without her everything was natural. We opened the presents and just did what we felt like doing. It was really nice. Now, here is a drawing with the eye in the middle and these wavy lines one after another making bigger and bigger circles. Suddenly I was like that eye observing, seeing for the first time how my sister and other people acted. I was able to be in the room but be *separate from them!* I felt I had been taken advantage of. It angered me that I was so gullible with my generosity. I realized that I wanted to please! I guess that's what I do sometimes to be appreciated."

From what Lori reported, it was apparent the daily art and writing acted as a concrete form with which to visually and psychologically explore herself as a person. Her insight was also recorded through the artwork, giving her additional reinforcement toward her struggle for individuation, and enabling her to literally act upon the separation from her sister.

Following this monumental event, Lori painted pictures and wrote about the "surprising and marvelous relief" she had undergone. She expressed a desire to continue the meaningful experience of painting and writing at home. In addition, plans were made whereby the author and Lori would first meet to go over the artwork which was done at home. Then, during the next hour Lori used an empty room as a private studio, where she painted by herself. This was followed up with a 45-minute session where the art therapist and the patient reviewed the artwork. This arrangement was of great value, for it gave Lori an opportunity to stretch out her autonomous art therapy time and lessened her dependency on the therapist.

The quotations cited in the second portion of this case history were written by Lori in relation to her artwork. These were created during the last eight months of clinical art therapy.

Lori's dramatic progress began with her description (Figure 73) of the "Relief I felt after I got mad at Frances. The only way I could get out my angry feelings toward her was to let loose and release it at once. Once I got mad at her, it seemed as though something had been lifted and my body felt free. The *dark figure* meant that I was feeling low. Then it was soon lifted once I got angry. Black rings represent pressure lifting from my body. The *yellow figure* is me outside of that feeling. Yellow means light, free figure."

After New Year's Day, Lori had her first date. At that time, and for the next six weeks, many paintings were produced which referred to a "state of confusion." Other pictures related to the fear of dating as well—an "uncertainty" and "need to explore" were common themes. At the end of January Lori drew a *self-portrait* and she declared, "I see a change in myself; I see confidence; I express my ideas more; I have been standing up for myself. I told Frances how I felt about her and I also told a fellow I dated that he was

Figure 73.   Ventilation and relief

rude. I stuck up for my dad when I thought he was right about something."

During the twenty-seventh month of psychotherapy, Lori painted a picture (Figure 74) which she described as "The different lines and shapes seem to mean there is no definite pattern. Things are going in all directions; things seem to be suspended. There is a phase of monotony. I see nervousness, a lost state. There is also confusion, which is expressed by the different colors and erratic design."

Another image (Figure 75) was interpreted as, "I have been sheltered so long. Just in recent years I have come out of my shell and out of that shell came a warm heart. I really feel for people. Before, I really couldn't care one way or another—or perhaps it was because I was unable to distinguish my feelings."

In a later painting, Lori stated, "I want to come out of my own small world and explore new things. I feel there are so many things around and I'm sheltering myself from them. I want to find my way out of this shelter and really look at the world around. Don't know where to start."

Figure 74. Adolescent confusion

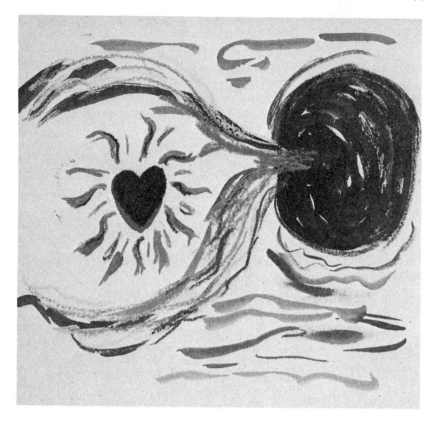

Figure 75.   In touch with emotions

All of the artwork was done in color, except for one pencil drawing (Figure 76) which showed two figures lying in the sand. The heavily sexual emotional content was subdued by the pale use of the monochromatic media. The contents related to Lori's first date. She explained the picture, "met two guys and went out. I fixed up a girlfriend." She went on to declare, "He didn't force me to do anything. I just did it of my own free will." She described how before leaving for the date she looked into the mirror and said to herself, "'Lori, I think you're going to say goodbye to your virginity.' When I think about it now, I did it because I was envious of my friends and Frances. Also I guess it could be an act of rebellion, because I'm sick and tired of hearing my family say what a good head I have on my shoulders." As Lori and the therapist talked about what the intercourse experience meant to her, she said she found having sex to be very natural and enjoyable and was delighted with her newly realized femininity.

Figure 76.   Sexual experience

A few weeks later, Lori stated, "I knew what I wanted to paint. This weekend, it seems I experienced things I was curious about and a little afraid and hesitant about. I made a girlfriend, which is new. I had intercourse with this guy I met. I even associated with people who I usually considered the least likely I would have associated with, namely, marijuana smokers, drinkers and bums (as they call themselves). What I feel about the whole experience is a sort of satisfaction. In a way, this seems to answer some questions. I have a girlfriend with whom I am able to talk freely. Intercourse—I found out some of my reactions towards it. Also I can now see how I feel about family situations. My associations with these different people—I never realized that I could really be able to see some of their points of view. Also, it's the first time I hitchhiked. I saw two different sides —it's cheap transportation, but it can be unsafe. Not that I didn't know this before, but I guess I wanted to see for myself."

Lori reported that during intercourse neither she nor the boy used a contraceptive. The therapist pointed out to Lori the necessity of taking care of herself and to prevent becoming pregnant. When Lori came in for the next appointment, she had already gone to the free clinic and picked up contraceptive pills, to protect herself in the future.

Shortly thereafter, Lori painted a picture which evoked the following,

"I'm in the middle of the ocean. There is no way to turn. I'm confused about sex and marriage. Then there are decisions I must make and things I must think out, but I'm having difficulty with both."

Several sessions later, Lori recorded, "I knew what I wanted to paint. My mood has been very changeable lately. I was feeling happy at times and others I felt depressed. I was happy when I was going to see John. I also figure that I have morals still. They have changed somewhat, but they are still morals. I'm also beginning to understand my actions for what I've been doing; I'm upset because of my parents. I figure I do want to stir things up at home. An example is that on Friday night I didn't go home. I stayed with John. I didn't bother to call my parents. I got home the next afternoon and nobody said anything to me. They didn't even care. After I got home, I thought about it. I was really upset. I actually felt like crying. Besides that, I became very angry with my parents and I felt very rebellious towards them. I was saying all sorts of mean things about them. So, that night I was so glad to get out of the house, but I was puzzled about certain things about John. I'm beginning to wonder what I really do feel about him. I think I like him more than I thought I did or something. I feel wanted when I'm with him and his friends. *Maybe I'm using him as a substitute for the lack of love at home. I don't know.*"

In response to Lori's disappointment and hurt regarding her parents' ignoring her night away from home, the therapist discussed Lori's mother's inability to cope with life on any level and how unrealistic it was of her to expect to receive an appropriate response. Although Lori's father was never able to show any emotion, he was and remained a steady and consistent figure in her life. The therapist suggested the possibility that Lori's father may have been so deeply wounded by her actions and words that he was unable to say anything. Lori was able to take this in and a few weeks later both she and her father spent an entire weekend making a welded sculptured lamp. She designed the lamp and Mr. Walters, following instructions, welded the pieces together. Then Lori sprayed it gold. Her father added the harp and the light bulb. The creative lamp was a symbol of their conscious effort to bring light to their relationship. In addition, so much pleasure was derived from this mutual creativity that they planned to make other objects together.

During the twenty-eighth month of art psychotherapy, Lori said, "I knew what I was going to paint" (Figure 77). "It had to do with 'How I felt about telling Mrs. Landgarten about my experience with intercourse.' I thought she would be disappointed in me, I had a hard time telling her; it was a very touchy subject. I was surprised the way Mrs. Landgarten reacted; we both spoke very openly and it made me feel good to be able to discuss the subject of sex. Here in the picture is the free circular mass with an enclosing circle

Figure 77.   Discussing sex with the art psychotherapist

around a square indicated my feeling or my fear to tell Mrs. Landgarten what I did with John. The green mass then flowed into a variety of colors which indicates my good feeling after discussing the situation.''

The following week, another abstract painting titled "Analysis" was completed. The writing stated, ''I see life. I see a change. The life I see is the line and curves. The change is in the color. The curves are swirling in a circular rotation which centers around a change.''

At this time Lori was evolving as a young woman who began to make her life and her surroundings more comfortable and enriched (Figure 78). She sewed curtains, painted her bedroom and hung up pictures. Aside from therapy artwork, an interest in creating aesthetic products developed. Lori's sculpture gave her much pleasure and increased her self-esteem. Lori began to give some of her art to special people as gifts, realizing their appreciation of her talent and her willingness to share a facet of herself.

During the next few months there was a period when Lori began to explore the female form in clay. The three-dimensional aspect of the medium helped her to investigate and gain a fuller understanding of her sexuality. In addition to the female forms, the client continued on to make vessel shapes

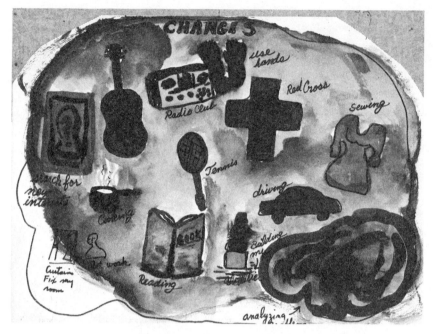

Figure 78.   Changes instituted

of one sort or another; these symbolized her integrated femininity and her ability to be a person who could be open and also to contain the emotions appropriate to the stage of late adolescence. Lori gave the author a gift (Figure 79)—it was a female clay vessel sculpture in which flowers had been placed. It was accompanied by the following poem:

> Life—I have found life
> I had learned to see, to feel,
> to hear and to love.
>
> I discovered the life within me,
> the life within my mind
> and the life of my body.

During the twenty-ninth month of art psychotherapy, Lori drew a picture of a date which she had with her boyfriend. It showed her standing aside watching the boy. She spoke about the meaning of the picture, "I was able to look at him and stand back and know who I was. I felt sorry for him and I realized that I could have been where he was and I was so glad that I was

Figure 79.   Self-discovery

where I am. I didn't want to hurt his feelings, but I knew that it was important for him to know that I didn't want to see him again. All of that is over. My experience with drugs was not good, but it's good to know that I could try all that and be strong enough to know that it isn't what I want. What I do want is a real relationship that grows by getting to know someone through the course of time. I want more than to be used as a sexual object. I want the kind of love that means understanding and the sharing of all kinds of thoughts, feelings and interests." Lori added, "There are still lots of nice people around to meet and with whom to make friends and to enjoy, to get to know on a deeper, richer level."

As Lori realized her potential, she became more discriminating of the friends she chose.

After 30 months of treatment, Lori drew (Figure 80) her final *tree*. She analyzed the picture, "This symbolizes the mood I am in today. I'm really rather happy, I guess, because things appear to be going well. I filled the picture with bright happy colors. The tree symbolizes that I'm in full bloom so to speak, and the apples represent the life I have within myself."

During the terminating phase of therapy, a videotape recording was made

Figure 80.   Final tree image portrays improved self esteem

of one of her sessions. At that time, Lori looked over the art which she had created during treatment. While looking at her initial pictures, she said, "I remember how unsure I was of myself. I never knew what to draw or paste." The various phases of "tree images" (five in all) gave her concrete examples of her personal growth; she was sad while she looked at her first, barren, confused tree, and showed pleasure and pride upon viewing the "tree full of bloom."

As she reviewed her portfolio, Lori saw how she had been unable to write appropriate thoughts or feelings to the "angry people" collage. The contrast was tremendous as she viewed the later art, which expressed not only anger, but also pain, loneliness, femininity, sexuality, love, etc. The alive expression on Lori's face as she identified with her recent images was a far cry from her blank expression at the outset of therapy.

The review recapitulated the therapeutic process. Lori could see for herself what kind of person she had been and visually perceived her growth. This videotape, plus one made in the early part of treatment, were played back for Lori to view. They were powerful media for the reinforcement of gains.

After 34 months of art psychotherapy, during the terminating session, Lori made a collage. Underneath she wrote about the difficulties she had in making up her mind during the beginning months of therapy. She was delighted with the contrast where she could currently be creative with speed and ease. Lori related this change to the growth she had made, as she stated, "Now I am a person with a mind and rights of my own."

The last piece of art, like the first, was a collage (Figure 81). She quickly selelcted and pasted an image of a head of a blindfolded female, then she superimposed an open eye on one side of the blindfold. Beneath it, she rapidly wrote the following poem:

> There stands one child alone and blind,
> She has no lack of sight,
> but yet she cannot see.
> Then in her life there appears a light,
> It is the inner glow which grows within her,
> giving warmth, love, hope, desire.
>
> As she stands she begins to move
> at a pace slower than many.
> But she keeps pushing forth
> till she's pacing near,
> Equal to those around.

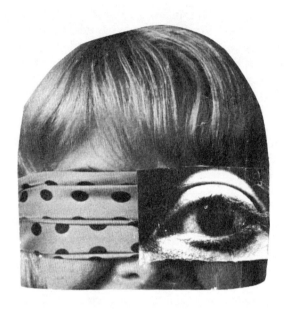

Figure 81.   Sight

The child has grown to near womanhood
but she still has limits of sight.
So pushing still,
she'll continue till,
she sees past these limits of light.

SUMMARY

Lori was an adolescent who was in art psychotherapy treatment for 34 months. The client is portayed in her isolated and depressed state at the beginning of therapy through her struggle to become a functioning person with healthy adaptive coping skills. Lori created art forms and used them as a means for gaining insight and integration. The client's imagery and written records revealed her emergence as a creative and growing individual, in touch with herself and the world around her.

CHAPTER 13

Emphasis on Media: An Adult in Long-term Treatment

INTRODUCTION

Iris was in clinical art therapy for a period of 20 months. She was 21 years old when treatment began. After a brief marriage she had been divorced, leaving her in a state of depression and fearful of having a complete breakdown. Resistant to psychotherapy, she claimed she knew all about herself; she did not like sharing personal information and said a therapist would be unable to "take away the pain." However, the client's mother, concerned about her daughter's mental health, insisted that Iris seek psychological help.

In the initial interview the client complained of headaches and backaches, continued fatigue, and inability to sleep or to concentrate. Iris persisted in using rationalization as a defense and the only emotion she showed was "anger," claiming that she was angry with herself for being dependent on her mother and friends. Due to Iris' resistance, art psychotherapy appeared to be the treatment of choice; within that approach the usual defenses would be less available and unconscious material would surface in the art.

Clients who are extremely resistant to treatment and refuse to talk about themselves or their problems tend to activate countertransference in the therapist. It is the author's belief that many art psychotherapists have less difficulty with this type of person, for the client engaged in the art task is communicating on a symbolic level. It is this factor which often enables the art psychotherapist to remain interested in the silent or defended client.

The case history of Iris emphasizes the cognitive approach to the media, which played an especially significant part in the treatment. The goal in therapy was to encourage the client to give up her rigidity. Therefore, media, style, color and space considerations were given to art techniques focusing on "gaining freedom." However, due to Iris' reluctance to involve herself in the artwork, a media desensitization process was instituted. Attention was also paid to Iris' fears of making mistakes and her intolerance of messiness. Work on adaptive coping mechanisms included symbolic risk-taking opportunities, presented through a gradual series of less structured media explorations, such as: drips or blotches of paint used to suggest abstract images; colored tissue paper superimposed one upon the other to stimulate creativity; poster paint sponge paintings to simplify the art process; oil pastels with turpentine to loosen up a structured style; plasticene for its three-dimensional quality; wet grey clay, then finally terra cotta clay for regression and a freeing experience; and plaster, a medium for extended work. Through this process Iris also learned to recognize that "the mistake" could be a "happy accident" which sparked creativity.

Symbolic expansion for Iris was implemented through specific uses of space. Initially, small-sized paper was used to match the client's need for containment; later, use of increased space was encouraged as development progressed. At the end of treatment, final drawings and paintings were created on huge pieces of brown wrapping paper. Sculptured pieces expanded in spatial dimensions through the use of multiple forms.

The nature of the art tools also dealt with the "expansion concept" through the use of thin to wide tips for felt pens and brushes.

The illustrations place an emphasis on the art media during the art psychotherapy diagnostic evaluation, as well as during the 20 months of treatment. Iris attended art psychotherapy sessions two times a week for the first six months, then once a week for the remaining 14 months. The art therapy directives are stated, along with the goals of their application and comments regarding the use of the media.

DIAGNOSTIC EVALUATION

As part of the diagnostic evaluation, Iris was asked to *create a house, tree and person.* The Landgarten version of Buck's (1970) H-T-P projective test was given. Iris was instructed to: 1) *Select colored felt markers to draw a house.* 2) *Select colored pencils to draw a tree.* 3) *Use a pen and watercolors to paint a person.* 4) *Select the media of your choice and create whatever you desire.* The way in which the client approached the problem, handled the media and created the pictures offered data useful in assessing her ego strengths and weaknesses.

1) For the *house,* Iris was offered a full set of colored felt markers. She chose to use the brown marker only. The house looked like two houses stuck together. It was a double A-frame with a double door, both on the house and garage. The brickwork was extremely detailed. Two trees were drawn on each side of the house and a profusion of flowers whose height covered up three-fourths of the front windows. The entire picture was painstakingly drawn. Iris mentioned if she could have selected her own medium she would have chosen pencils, since she liked fine details which were difficult to draw with wide-nibbed markers.

The House oftentimes represents the client's family life, as well as aspects of the self. All of the house's double features indicated a possible symbiosis with mother, the profusion of flowers showed a tendency to deny what goes on inside, and the meticulous detailing of the brickwork suggested an obsessive-compulsive tendency.

2) The *tree* was drawn very carefully with a single brown pencil (although a full set of colors had been presented). The tree's stiffness and lack of leaves (especially significant in California) gave some clues to a possible lag in emotional growth and development; a knothole towards the top of the trunk revealed a trauma at the time of the client's divorce; the sun almost entirely covered by dark clouds indicated unhappiness and concern. When Iris was asked to "talk about the tree" she said it was "very stiff, old, and ready to die"; these were indicators to her inflexibility, depression, and possible suicidal ideation. The single brown color lent additional clues to the depression and perhaps a withholding or narrow mode of functioning.

3) The *person* (Figure 82) was started with a penned outline, then later filled in with watercolors. Iris used the medium with a minimum amount of water in an effort to control the paints. However, since the brush maintained more water than she intended, a struggle with the "looseness" of the paints showed her obvious frustration. When Iris was asked to look at her picture and relate something about "the person," she said, "the girl is scared, she is stiff. Her hands are like a baby's and her feet too little to keep her up." She went on to report how uncomfortable she felt with the "paints running together or going outside the lines." Although unaware, the client revealed her fear, inflexibility, and inadequacy in handling adult life.

4) Free choice pictures were accompanied by a variety of media from which to choose. Iris volunteered to use black, brown or dark blue colored pencils to draw a single person in a landscape with twin trees, twin

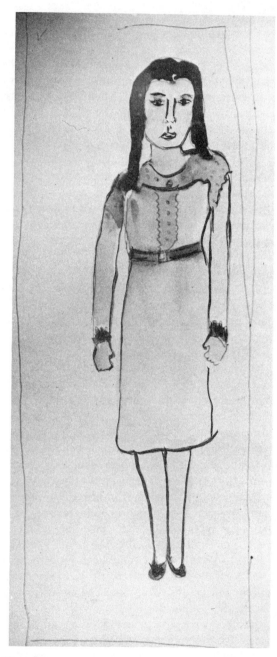

Figure 82.   The "person" as part of a projective test

mountains and even twin clouds. The client's depression, sense of isolation, symbiotic tie to mother, and rigidity were consistently implied in her artwork.

Iris felt a need to maintain limited parameters, and her harsh superego was immediately evident (insight into the source evolved later in her art therapy).

A long-range treatment plan included the following goals: increase self-esteem, work through maladaptive rigid defenses, dissolve the symbiosis with mother, and make progress toward individuation.

An essential part of the total treatment was the introduction of various goals as the patient progressed from one stage to another. The media and the directives always encompassed the immediate goal in order to facilitate development. Appropriate art materials were vital in meeting the client's needs during phases of transition. *It is realistic for the reader to remember that sessions which are not reported continued on plateaus; only milestones are reported herein. Therefore, the following illustrations are selected highlights of Iris' developmental progress.* Changes in the artwork parallel movement outside of the art psychotherapy sessions. Successful treatment takes place only when the art functions as a model which is acted out in real life situations.

ART PSYCHOTHERAPY

Colored Pencils: Structure

Colored pencils, a medium which the client preferred and which symbolically suited her compulsivity, was initially offered. This structured medium was introduced to make Iris feel comfortable and to help her trust the therapist's judgment. A *free choice drawing* was requested.

Iris was very meticulous. She asked for an eraser and a ruler (both of which she used). Her picture showed a girl standing outside, looking through the window of a supermarket. This single drawing took the entire session. The length of time seemed to be a part of her resistance to talk about herself and in this way Iris controlled the session. When asked to talk about the artwork, the client hesitated for a long time. Finally, she said the person in the drawing, like herself, was "hungry." She mentioned her intention to shop for her mother on the way home because "the refrigerator at home is empty."

Comments

It is not unusual for persons beginning therapy to express their oral needs with the underlying message of a desire for psychological nurturance. After the first session, the art psychotherapist slowly shifted the client away from the structured colored pencils by *combining* them with felt pens. After several sessions of using the mixed media, the pencils were eliminated.

Watercolors and Pen and Ink: A Loosening Agent

When Iris was first given the opportunity to work with watercolors and ink, her approach was a rigid one. She began with a penned outline, then used the paint in a controlled fashion to fill in the guidelines. In an attempt to reverse this procedure, the client was told to *wet the paper down first, then brush on several colors.* This procedure was followed with instructions to *relax, close your eyes, picture someone in your mind's eye.* After a brief time the therapist continued, *try to portray the fantasized image either in a realistic or symbolic manner. Use the pen and ink for the drawings which are to be placed on top of your watercolored paper.*

Following these instructions, Iris painted Figure 83. She was asked to make up a story about the two representational female figures. Onto the picture she wrote, "One woman is delicate, but big and is influenced by someone else. The other woman is a mother and an artist." Iris admitted this statement represented her positive transference to the art psychotherapist. After this technique was utilized for a number of sessions, Iris was asked about her reactions to the watercolor medium. She replied, "I'm beginning to get the hang of it. In fact, I seem to be more able to let the colors take control." With these words, Iris became aware of her relentless "need to maintain control."

Comments

During this phase of treatment, Iris maintained a meticulous, compulsive style during free choice picture. On the other hand, instructed techniques lent greater freedom to the artwork. The polarization offered Iris an opportunity to understand the feelings which each style elicited.

Watercolors: Less Structured Medium

To encourage freedom, watercolor paints were dropped onto white blotters. This was followed by the use of felt pens to draw into, around, and between the watercolor splotches. Iris was asked to title these pictures. At first the artwork was given negative titles, such as "Nothing," "Just blobs," "Messy," "Slob Dob."

Figure 83.   Free associations indicate positive transference

With the establishment of the therapeutic alliance between Iris and the author, the therapist humorously requested a "Nothing" picture, or a "Messy" one, or a "Blobby" one. Iris enjoyed the "in-therapy joke" as she began to respond to the paint by having fun with it. Within a few months, Iris' changed attitude towards the artwork was indicated by such titles as "Flowers," "Fruit," Starry Night," and "Loneliness."

Comments

The repetition of a "loose style" began to be an ordinary experience for Iris. This fact, plus the therapist's sense of humor, brought the client to the point of accepting and enjoying the procedure.

In reference to the media, white blotters were used since they absorb immediately and the flooding quality can be kept in check. For Iris this was especially beneficial, for the difficulty of controlling watercolors still evoked her frustration and anxiety. After several sessions, the watercolors were used on different, less absorbent types of paper, for example, construction paper, newsprint, and, finally, a slick, non-absorbing poster paper.

Felt Markers and Poster Paints: Transitional Experimentation

The client was instructed to *fold the paper in half. Take poster paints and dab some onto one side of the paper. Then fold it over (Rorschach style).* Iris was obviously uncomfortable as she complained, "Gosh, this is messy. It reminds me of my childhood." At this point it would have been premature to deal with the unconscious meaning of "messiness." In an effort to alleviate Iris' anxiety, the therapist offered her a method for a "symbolical clean-up," saying, *find a part of the design which you like, then cut it out and paste it onto colored construction paper.*

Iris discovered a small section of the picture which she found pleasing and placed it on a beige background. Surprised with the results, she told the art therapist, "Hey, how about that, something messy and something neat, it looks like a modern painting. I almost like it."

Comments

In the beginning, the Rorschach-type picture was introduced for its loose style. It is not as threatening as one which is intentionally made by the client. However, with Iris' anxious reaction, it was necessary to provide closure. The instructions to cut out a part of the picture which she liked gave the client symbolic structure and the opportunity to make changes.

Variations of this concept were frequently used to facilitate the art media experimentations.

Painting: Meaning and Autonomy

Iris was encouraged to keep an art therapy journal. Several times she brought it to the therapy session. One of her entries stated:

I'm beginning to like the use of watercolors, because I can see the effect they give on the paper is special—a wateriness, a surprising graduation of color—even an ordinary splash looks interesting—they almost automatically make all sorts of textures, light and space and nuances—it's become painless to use them. It seems to me, it expresses my emotional states and impressions better than representational figures where the heaviness of line is awkward.

This new thing for me of *allowing* myself to paint has been a very happy experience. I can do what I want, how I want. I like painting at home, too, but I wonder how much of the effect is also to have the "treasures" presented to me by someone else as a kind of a gift; will I keep on painting when therapy is over or will I give it up?

The joy of making something is exhilarating, but when it comes to keeping it, there is still too much critical faculty in check—I do know I always feel much better after I do the artwork!

Comments

The journal and the artwork functioned as transitional objects for Iris. They were important aspects of her treatment, proving that she could express herself and *give herself* a cathartic experience. This aspect was especially therapeutic in working with a client who tended to fuse with the mother figure.

Free Choice: Responsibility

After Iris learned to use the various art media with comfort, she was usually given the responsibility of choosing her own subject. Frequently, decisions regarding size, media and style were also made by her. This step was taken to help her with issues such as decision-making, problem-solving, and independence. With a client such as Iris, who is in a symbiotic tie with mother, the author believes it is crucial to the therapy that the transference

does not repeat the patient's dependency pattern. Therefore, the autonomous work within, as well as outside of, the session is stressed, except on
the occasions when it is therapeutically contraindicated.

Color Portrays Conflict

At the time when Iris stopped fighting the art media, she began to select
certain colors as an explicit tool for dealing with her internal conflicts. For
example, she painted and recorded the following:

On the left side is my painting of a crystal glass. I attempted to show
its many facets and at the same time its simplicity. The blue and aqua
color was the closest approximation I could make of the clear crystal
color. I see that I use *objects,* elegant *things,* to picture *my striving
after elegance* and what seems to me to be clear, cool perfection. It is
to a great extent *external,* that is, it is primarily a self that I am concerned with showing to the world. It is positively associated with beauty and a taste for fine things, and negatively associated with snobbishness and affectation.

In contrast to the left elegant crystal glass external self of mine, I
have this brown, grey and dark gold colored right side. In these colors
I show my limited, complex, but essentially "uninteresting" self—the
person that people don't remember and who lets herself be pushed
around, who is confused. *I don't like the color combination so I added the purple and yellow on purpose because I wanted to show my
negative feelings about myself. It is my tasteless, "poor folks," insecure, unhappy side.* In the middle I again chose a round thing, with
warm colors, light, warmth and completeness. This center reaches out
and embraces the rest, with varying success.

Comments

The client began to formulate the meanings of her own colors. At times
she would intentionally use them to portray a special meaning (as in this session). At other times she painted and analyzed herself, using the colors as a
clue to her unconscious.

Symbolic Identification

Iris began to paint the "Poppy" theme as a means of projecting her emotional state. After her first Poppy picture, she wrote, "Poppies are

beautiful and very fragile, and their stems and leaves are spindly in comparison to the richness of the petals. Poppy leaves have a particular way of wilting and getting saggy, which in turn reminds me of my own sadness. I used to want to pick giant bunches of them, but they always wilted and died. You can't, or mustn't, pick poppies.''

Comments

Iris did not connect her own flower name with the poppy until later in treatment. Her continued use of this theme served the purpose of identification and mastery.

Acrylic Over-painting: Concretizing Changes

To provide Iris with a medium where corrections could easily be made, acrylics were introduced. Instructions were given to *paint a symbol of an important goal, on top of a paper carton, and on the sides paint symbols of what you want to change.*

On the top of the carton, Iris painted a singular design. She said it represented *independence.* On the four sides of the carton she displayed: 1) *a fat woman;* 2) *a wild hairdo;* 3) *a telephone;* 4) *a hand with handcuffs on the wrists.*

Iris blocked off the sides of the obese woman, slimming the figure down; she used the same approach for the hairdo (Figure 84), giving it a neater ap-

Figure 84.   Possible changes

pearance; an X was placed over the telephone, symbolically negating a need to talk to her friends daily; finally she painted out the handcuffs for they represented the symbiotic tie to her mother.

Comments

Changes in the artwork symbolically reinforced the messages of one's ability for modification. Acrylic paints dry quickly and overlays can be made quickly. The use of the carton diminished the "precious" quality of the paint. Visual and psychological overload can sometimes be reduced by using a carton, where the focus can be on one side at a time.

The acrylic carton project gave Iris the impetus to get a haircut. She related that the "symbolic change" technique helped her decide to "cut something away instead of hanging on." Iris claimed, "I hang onto my weight—before it was my hair, my friends and my mother. Although painting those pictures on the carton was easy, doing something about it is quite different! Anyway, cutting my hair seemed to me to be the easiest thing I could manage; I've even gotten some compliments out of it!"

Collage: Lends Structure, Assists Expression

During treatment, there were sessions when the stress on media exploration was an inappropriate pressure. At that time it was necessary to back off and to simplify the art task. On one such occasion Iris was given magazine collage material. She was told to *pick a picture which catches your eye. Paste it down and write your free associations.*

Iris selected two pictures (Figure 85), a shovel and an elegant plate, which she pasted together into a single image. Iris explained the collage as follows:

I saw the part of me which I deny—simple undistinguished background, lack of brilliance or specialness—I run from this and become very vulnerable if people put me in the nobody category—yet sometimes I reject what I see in the "white plate self"—snobbishness and weakness—trying to run from the real me. As far as the meaning of the plate goes, I see this as the part of me which wishes to distinguish myself. I do so by my association with gourmet cooking which shows my taste for the delicate and the refined. But by doing this I am somehow trying to escape from the insecurities I feel about my background, about my lack of distinction.

Comments

The simple task of collage was a creative respite for the client. Yet at the

Figure 85.   Conflict in values

same time she was able to use the art to validate insights. Although collage is often used for structure or for clients who are resistant to art media, in Iris' case it was used to relieve her from the feeling of being inundated by the "art" aspect of treatment.

Photo Collage and Painting for Involvement

After the media became an easy process for Iris, her resistance was observed through the "manipulating reporting device." Although a certain amount of reporting is necessary, it can be used for avoidance; then it is important to re-engage the client in the art process where repressed material may surface. The art therapist involved Iris by asking her to *establish a scene with the magazine pictures. When it is finished use the acrylics to paint some human figures into the scene.*

Iris created the interior of a child's nursery; onto it she painted the picture of a mother and an infant. She reported:

> I wanted to express the warm feeling that the mother has towards the child, the freely-given affection and surrounding warmth. I find myself, though, getting very stuck on this subject, as though *somehow the mother-child relationship is too complicated for me to handle.* But anyway I wanted to express the givingness of the mother and her solidness too in her own self—she loves the child but remains herself.
>
> I had problems drawing the figures—the child looks totally unreal. I felt cramped by my inability to draw well, but I think it was also my very mixed feelings towards maternity that made me paint such a representational and essentially unconvincing picture. Originally, the child was supposed to be looking at its mother, but in actuality it looked sideways, or up at the ceiling. It (the child's face) looks like an Indian mask. I intended the mother to be looking at the child and smiling at it.
>
> The mother looks as though she were looking at the floor. I in tended her to have a natural warm smile, but she simply looks vacant—her mouth is not like a real mouth.
>
> The mother looks glassy-eyed and the baby looks creepy. This whole picture and the idea of the loving mother really brought out a lot of feeling in me. I hated myself as a child—I thought I was bad and mean and manipulative.

Several weeks later, Iris told the therapist she had had an abortion as a teenager. With reference to the picture, she addressed herself to the past guilt and future ambivalence which childbearing evoked in her.

Comments

The combination of magazine pictures and painting is a stimulating technique for creativity. The content is consciously and unconsciously presented; further, this method seems to be a motivating factor for bringing repressed material to the surface.

Crayons: Regression and Ventilation

Iris, who originally had been unable to distinguish her emotions, was often encouraged to express her feelings. On one such occasion, she reached for the crayons and in a regressed posture she scribbled until she had obviously experienced catharsis. She titled the image "My Angry Picture." In describing the process, Iris said, "I just drew scribbles, harsh lines in brown, blacks and then some green squiggles—I cut the page and tore it. At first I just felt the anger, and twice I broke the crayons—but afterwards I began to laugh. It all felt good. The green squiggles (which slightly resemble gnashed teeth and a snarling face) came after; I felt much less concerned about them than about the first angry picture. I didn't have anything specifically in mind when I drew the angry picture—at first it was just anger directed at the page, then I realized it was because my mother still treats me like a child."

Comments

Crayons are often associated with the elementary school years. For that reason, the author seldom uses this medium with anyone over the age of eight. It is not the medium itself which elicits regression, but the associations which are sometimes made to it. In the case of Iris, the self-selected crayons facilitated a regressive, child-like act.

Plasticene on Collage: Transition to Sculpture

Iris had decided to get her own apartment. However, her mother wished to keep her daughter close by and did not support the move. The two women had a heated argument. The client came into the art therapy session feeling angry with her mother and needy of the therapist's attention.

To help Iris express her anger, red, brown and green plasticene was offered because of the energy which needed to be expended while using the medium. But Iris refused to attempt a three-dimensional form. Therefore, the art psychotherapist decided to introduce an innovative way of using the plasticene. She gave Iris instructions to: 1) *Select a portrait from the collage box and paste it on the paper.* 2) *Mold some accessories out of the plasticene. Then press them onto the portrait or background.*

Iris began by cutting out the picture of a woman (Figure 86). Although unconsciously selected, it resembled her mother. She then rolled out small red plasticene balls and pressed them down onto the picture around the neck to represent tight fitting beads. The brown color was squeezed and rolled out, then shaped into eyeglasses which were also pressed onto the portrait. With the green plasticene she created a flower pattern and placed it onto the woman's blouse. Iris was delighted with the effect. The magazine photo took on a relief sculpture quality. This technique was used only a few times

Figure 86.   Mixed media facilitates transitions

before the client decided to use the plasticene to create a three-dimensional sculpture.

Comments

Red, brown and green plasticene were selected for their quality of hardness. To help Iris deal with her anger towards her mother, a tactile medium which required manipulation was most beneficial. The quality of the medium provided a kinetic experience where squeezing, pounding, pushing and pulling offered an emotional release. However, with Iris' initial resistance to handling plasticene, its use as an accessory gave it less importance and was not too threatening.

Iris interpreted the tight beads as her fantasy of strangling her mother. Well aware of sublimation, she gave herself permission to express her hostile thoughts through art.

Plasticene Sculpture: Role-Playing

Sculptures are particularly useful for role-playing, since they can be moved around to display confrontation, distance, etc. To give Iris a technique for understanding herself, she was offered white and gray plasticene, along with instructions to *model two heads—first, a soft-featured one from the soft white plasticene and, second, a severe one from the harder gray plasticene.*

After Iris molded the two heads, she was asked to give each a voice which matched its character. The gray head had a stiff appearance; the voice she gave it said, "I try to do everything perfect but it's never good enough." The white pliable head said, "I do only what gives me pleasure." Iris was instructed to play out a dialogue between the two heads. Each one complained that the other saw things in extremes. The therapist then asked the client to use white and gray plasticene together to create a medium with an intermediate quality, one which was neither so rigid nor so pliable and to *use this to form a third head.* When Iris finished, she gave the head a voice. It said, "I don't have to be so perfect, I don't have to seek only pleasure. Guess if I relaxed I wouldn't worry so much about the outcome—I'd be better off. Then maybe I could get myself going!"

Comments

Iris' dialogue portrayed her conflict between the superego (gray) and the id (white). Her fear of acting out her impulses exposed the source of her rigid reaction formation.

It is valuable to the readers to be aware of the hardness properties of the plasticene. Although they vary with the manufacturer, the tendencies are toward the following (going from soft to hard colors): white, yellow, pink, blue, red, green, brown, gray.

Artwork Review: Validation of Gains

A review of the artwork is a technique for reinforcing the client's gains. Styles, media and subject matter are compared. When Iris looked over her products, she was struck with the content as a mirror image of herself. She recognized her first person picture with its "stiffness and insecurities" as the way she had felt. She was pleased with the way she had adapted to the variety of art materials. The media and styles were perceived as parallel to the way she functioned. Iris tied together her "willingness to try out new things in the sessions" with making an effort to meet people, paying attention to her personal appearance and returning to school.

Colored Paper Base: Unified Appearance

Although Iris made progress, she had periods of regression. There were times when the client became discouraged, stating, "It was a bad week," or "The artwork just isn't right—for a while I had the knack of this medium," or "If I go backwards, that's when I get depressed or immobilized. I'm afraid I'll go back to where I was before I came to art therapy." On one such occasion, when Iris complained that her artwork appeared fragmented, the art therapist gave her colored construction paper to serve as a background for *a painting of your choice*.

Iris selected blue paper and white poster paint for an abstract design. Although the forms were scattered, the blue base held the composition together. She claimed, "I think it's a nice, cool-looking picture." She laughed as she associated it with a reminder "to keep my cool." Iris decided to made a series of paintings, each on a different colored piece of construction paper. When she finished, she associated thoughts to the paintings, for example: "The orange painting stands for my good feelings about things in general—I'm not as blue as I used to be." The green picture "implies growth. I can see leaves and plants all over it. Maybe it's also a green light with the message to *go ahead*." The lavender is "a pleasant color. I wore a lavender dress last night when a fellow student asked me out for coffee—he was very nice. Light gray always reminds me of the gray plasticene sculpture which is my 'new self.'" Iris complimented herself on the aesthetic quality of the artwork.

Comments

Iris' remarks about seeing her artwork as "fragmented" indicated a clue for symbolic unification. The colored construction paper served the purpose of holding the design together.

Space: A Delineation of Priorities

After 18 months of treatment, Iris was living in her own apartment, working at a school as a part-time typist, and attending several psychology classes at night. She had also joined in the Sierra Club activities. At times she felt overwhelmed by all her new experiences. To help her separate out her thoughts and to deal with them one at a time, Iris was given a five-foot piece of paper, window sash brushes, and rubber cement. She was asked to *paint three horizontal bands of color, then select collage images to portray the various aspects of your social life. Paste them down onto the painted surface with rubber cement.*

Iris' three horizontal bands of poster paint displayed yellow-green at the bottom, dark green in the middle and blue at the top. Then with rubber cement she placed photos of people all along the bottom row. Upon completion Iris said, "See, I'm moving too fast—all of a sudden I have all sorts of social demands put to me. Before I used to call my friends all the time, now people are calling me. I know it's good for me, but I really feel overwhelmed."

In order to give Iris some distance from her situation, the art psychotherapist suggested the following technique: *Pull off some of the people images and rearrange them. Place the least important persons on the blue far distance space, the most important persons in the yellow-green front row, and the rest of the images can be placed in the dark green middle ground.*

Iris proceeded to rearrange the collage (Figure 87). When finished, she claimed, "That's better, now I can see that everyone isn't right on top of me. I have to start sorting out my priorities and decide where I want to put my energy."

Figure 87.   Delineating priorities

Comments

Rubber cement lends itself to the ideas of changes. However, the idea of separating out elements to prevent overload could also have been managed by cutting out the people clusters and pasting them onto separate *panels*. In this way they could also be viewed in individual groups. The technique of separating out a mass gave Iris a visual means for sorting out her priorities and relieving social and psychological overload.

Clay: Regression and Insight

When Iris' ego was strong enough to tolerate the possibility of regression in service of the ego, gray clay was introduced.

The author suggested *play with the clay, let it dictate its own results.* Iris immediately complained about the mushy feel of the clay. With difficulty in experiencing the potential of the medium, she became frustrated and angry as the forms she tried to create collapsed. After a while, Iris began to pout, as she recalled a memory of "messing up" her pants and being punished by her mother. As the clay started to dry up, water was added to it. However, the consistency became too thin and out of desperation Iris decided to make ocean waves by smearing her fingers in the clay. Then she was asked to free associate to the waves, she talked about her daily habit of watching her feces flush down the toilet; then she continued to recall, "I remember when I was a little kid I swallowed a penny; my mother had to examine my bowel movements as proof of its being dislodged from my insides, but it never was discovered. I think I defecated at school so my mother wouldn't get a chance to look it over." Iris, now taking a course in psychology, wondered if that was the source of her neat and compulsive behavior. The process of free association led to a major insight for Iris. However, this event happened only after the patient had developed a trust in the therapist, become involved in a psychology class, and become ready to be aware. Together, these factors created the appropriate timing for understanding her controlling personality.

Comments

Wet clay is a regressive medium. The therapist used the clay *when Iris could regress safely.* The clay's tactile quality helps to elicit free associations. In this case, both the regressive tactile quality and the theme (waves) triggered memories of the past.

Carved Plaster: Delayed Gratification and Continuity

Towards the end of therapy, Iris created numerous images, many of which portrayed a more complete self. Although the usual conflicts which are a part of life were still expressed, they lacked the painful polarization which had formerly plagued her. It was time to give Iris an opportunity to do a sustained carving. Plaster previously prepared was mixed and poured into a milk carton; after it hardened, the paper was torn away and the remaining block of plaster was ready to be carved.

Iris worked on this project for several sessions; she carved an egg with a wavy lines across its girth (Figure 88). She described her experience as follows: "I loved carving the plaster; it was somewhat hard, but yet malleable. It's a heavy stable form—its oval shape is appealing and soothing to the eye—the shape is solid. I made the line in the middle to give it a sense of two parts—the two parts complement each other. The form is perfect, it's rich." Later she added, "I don't know why this image came to me. I see eggs every day, but this is the first time I sensed it as a form of wholeness."

Figure 88.   Wholeness

Comments

The plaster medium lends itself to sustained work. For some clients it is especially useful for dealing with the issue of "delayed gratification." However, in this case it was also used to give Iris a sense of continuity and mastery over a new medium.

Figure 89.   Movement

Paintings Series: Proof of Growth

During the last few months of clinical art therapy, Iris made numerous watercolor paintings of an individual in motion. At times the person was walking or running, skating, swimming and/or dancing. All of these symbolically portrayed Iris' movement and growth (Figure 89).

Just before therapy ended, Iris began to choose smaller-sized paper; her style began to tighten. It is not unusual for clients' artwork to show regression just before termination. This was interpreted by the author. However, to give Iris positive reinforcement, the art psychotherapist handed Iris her "Movement Paintings," suggesting that she might like to *put the movement images together.* Iris trimmed these pictures into free forms and pasted them onto lavender poster paper. The finishing touch was painting in a landscape background. The product was most impressive, for it clearly displayed the vast change from the tight, rigid pictures which symbolized herself at the beginning of treatment to the mobilized person she had become.

Although Iris thanked the therapist for her progress, the author could in all honesty put the credit right back to the client, as she stated, "Look at all the artwork. You did it; you worked hard to change what you were, what you did, how you are now! All your progress is recorded through your own hands!"

Comments

The following month, Iris reviewed her work. It took five sessions, for many of the artworks brought back memories which needed to be explored during this final phase of termination.

SUMMARY

Iris, a resistant and rigidly defended adult, was treated through art psychotherapy for 20 months. The art tasks and their exploration were essential in making adaptive gains. *Special emphasis was placed on the media, style, color and spatial qualities. Art directives* were implemented to complement both immediate and long-term goals of treatment. An *art desensitization procedure* was used to deal with the client's resistance to the involvement in art. The role of *symbolic risk-taking* served as a vehicle for change; its prerehearsal function gave Iris experimental and integrative opportunities.

CHAPTER 14

Group Art Therapy
Format With Children
of Holocaust Survivors

The group art therapy format was used with Holocaust survivors' children for consciousness-raising and data collection and assessment. The participants' artwork provided a viable means for self-exploration in regards to value systems, personality strength and weaknesses, coping responses to crises situations and self-perceptions. These were examined in relationship to the participants' survivor parents. The artwork poignantly portrayed family roots and led to an *awareness of the influences which Holocaust survivors transmit to their children.*

At Cedars-Sinai Thalians Community Mental Health Center in Los Angeles the author, a staff member of the outpatient Family and Child Guidance Unit, Department of Psychiatry, treated past concentration or labor camp victims and their children. Unlike the participants in the exploratory study, the majority of the clinic clients were of a low-middle-class socioeconomic status. Case studies of this unique clinic population frequently showed a father with low self-esteem and paranoid tendencies, struggling to make a financial living. The youngsters often included a latency-age or adolescent son who identified with his father and whose predominant defense mechanism was acting-out behavior; daughters tended to be symbiotically tied to their mothers and often displayed schizoid features, sometimes selective mutism and frequently school phobia.

LITERATURE REVIEW

The literature on children of Holocaust survivors is relatively limited. However, there has been a recent resurgence of articles and research is now being conducted by the survivor children themselves. The following literature review is written within a categorical framework as an attempt to simplify issues which have been presented.

Overprotection

Survivor parents have found to be overly involved with their sons and daughters. Newman (1979) says that the interest in the child's health and success takes on "pathological porportions." In agreement, Trossman (1968) notes that parental overprotection is played out through constant warnings against impending dangers.

Hoppe (1968) noted that life-styles of survivor families are characterized by pressures to maintain cohesion, mutual overprotection, interdependence, avoidance of conflict and a suspicious outlook towards authority figures outside of the familial milieu.

Parental Over-Identification; Inhibition of Autonomy

In his studies, DeGraaf (1975) found that parents who had lost relatives displayed a marked tendency to "be needed" by their children. They maintained "loving control" over their daughters and sons and managed to sabotage the separation-individuation process. This phenomenon was due to parents' unfinished separation from their own mothers and fathers, which activated their *restrospective trauma.*

Rosenberger (1973) referred to a group of parents who identify with their child by reliving their own past or acting in identification with their deceased parents. Inhibition of autonomy is referred to by Wanderman (1976) as a mechanism for parents to secure their own identity.

Introjection and Reenactment

Axelrod, Schnipper and Rau (1978), in a New York study of 30 hospitalized children of Holocaust survivors, discovered patients had symbolically reenacted their parents' camp experience. DeGraaf also addresses himself to the issue "reciprocal identification." He discusses the parents' masochistic tendencies, which have been externalized and projected onto the child and which are often manifested as a psychosomatiç illness and/or suicidal ideation.

Limit-setting

In discussing limit-setting, Rakoff (1969) described polarized approaches. Where some Holocaust survivor parents described ineffectual attempts to "control" their children, others approached this issue in a strict, rigid manner.

Sigal et al. (1973) pointed out that survivor parents preoccupied with unresolved grief have difficulty with their children's robust activity. They correlate the child's activity with the interruption of the parents' mourning process, and this is perceived as an extra burden on the depleted parent, who is without available energy resources. Sigal believes these parents are unable to give appropriate feedback to their children; therefore, the lack of limit-setting arouses anxiety, disruption and problems in the area of identification.

Aleksandrowicz (1973) found fathers, in particular, needed to assert a great deal of control over their children to deny the enforced passivity of their concentration camp life.

Expression of Aggression

Significant psychological differences between Israeli and American children's psychodynamic responses were reported by Klein and Last (1978). The Israeli children of survivors were relatively direct in their hostile and aggressive expressions, while their American counterparts revealed massive denial of hostility and an emotional inhibition or negative affect toward the persecutor. Klein (1971) claims that these findings may be "interpreted as a continuation of parents' attempts to cope with the hostility and aggression toward the persecutor. In some instances this could serve as an antecedent condition of psychopathology with auto-aggressive components."

Both Karr (1973), from the United States, and Klein, from Israel, address themselves to the legitimatized mode of aggression which is ventilated through war and political ideology. These factors provide an appropriate expression of rage onto an external enemy and reduce both the need to internalize anger and the frequency of depression.

Barocas and Barocas (1973) noted, "The survivors, being terrified of their own aggression and unable to express it, may broadcast explicit or implicit cues for their children to act out."

However, many authors cite the blockage of aggression directly toward the survivor parent on the part of the child. This trend is due to the guilt at adding even more pain to their suffering parents.

Parental Pressure to Perform

Passivity is displayed by the survivors' children in response to excessive parental expectations and demands. Authors are in agreement that the parents' pressure for performance is due to their own need to justify their existence and assuage their survivors' guilt. Gratification from children is also intensified as a compensatory measure for the family losses. The "princeling phenomenon" postulated by Rakoff, Sigal and Epstein (1966) and Sigal, Silver, Rakoff and Ellin (1973) states that parents need to have their children succeed as a means to increase their own self-esteem; this vicarious aspect was correlated by Klein and Reinharz (1972) with survivor parents who held little regard for their own personal ambitions or needs.

Maladaptive Coping Mechanisms

Greenblatt (1978) believes survivors utilize the same coping mechanisms which they used during their concentration camp internment. The maladaptive forms of coping with stress are passed onto a second generation, who perpetuate their parents' behavior.

Russell (1974) states, "Every major life crisis—decisions on careers, even on vacations, on moving, on whether to marry—brought old conflicts to the surface and paralyzed the family into inaction."

Karr (1973) observed that where both parents are survivors there exists, "a passive resignation which seemed to have occurred within the concentration camps." However, Sigal et al. (1973) postulate that parents, because of their "survivor guilt" and inability to show their own aggression, unconsciously encourage their children to act it out.

Pathological Family System

Russell (1974) observed that the survivor family tended to convey a depressed, gloomy and empty demeanor. He found that these families lacked involvement in their relationships and in their daily lives. Russell declared, "As family units, they presented even more than the expected double binds, skews and schisms, destructive dyadic and triadic alliances, incongruencies, dysfunctional communication patterns and maladaptive behavioral sequences."

Resistance to Treatment

Difficulties in getting families involved in treatment were reported by Kestenberg (1972, 1973) and Trossman (1968). Rosenberger (1973) reported that parents interfered with their child's analysis as "separation was taking place." Lipkowitz (1973) reported a case which ended just as an adolescent patient began to "walk on his own." This is similar to the author's clinic experience, where the fathers, in particular, implicitly sabotaged or explicitly terminated the designated patient's individual and/or family treatment. For latency-age children this took place at a time when positive changes were being made and the family system was in a healthier state of flux. With adolescents, especially girls, therapy was prematurely ended when individuation was in process. The author found some fathers resented the family's positive transference to the therapist, experiencing this phenomenon as a conspiracy to devalue his authoritarian position.

Observations on Functioning Families

Although meager, findings regarding the nonpathological aspects of the survivors and their children have been reported. Where some clinicians see the parents' enormous involvement with their sons and daughters as a symptom of psychopathology, the Israeli author Klein declared that survivor families have a unique life-style which is characterized by a great deal of affection, protectiveness and openness among family members. Klein believes, due to the Holocaust survivors' reconstituted love objects and recathection, affect is exhibited. Klein (referring to Israelis) says in adjusted families the parents' over-attachment is a coping mechanism; it is a response to a need to replace familial losses and a defense against anxiety about additional losses. He compares this to the neurotic families' pathology where the over-attachment stems from a reaction towards death wishes. Klein said he found survivors' children able to find continuity and capable of accepting and exercising authority. He also noted their capability to "develop social skills as well as responsibility, with positive experiences in leadership and in the spheres of sexuality and their own competence." This statement is in accord with another Israeli, Rosenberger (1973), who found no distinctive psychopathology of children of survivors.

Family situations in which one or both parents maintained a healthy, vital, emotional equilibrium in the family were described by Sigal (1971). Kestenberg (1972) also stated that even though "survivor parents can and do behave pathogenically, they can also manifest a surprising vitality, stability and strength in the upbringing of their children."

In spite of acknowledged similar patterns between children and their parents, Trachtenberg and Davis (1978) declared, "Let us not forget that like their parents, children of survivors are unique and distinct individuals; and as a group, they have generally found healthy ways of dealing with their lives."

THE STUDY

The exploratory pilot study described in this chapter was initiated by Judy Flesh (1979) and conducted by the author. The art therapy directives created by the author were utilized for this study and with a follow-up control group led by Maxine Junge.

The members of the art therapy pilot study group agreed to participate out of their interest in providing information about children of Holocaust survivors. They also viewed the group as an opportunity to raise their own consciousness.

The selected participants were individuals who did not feel the necessity to seek help for any emotional problems or concerns; functioned well in society, in middle- or upper-class socioeconomic levels (unlike those in the author's clinic practice); resided in Los Angeles or Beverly Hills, California; and were children of parents who were both Holocaust survivors (defined as concentration or labor camp victims or in hiding). The group consisted of six females and two males, ages 17 through 31 years. The group met for four weeks, two hours a week.

The art therapy format enabled the therapist to gain both conscious and subconscious data in a brief period. Subconscious data observed in the drawings provided correlations and greater validity to this exploratory investigation.

The author created art therapy instructions which elicited information from the survivors' children regarding the following areas: 1) personality traits; 2) value systems; 3) fantasized parental attitudes towards the participants' value system; 4) imagined family roles in coping with crisis stress; 5) participants' perception of themselves and their parents; 6) characteristics of strengths and weaknesses in parents and themselves; 7) aspects of themselves which participants and their parents display in society, versus those which are undisplayed; 8) perception of parents' past, present and future in contrast to the participants' past, present and future; 9) parental influences on participants' strengths and weaknesses; 10) personality projective tests.

Details of each session described here, include the *directives, artwork* and *verbal responses,* followed by discussions carried out by the participants, and the author's conclusions based on the findings of the exploratory study.

FIRST SESSION

The art therapist introduced herself and the recorder. She explained the art therapy format and the intention to gather data on Holocaust survivors' children. Ground rules were as follows: People would use simple art materials to make symbolic statements regarding themselves and their families; participants would share the artwork only if they chose to do so; artwork would be interpreted only by its creator; group members could relate their own associations to the artwork of others; and the group would not function as a vehicle for confrontation or encounter. The author offered herself for contact, in between sessions, if any member felt this need due to emotions which were stirred up in the art therapy sessions.

Warm-up

To introduce the members to each other, a warm-up exercise was first presented.

The participants were asked to *draw something you like about yourself. It can be a design or a representational symbol. When you are finished, give it a title.*

Five participants (62 percent) displayed symbols which represented a relationship to people. These were seen in portrayals of body parts such as hearts, an ear and hands touching.

Comments

The group was stimulated; a friendly excitement permeated the room. Everyone was quickly involved. Resistance to sharing was not evidenced.

Value System

To understand the values which may have been transmitted by the Holocaust survivors to their children, a three-part directive was given.

First Part: A 16" x 24" folder was handed out to each group member. These folders represented "suitcases." The participants were told to imagine their home was endangered by fire and evacuation was necessary. Instructions were given to *draw or make a collage which symbolizes items which you will pack. These will be put in your suitcase. Put on an address where the suitcase will be sent and a return address.* (See Figure 90.)

In Table 1, the participants' responses to this directive are shown.

In the suitcases, all respondents included monetary items; photographs

TABLE 1
Suitcase

CLASSI-FICATION	ITEMS	PER-CENT-AGE	NUM-BER	SUIT-CASE SENT TO	PER-CENT-AGE	NUM-BER
Monetary	money, stock, jewelry, silver	100%	8	Family	37%	3
Photographs		87%	7	Self c/o	37%	3
Sentimental	diary, porcelain, music box, special poster, painted egg.*	62%	5	Friend School	12% 12%	1 1
Artwork		37%	3			
Practical	identification and credit cards, check book, tax returns, eyeglasses, passports, clothes	37%	3	RETURN ADDRESS		
				Self at home	100%	8
Other	diploma	12%	1			

*One person was robbed, otherwise would have included sentimental item (not included in percentage).

were packed by seven (87 percent); and sentimental items by five (62 percent). Other items are charted on Table 1.

Although the art therapist stated that the house was endangered, seven of the group (87 percent) took it for granted "the worst would happen, and the house would be completely destroyed."

In spite of thinking their homes would be demolished, it was interesting to note that all of the group members used denial as a defense by using their home for the return address. Most participants openly stated "I wrote the return address to myself, to a place that had burned down!"

Comments

Since the majority of people included jewelry (a monetary item), the therapist questioned if this had anything to do with stories of fleeing im-

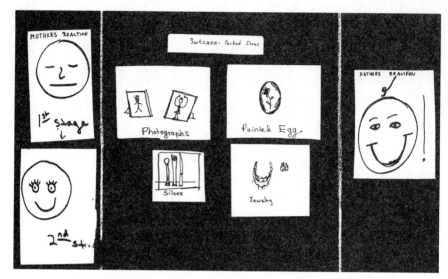

Figure 90.   Packed items reveal values and parents' reactions

immigrants taking jewelry due to its value and small size. Everyone admitted
that their families tried to take jewelry, although often it was hidden. Mary
volunteered, "I was brought up to think little things were valuable."
However, pessimism was expressed by Eve, who said, "I took very little; I
knew from my mother it was all useless."

Parental Attitude Towards Participants' Decision

   Second Part: The next art therapy technique involved the parental attitude towards their child's value system. The author asked group members
to *write "my mother" on the right side of the page and "my father" on the
left side.* The following question was asked, "If your mother looked inside
the suitcase, would she think your choice was good, bad, indifferent, etc.?"
They were instructed to *make a drawing under mother's side of the page
which is a symbol for mother's response. When you are finished, do the
same for your father's response.*
   In the beginning, all group members stated that their parents approved of
their choice. Gerta said the parents, "just wanted our bodies to be safe." It
became apparent that it was difficult for the participants to deal with a crisis
situation in terms of a difference in values between themselves and their
parents. As they spoke, five members of the group (62 percent) made
statements showing some second thoughts about their parents' reaction.

For instance, Pauline said, "Mom would say don't take anything, but taking the silver was okay." Clair added, "My father would be happy"; however, later she said, "My mother would think I needed to take the jewelry." As an afterthought, Lenore decided that neither of her parents would think she had made such good choices. Mary began by saying, "Dad at first would be happy, then he wouldn't care about what I did or didn't take." However, later on she remarked, "Maybe he would want me to take certain paintings or jewelry." Josh was certain his mother would complain, "Why did you take this? You should just get out and put nothing in." After everyone had spoken, Clair changed her mind about her father's response, stating, "He probably would say I should have left out the picture albums and have taken statues instead." For the majority, comments about selection dissatisfactions revolved around father's desire to include more monetary items.

Comments

In general, participant consensus was that parents' approval on suitcase choices was not a critical issue (as indeed it was not meant to be on the part of the therapist). At first, all of the participants portrayed their parents' approval of their choices. They denied a difference in values and a resistance to exploring disparities. As one group member rationalized, "Our parents have gone through so much that we are not going to put them through any more." This implied that "differences" were seen in a negative light within the family system.

Body Awareness

Third Part: The art therapist put the participants through a body awareness exercise to help them understand the emotions which were evoked by the topic of "crisis" and their value systems. A relaxation induction technique was implemented, along with instructions to pay attention to their bodies and what they were experiencing. Group members were told to allow themselves to relax and to fantasize. Afterwards the participants were instructed to *draw the imagery of your body awareness through an abstract or representational design.* Table 2 shows participants' pictorial responses to this exercise. The significance of these data is unclear.

Comments

The body awareness exercise relaxed the group members. They then discussed the art therapy experience. Gerta noted, "We have a lot in common;

TABLE 2
Pictorial Response to Relaxation Exercise

Relaxed	Excited	Tense	Tired	No Emotion
12% (1)	25% (2)	25% (2)	25% (2)	12% (1)

it seems none of us has ever shared these types of experiences before." Josh remarked, "There is a lot of trust in this group. We must have wanted to deal with being children of Holocaust survivors or we wouldn't be here."

SECOND SESSION

The art therapy group started with the therapist's asking members if they had given the last session any thought. Clair quickly responded, "I thought about it all week; it made me feel good. I asked my family about the suitcase." Josh responded, "I asked my parents what they would take. My dad surprised me—he said he would take documents." Noah reported, "I was surprised that everyone thought the result would be a disaster; it sneaked up on me. I was stunned." Eve remarked, "My strongest reaction was surprise about how many of the little sentimental things were included in the suitcase."

Family Roles in Coping with Stress

To understand how participants imagined family roles would be played out at a time of stress, the group members were instructed to look through the magazine collage material and then to *select four pictures of people: Two adults and two children.* The pictures were to be pasted down on a large sheet of paper. When this was completed, the members were asked to *imagine these four people in a cabin in the snow. During their stay an avalanche occurs. Write next to each person what he/she is thinking and saying.*

For the simulated role responses to crisis situation, *adult male* responses showed passive or non-action-oriented men with a rating of 77 percent (seven out of nine). The two action-oriented men demanded that the family leave. *Incongruencies* between the adult males' thoughts and statements were shown in a 77 percent (seven) frequency. Lower scores are shown in Table 3.

TABLE 3
Avalanche: Simulated Role Responses to Crisis Situation

| AGE-SEX NUMBER | ACTION ORIENTED | ACTION TOTAL | NON-ACTION TOTAL | STATEMENTS — NON-ACTION ORIENTED | | | | | | | | | | | INCON-GRUENT |
				anger towards parents; calm parents'	assurance given	calm	danger ignored	excited positive	family check	fearful	paused to think	questioned	resentful	requested death	thought vs. statements
Adult Male Total: 9	22% (2)	22% (2)	77% (7)		22% (2)	22% (2)	11% (1)				11% (1)	11% (1)			77% (7)
Adult Female Total: 7	14% (1)	14% (1)	84% (6)		28% (2)				14% (1)			14% (1)	14% (1)	14% (1)	84% (6)
Adolescent Total: 6			100% (6)	17% (1)	17% (1)			17% (1)	34% (2)			17% (1)			34% (2)
Young Child Total: 10			100% (10)					40% (4)		60% (6)					30% (3)

Adult women responses were passive or non-action-oriented with a rating of 86 percent (six out of seven). Lower scores are shown in Table 3. Examples of statements made by the passive or non-action-oriented women were as follows: "At least we are all safe; I went to the market yesterday." "I didn't need this." "Go, leave me behind. Shoot me—I'm too old to get out." The one woman who was action-oriented had the husband who insisted that "everyone get out." *Incongruencies* between thoughts and statements were displayed by six responses (86 percent) of the adult women.

Responses of *adolescents* were all passive. *Incongruencies* between thoughts and statements were displayed by two (34 percent) of the adolescent responses.

Responses of *young children* showed that 60 percent of the children (six) were "scared" (although one voiced an opposite feeling, as well); they cried out, "Don't leave me behind" or "Hold onto me, grandma; I'm scared." Four children (40 percent) had fun or were stimulated (although two said they were also scared). *Incongruencies* between thoughts and statements were displayed by three (30 percent) of the responses of young children.

It was noted that five of the male adults included in the collages were pictured in their fifties (similar to the ages of participants' fathers). Five participants also included grandparents aged 60-70.

The art therapist asked the group members, "Does anyone identify with the pictures in some way?" Seven respondents said they identified these pictures with themselves and/or family members. Clair went on to say, "It answered all parts of my personality, the way I react in a panic situation—fear, take care of me." Josh replied, "It was patterned after my family and responses which I perceived my parents would give." In agreement with Clair and Josh, Pauline said, "My mom, dad and sister would be like the person who gives comfort and deals with reality."

Seven of the respondents stated they compiled pictures which constituted "a family group."

Literature on Holocaust survivors' coping mechanisms suggests that crisis responses in everyday life are similar to those which were utilized in the camps. If this postulation is valid, then the responses to the "Avalanche Crisis" is understandable in light of Holocaust victims' inability to control their situation.

Incongruencies between thoughts and statements had a high frequency for both parents. This tends to correlate with the literature regarding survivors' being overprotective of their children. The young children's incongruencies stemmed from a different source, one in which their thoughts would provide shame if revealed (for example, enjoying the crisis).

Comments

The participants discussed similarities between their selections and their own families. The group members all began to share and compare their parents' backgrounds. There was a general consensus about the benefits of hearing others' stories. For example, Pauline told the group, "This has been a good experience. I always thought my background was unique—now I know it's a drop in the ocean."

Participants also related that the survivors participated in closely knit organizations or clustered groups of their own making.

Perception of Family Members

To gather data on the perceptions of the weaknesses and strengths of family members, a distancing device was used to lower the defense of group members. The art psychotherapist asked everyone to *think of your family in terms of animals. Draw an animal which depicts each family member. Label each animal mother, father, sister, brother, me (omit your name). Next to each animal write its greatest weaknesses and strengths.* (See Table 4 and Figure 91.)

Participants' strength response was 62 percent (five) for flexibility/energy/movement. See Table 5 for low frequencies. *Weaknesses* response was 37 percent (three) for worried. Lower frequencies are charted on Table 6.

Half of the participants said that their *fathers'* predominant *strength* was in being "strong." *Weaknesses* received low frequencies only (see Tables 5

TABLE 4
Animal Symbols: Pictorial

	MOST POWERFUL						LESS POWERFUL						LEAST POWERFUL					
	BEAR	GIRAFFE	LION	LIONESS	WILD	COUGAR	DEER	FOX	HYENA	WOLF	CAT	COW	MOUSE	OCTOPUS	PANDA	PEACOCK	PORCUPINE	SHRIMP
Self	12% (1)		12% (1)	12% (1)			12% (1)	12% (1)		25% (2)								12% (1)
Father	37% (3)		25% (2)		12% (1)										12% (1)	12% (1)		
Mother	12% (1)	12% (1)	12% (1)							12% (1)			12% (1)	12% (1)	12% (1)	12% (1)		

Figure 91.   When contrasted, parents are more colorful than participants

TABLE 5
Animal Symbols: Participants' Interpretations

STRENGTHS

| | PSYCHOLOGICAL | | | | BEHAV-IORAL | MISCELLANEOUS | |
	affectionate kind-warm	flexible energetic movement	insight	strong	well rounded	beauty	survivor
Self	12% (1)	62% (5)	12% (1)	12% (1)			
Father	25% (2)			50% (4)	12% (1)		12% (1)
Mother	50% (4)			37% (3)		12% (1)	

TABLE 6
Animal Symbols: Participants' Interpretations

WEAKNESSES

	disciplined	domineering	pessimistic	sensitive	temper	unrealistic	weak	withdraws	worried	preoccupied	quiet	slow	stifling	stubborn	unpredictable
	PSYCHOLOGICAL									BEHAVIORAL					
Self	12% (1)		12% (1)	25% (2)	12% (1)			12% (1)	37% (3)						
Father		12% (1)		12% (1)	12% (1)	12% (1)				12% (1)	12% (1)	12% (1)			12% (1)
Mother			25% (2)	12% (1)			12% (1)				12% (1)	25% (2)	12% (1)		

TABLE 7
Animal Symbols: Pictorial Elements

APPEARANCE

	Size: largest figure	Color: more than one	Details: greatest number
Self	12% (1)	12% (1)	0
Father	62% (5)	25% (2)	62% (5)
Mother	25% (2)	12% (1)	37% (3)

SPATIAL RELATIONSHIP
OF SELF TO PARENTS

off to a side	between parents	on separate page
62% (5)	12% (1)	25% (2)

IDENTIFICATION

similar to parents	unique
50% (4)	50% (4)

and 6). *Mothers'* predominant *strength* was seen by half of the group as being warmth, kindness and affection, while strength itself was seen as the mothers' strong area by three participants. *Weaknesses* received low frequencies only.

Pictorial elements are shown in Table 7.

Comments

Group members gained insight through their visual responses. Several persons realized a common identity with their parents. However, none of the participants made a conscious effort to draw similar types of animals for purposes of identification.

THIRD SESSION

Covert and Overt Expression

To further understanding of the participants' and the survivors' extroverted and introverted personality traits, the group members were told: *You have three large paper bags. One will be used to symbolize yourself, another your father and another your mother. On the outside of each bag draw or paste magazine photos to show what parts of yourself (or your parents) are shown to the world. Then, on separate pieces of paper symbolize what is kept inside. Place the concealed aspects inside the bag.* (See Figure 92 and Tables 8 and 9.)

On the *outside,* five participants (62 percent) showed a happy appearance. Four (50 percent) portrayed themselves as intelligent or educated, or friendly; all the *inside* aspects showed only low frequencies (see Table 9).

Portrayals of *father's outside* showed five responses (62 percent) in two areas: patriotic and hardworking or ambitious, or with an ability in business. Four responses (50 percent) revealed father as a warm or loving person (see Table 8 for low frequencies). There were five responses (62 percent) with *father's inside* as vulnerable or too sensitive, and four (50 percent) for shy or quiet.

Six responses (75 percent) contained *mother's outside* as hardworking or ambitious, or with working ability. Five responses (62 percent) were given in each of two areas: friendly, warm or loving. Four responses (50 percent) included family oriented. Portrayals of *mother's inside* revealed six responses (75 percent) as vulnerable.

Participants portrayed the largest number of concealed traits, with a

TABLE 8
Outside Bag: Displayed Aspects

	PSYCHOLOGICAL		BEHAVIORAL				MISCELLANEOUS	
	happy*	warm* loving	friendly	generous	patriotic	works hard ambitious ability	educated intelligent	family oriented
Self	62% (5)		50% (4)	25% (2)	37% (3)	25% (2)	50% (4)	
Father		50% (4)	37% (3)	37% (3)	62% (5)	62% (5)		25% (2)
Mother		62% (5)	62% (5)	37% (3)	12% (1)	75% (6)		50% (4)

*May also be behavioral

TABLE 9
Inside Bag: Undisplayed Aspects

	PSYCHOLOGICAL				
	confused insecure	enjoys privacy	lonely isolated	quiet shy	sensitive vulnerable
Self	37% (3)	25% (2)	37% (3)	37% (3)	37% (3)
Father				50% (4)	62% (5)
Mother	12% (1)			12% (1)	75% (6)

Figure 92.   Happy self is shown to the world

score of 14. This is in contrast to *fathers* (nine) and *mothers* (six). This may be due to group members' guilt over disappointing or worrying their parents.

Considering their past, it is little wonder that the Holocaust victims are seen to be overly sensitive or vulnerable. However, in spite of this, survivors have made tremendous adaptations. The Holocaust survivor parents are perceived as being warm and loving persons, who sublimate through hard work and achievement. It is interesting to note that being overly sensitive or vulnerable is not a major feature for the participants themselves.

Comments

The author asked the participants the following questions: 1) Were your general responses unique, or did you identify with either or both of your parents? 2) Are you and your parents at all alike? 3) Where likenesses exist, do they pertain to displayed or concealed parts of yourself?

For *outside,* the exposed parts of one's personality, five persons expressed an identification with one or both parents; three saw themselves as unique.

Participants voiced many ways in which they identified with their parents. Half of the group members realized they presented themselves as similar to their parents, although they wanted to be different. Eve declared, "It might be easier to model ourselves after our parents on the outside; for the inside I know I haven't had their experiences." Polarities between the participants' inside and outside portraits were repeatedly portrayed; this is illustrated through Gerta's comment, "Here, outside the bag, I show myself self-assured, confident, studious, serious, intelligent, and on the inside I'm lonely, insecure, invisible, scared of death." Most members admitted an identification with their fathers, although it was not portrayed in or on the bags.

All agreed to one family dynamic which they had in common—the tendency for family members to "suppress sad feelings." Several people emphasized that it was outstandingly true of their fathers.

Denial of the Holocaust experience was seen by the "lack of pain" about the past on the part of their parents, either on the outside or inside of the bag. During the discussion, several participants said their parents did not talk about their painful past, while others said they realized they had failed to portray this aspect on the inside of the "bag."

There was unanimous agreement to the fact that group members would not tell their parents their problems. Although the reason was not voiced, the author believes it was due to the guilt of adding another burden onto their parents.

FOURTH SESSION

Perception of Parents' Past-Present-Future in Contrast to Participants'

The goal of the next technique was to gain an understanding of how the Holocaust experience affected the life stages of the survivors (as perceived by the participants) and a comparative view of their children's lives. The members were given three sheets of paper, each of which was divided into three parts. On sheet #1 the participants were instructed to *write the following headings: a) Where I Came From; b) Where I Am Now; c) Where I Am Going.* On sheet #2 they were instructed to *write: a) Where My Father Came From; b) Where He Is Now; c) Where He Is Going.* On sheet #3 they were to *repeat a similar page for your mother. Then proceed to draw symbols under each heading.* The author added, "The terminology may sound vague to you. It means different things to different people. Draw whatever comes into your mind." (See Figure 93.)

As shown in Tables 10 and 11, no predominating items are revealed by participants' *past* or *present* data. The *future* predominant feature, with a 37 percent (three responses) frequency, was growth; lower frequencies are charted on Table 12.

Father's *past* was represented in six responses (75 percent) by a country.

TABLE 10

PAST

| | LOCATION | | | | PSYCHOLOGICAL | | | MISCELLANEOUS | | |
	city or country	concentration camp or war	hospital	hate for jews	love	pain struggle	family	single	vacation
Self	25% (2)		25% (2)		25% (2)	12% (1)	12% (1)			12% (1)
Father	75% (6)	25% (2)		12% (1)		12% (1)	12% (1)			
Mother	50% (4)					12% (1)	12% (1)	12% (1)	12% (1)	

TABLE 11
PRESENT

	LOCATION				PSYCHOLOGICAL			MISCELLANEOUS			
	art therapy	at home	city or country	vacation	love	growth	positive emotions	dead	question mark	success	work or works hard
Self	12% (1)	12% (1)	25% (2)		25% (2)	12% (1)			25% (2)		
Father			12% (1)	12% (1)	12% (1)		50% (4)	12% (1)			37% (3)
Mother		25% (2)	12% (1)	12% (1)	12% (1)	12% (1)	25% (2)			12% (1)	

TABLE 12
FUTURE

	LOCATION			PSYCHOLOGICAL		BEHAVIORAL		ROLE	MISCELLANEOUS	
	at home	city or country	grave	growth	positive emotions	advocation leisure	work	family	dream come true	question mark
Self		25% (2)	12% (1)	37% (3)		12% (1)		25% (2)		25% (2)
Father	12% (1)				50% (4)	12% (1)			25% (2)	
Mother	12% (1)			25% (2)	37% (3)	12% (1)	12% (1)	25% (2)		

Figure 93.   Denial of parents' holocaust past

The *present* and *future* highest frequency was (50 percent) four responses for positive emotions (relaxed/happy/enjoy/content/secure).

Mother's *past* was represented by four participants as a country. There was no predominant item among *present* representations, although three saw positive emotions in the *future* for the mother.

It appears that participants perceive their fathers' current and hopefully future adjustment as a portrayal of their capacity to enjoy life in spite of the Holocaust ordeal. This may be an important factor in the participants' own future due to the concept of identification. It may also be an indication of the fathers' use of sublimation.

In regards to the participants' self-image, drawings pertaining to themselves were drawn predominantly at the top of the page, in contrast to those about the parents, which utilized the total page. Similiar to other drawings in this study, self pictures contained a minimal use of color, while parents were more colorfully portrayed. This correlates with other clues about the participants' "paled" perception of themselves in contrast to their fathers and mothers.

Comments

"Denial" is indicated by the fact that in 16 responses (both mothers and fathers) regarding parents past, only five indicated the painful past of the

Holocaust survivors. During the discussion, Clair said, "My father came from a resort town in Europe; it was pretty, lots of land, large family." The author silently noted that this drawing was created in spite of the fact that the father spent time in a forced labor camp. The height of denial was evidenced by Clair, who referred to her mother's "past" through a drawing of her parent on her recent vacation, while Lenore drew her mother's past as a "single woman." Others portrayed the country of origin. The therapist suggested the group members might possibly be having difficulty in confronting the heinous crimes which were perpetrated upon their parents. In response, Eve defensively volunteered, "My mother was in a camp but she has never talked about it. That's why it's not in here." It seems the parents' denial and/or suppression have influenced the manner in which participants cope with painful material. Some people did admit their parents' past "was painful and kept very much a secret"; it was also mentioned that "it just had not been talked about."

From the pictorial statements it would have been impossible to detect that the artwork symbolized portrayals of Holocaust victims. The literature on survivors' children's psychopathology often refers to the Holocaust survivors' rumination and repeated reporting of their life in the camps. It seems that among this group withholding or giving limited information may have caused a positive effect on the children's ego strengths and lessened or eliminated the survivors' guilt complex.

Parental Influence on Strengths and Weaknesses

To gather data on the strengths and weaknesses in the participants, in relationship to their parents, the following directive was offered: *Divide the paper in half. On one side draw the strengths, on the other side the weaknesses, which you believe you have received from your parents.*

The most frequently cited *strength* from parents (seven responses) was loving/warmth; six responses referred to caring for others; there were four each for ambitious/hardworking and desire to learn or intelligence. (See Table 13.)

Weaknesses from parents included six responses as suspicious, and five responses as over-emotional and sensitive. (See Table 14 and Figure 94.)

Participants gave 35 responses for the *strengths* which they received from their parents, in comparison to 22 for *weaknesses*.

Comments

Strengths which participants said were integrated from their parents were

TABLE 13
Parental Strengths Transmitted to Participants

PSYCHOLOGICAL								BEHAVIORAL			MISCELLANEOUS		
caring	character	flexible	loving warmth	optimistic	pride	secure	strength	ambitious hard-working	energetic	generous	common sense	honorable	intelligent learning
75% (6)	12% (1)	12% (1)	87% (7)	25% (2)	25% (2)	12% (1)	12% (1)	50% (4)	12% (1)	12% (1)	25% (2)	25% (2)	50% (4)

TABLE 14
Parental Weaknesses Transmitted to Participants

PSYCHOLOGICAL								BEHAV-IORAL
drives to succeed	gives in	hard to separate from parents	insecure	over emotional and sensitive	out of it	pessimistic	suspicious	materialistic
25% (2)	12% (1)	12% (1)	25% (2)	62% (5)	12% (1)	37% (3)	75% (6)	12% (1)

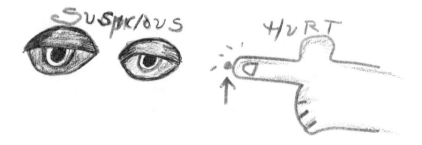

Figure 94. Hurt, sensitive and suspicious; weaknesses transmitted by parents

indicated by such statements as: "Strength of heart, I got it from my parents—also an ability to love and intelligence." "Wisdom, common sense, warmth and loving—I got all of them from them." "Trying my hardest, doing my best, commitment to others, caring."

The major strengths related to both relationships (loving and caring for others) and intelligence, learning and ambition and hard work. The weaknesses of being hurt, over-emotional and sensitive, along with a suspicious nature, rated top scores. Together these traits give a picture of the effect which survivors of the Holocaust have upon their children. The predominant single symbol, the *heart*, portraying "love and/or warmth," was drawn by seven of eight of the participants. Weakness symbols predominantly displayed were question marks and/or impinging arrows.

The highest score on *weaknesses* which participants received from their parents was their "suspicious" outlook. Statements included: "Not completely trusting." "I'm distrustful." "Mistrust of people." "Paranoid stance." "Not trusting." It is little wonder that "distrust" has been transmitted to the Holocaust survivors' children. Certainly, the pain which the survivors have undergone contributes to their high score of being easily hurt, sensitive and/or over-emotional. Once again, these emotions have served as a model for responses in their offspring.

Although only one respondent listed "hard to separate from parents" as a weakness which has been transmitted by the survivors, a group discussion took place around this issue. Group members agreed to the common experience of "being too hooked into our family."

Projective Tests

The House-Tree-Person projective test (Buck, 1970) was given to gain clues into the participants' personalities and intrafamilial relationships. A full array of colored felt markers, oil pastels and newsprint was put forth, along with instructions to draw a house, tree and full length person. *When you are finished, write on the back of the page what is the worst and best thing that could happen to each—the house and tree and person.* (See Table 15.)

Buck (1970) states, "The House, a dwelling place (and usually the site of the most intimate interpersonal relationships), tends to arouse associations concerning home and those living in the home with him." Therefore, in children it often reflects their attitude regarding their parents and/or siblings and home situations. For married persons it may portray their family of origin or their relationship to their spouse.

The *House* was shown with a single view by four (50 percent) of the par-

TABLE 15
House-Tree-Person: Predominant Responses

HOUSE	
single view	walkway included
50% (4)	62% (5)

TREE		
equal to or higher than house	many leaves	fruit or blossoms
87% (7)	87% (7)	50% (4)

PERSON			
equal to or higher than house	appears 5-13 years old	smile on face	firmly planted stance
100% (8)	100% (8)	75% (6)	75% (6)

ticipants. Jolles (1971) postulates that this feature "represents expression of great need to maintain acceptable façade in interpersonal relations." In the author's experience, this may also reveal the "ideal family myth" which lacks reality substance to family dynamics. The walkway was easily and proportionately drawn by five (62 percent) of the participants; Buck says this feature implies that "the person exercises control and tact in contact with others."

Buck presents the *Tree* as a drawing which stimulates associations concerning one's "life-role and ability to derive satisfactions in and from the environment in general." Hammer (1971) claims the Tree drawing reflects unconscious information regarding self-concept and body image. Seven of eight participants drew trees which had solid trunks, appropriately proportioned, and full branched with leaves, indicating the respondents' ego strength and developmental growth.

Machover (1949) claims the *Person* drawing "provides a vehicle for the expression of one's body needs and conflicts." The Person drawing is a self-portrait, which reveals physical and psychological self-perceptions. It may be reflected in a realistic or ego ideal compensatory manner. The face, which represents the social characteristics of the Person, was drawn in full view by seven of the participants; Buck (1970) postulates that this indicates a "façade." Another façade indicator is the upturned smiling mouth, presented by six of the participants; Machover says, "This is seen in children's and other infantile representations of the human figure." It has been interpreted by her as "forced congeniality, an effort to win approval." Figures with a very young appearance (approximately five to 13 years of age) were displayed by all of the participants; this gives evidence of the respondents' dependency needs. A firmly planted figure stance was scored by six of the participants, portraying ego strength and self-esteem.

   In viewing the House-Tree-Person on the single page, the outstanding feature was the person's disproportionate oversize, drawn by all of the participants (See Figure 95). All of the persons were at least as tall as the height of the house; in fact, the majority were taller. This feature may indicate how large the participants loom in their homes. It is interesting to note that,

Figure 95.   H-T-P projective test indicates overprotectiveness on the part
             of the parents

of the three married participants, two of them drew the person on a separate page, possibly as a psychological attempt to separate themselves from their family of origin.

Comments

Indicators found in the House-Tree-Person test were consistent with findings in the artwork created with other media techniques and directives. The composite picture for the majority of participants is: good ego strength and self-esteem, flexibility and growth-orientation, dependency needs, a friendly cheerful façade, along with control and tact in social relationships.

Participants were asked to record their free associations to the "best" and "worst" things that could happen to the house and tree and person. Their responses are shown in Tables 16, 17 and 18.

For the *house,* the highest scores for the *best* association were for "positive physical condition," rated by 50 percent (four), and being "inhabited," rated by 37 percent (three). The *tree's best* association highest score was to "bear fruit" or "blossoms," rated by 50 percent (four). Although Buck and Jolles claim "apples" on trees indicate children's

TABLE 16
Written Responses H-T-P Best and Worst Associations
House

BEST			WORST	
positive condition	inhabited	paid off	destroyed	empty room family moved
50% (4)	37% (3)	12% (1)	75% (6)	25% (2)

TABLE 17
Written Responses H-T-P Best and Worst Associations
Tree

BEST				WORST	
bear fruit or blossom	positive environment	stay young	noticed	destroyed	diseased
50% (4)	25% (2)	12% (1)	12% (1)	62% (5)	37% (3)

TABLE 18
Written Responses H-T-P Best and Worst Associations
Person

BEST			WORST				
happy	fulfilled	positive self-image	unhappy	die	sick	beloved's death	rejected by college
62% (5)	25% (2)	12% (1)	25% (2)	25% (2)	25% (2)	12% (1)	12% (1)

dependency, the author has also found fruit to be significant as an expression of growth. The *person's best* association is scored at 62 percent (five) for being happy.

ADDITIONAL DISCUSSION BY GROUP MEMBERS

Art Therapy Benefit to Group Members

A great deal of discussion evolved out of the various art tasks. It was evoked by the participants' own artwork, as well as by identification or associations elicited by another member's artwork. Seeing the artwork and responses together gave participants a sense of group identity, empathy and insight. In each session, some participants mentioned the surprising ease with which they were able to share extremely personal information.

Motivation for Art Therapy

Conversation evolved around the art therapy experience and what it meant to the participants' parents to have their children attend. On the whole, parents felt psychotherapy was for "crazies" (two mental health professionals were the only participants who had been in psychotherapy). Participants reported their parents felt the art therapy attendance would be good for research on children of Holocaust survivors.

Response to Literature on Holocaust Survivors' Children

Discussion around articles about children of Holocaust survivors showed the participants to be resentful of the references to these children as being "abnormal." Early in the group's formation Pauline declared, "Articles I read said the children were neurotic." Josh reported, "I resented reading children were having problems because parents were too strict because of the Holocaust." Clair expressed, "I resent that people expect our parents to be different, odd, maybe think they have problems." She went on, "A friend had a nervous breakdown. She was wacky. They blamed it on her parents' going through the Holocaust. It made me wonder if, since my parents went through it, should I have troubles too?"

Survivor Children Perceive Themselves as Different

The therapist asked the group, "Do you think you are different from other people your age whose parents did not go through the Holocaust experience?" All the participants agreed to their "differentness." To testify to this fact, Gerta said, "I'm a teacher. Like Anne Frank I'm more sensitive to minority problems. My students keep diaries in class. My interests are in the reflection of differences." Josh offered his opinion, "My own political views and my parents' are that this is a country where it could never happen. I vote every election, very liberal on civil rights." All the participants who were eligible to vote emphatically related that they exercised that right.

This discussion led to the question, "How did you find out you were different?" Josh replied, "I always felt different. We had no extended family, my parents were older, they didn't have any teeth." Differentness was also referred to by the fact that their parents spoke with an accent. All agreed that, as children, they felt embarrassed about their parents.

Difficulty in Professing Parents' Weakness

The group members agreed that it was easier to do the transmitted strengths rather than the weaknesses. Clair, speaking for the group, said, "It's hard; it makes you feel like you're kind of betraying your parents." Although it was not voiced, perhaps confronting parental weakness was in itself overloading and guilt-provoking.

Survivors' Experiences Suppressed or Denied

The participants made different statements in various sessions pertaining to their parents' Holocaust experiences. On one hand there were statements about how parents never talked about what happened to them in the concentration or work camps. Eve claimed her parents "had not shared their past, but their pain was definitely there." Gerta said, "So much is withheld," and Pauline related, "I wanted to know about the past; I wanted them to share so I could feel I'm giving to them, just as they listen to me." Noah reported, "I had fantasies about their survival. Did my parents do heroic or terrible things to get through it?"

However, when the therapist mentioned, "There are several things we learned tonight. One is that bad or painful experiences are not talked about. Josh quickly defended his family by saying, "I feel I have heard the 'stories.'" Pauline added, "The gory details I've heard recently since I'm grown-up. My dad liked to tell funny stories, nothing gory. I have a tendency to stop him; it makes me uncomfortable."

As the group was coming to an end, the author asked the members if there were anything they wanted to say. In response, Clair stated, "In regards to talking about the past, well it's talked about in my family, but we do appreciate the present." In contrast, another member said, "I only know about the past because I'm asking; before I only saw my mother cry." The author's assessment indicated that a few members, heard "the stories" without asking. In general, the attitude seemed to be one of "unknowing."

Parental Expectations

Unanimously, parents wanted their children to date Jewish people; this was seen as desire to maintain their ethnic culture. However, distrust of the non-Jewish population as a threat to group closeness or to maintaining their identity was an essential factor.

Suppression of Sadness: Parents' Overprotectiveness

When a group member mentioned, "I was never allowed to show moodiness or sadness," six of the participants agreed with this statement, adding, "As a child I was not allowed pain, depression, or sadness."

Six also felt that their parents were "overprotective." Phrases mentioned were: "Don't talk to strangers." "Don't open up the door." "A man might be waiting." One father had advised his child, "Protect yourself, don't ever let yourself be vulnerable. We trusted—look what happened!" The messages of being distrustful of people seem indicative of their parents' horrific experiences.

CONCLUSION

Sublimation

The torturously painful experiences of the past will never be forgotten by the Holocaust survivors. Literature about this population has used such terms as "survivors' syndrome" and "survivors' guilt." Whether or not these emotions can be worked through is not yet empirically recorded. However, the issue of *how* guilt, rage and/or grief can be handled or worked through has received some attention in the area of aggression and its appropriate discharge through war or politics.

The author questioned why the group members of this exploratory study *did not* fit the children of Holocaust survivors literature. It became evident that economic status had not been mentioned in any of the previous research, and it seemed that this factor might have some bearing on the ego strength of the participants. However, it was noted that the characteristic of being ambitious and/or hardworking received extremely high responses as being representative of both fathers and mothers (this was not true of the control group). The author believes that, within this skewed Holocaust survivor populations, where parents were successful in their business ventures, rageful, guilty, grieving, depressive energies were productively redirected through the *drive to succeed in business.* These parents transformed pathological obsessive and/or compulsive tendencies into socially acceptable hardworking, ambitious and creative channels. It is the defense mechanism of *sublimation* which served to alleviate some of the tension and conflict and allowed survivors to succeed, to enjoy their children and the world around them.

Since many of the participants identified with their parents' qualities of ambition and willingness to work hard, it is feasible that they, too, will use sublimation as a means for self-esteem and success.

Double Message Communication

The overprotective pattern on the part of survivor parents may be the basis for double message communication. This tendency was observed through the *avalanche crisis technique,* wherein 13 out of 16 adults were portrayed as giving double messages through incongruencies between their thoughts and verbalized statements. The conflict between implicit and explicit messages is clearly seen in the collages. The double message assumption appears to be significant, as the control group exhibited only three out of 16 adults who displayed incongruencies. The divergent data seem to indicate that participants perceive the Holocaust survivor parents as being fearful of letting them know about dangerous elements. It was fantasized, on the part of group members, that their parents manage not to divulge this information by either denying impending danger or consciously withholding thoughts of crisis. This denying or withholding postulation correlates with the fact that survivor parents seldom or never shared their concentration camp experiences with their children.

Communicating double messages may be a trait which the group members have learned from their parents. This was indicated by the overabundance of "smiling faces" in the various techniques. For example, in the *bag technique,* for displayed traits, the vast and highest number of participants illustrated a "happy" self (Figure 92). It was not clarified whether this image portrayed a genuine state of emotions or a façade. Numerous clues in the House-Tree-Person projective tests suggested the latter. For survivors' children, this can be an attempt to compensate for their parents' losses and suffering. This correlates with the group members' mutual expression that they do not share their own sadness or pain with their parents, because the parents have had enough unhappiness. (In the control group, when doing the *bag technique,* only one person portrayed the "happy" characteristic on the outside.)

Suppression and Denial

Participants related that the Holocaust survivor parents shared little or no information about the concentration camp experience. This fact is in opposition to the literature on survivors and their tendency to obsess or ruminate. The horror stories are claimed to have damaging effects on the children who introject the pain, rage and guilt of their parents.

The survivors' avoidance of relating their concentration camp memories may have been a conscious decision to protect their children from the excruciatingly painful and frightening information or may reflect the defense mechanism of denial. In the cases where it is specifically a defense mechanism, it may have served the purpose of "psychological survival" for the parent. The participants in this exploratory pilot study seem to have benefited from parental suppression or denial of the Holocaust events. It is possible that children who are informed about their parents' concentration camp experience in early or middle childhood are more likely to be affected than those who are told in late adolescence or early adulthood. The developmental age of the recipient may have a direct bearing on how the Holocaust experience is perceived and handled.

The pattern of "denial" may be a transmitted trait, as demonstrated through the parents' *past-present-future technique,* where participants portrayed only two out of 16 Holocaust survivors with the concentration camp as a part of their "past."

Family Awareness

Participants' "family consciousness" was evidenced through discussions and in the *avalanche technique*. In that exercise, participants were asked to make a picture collage of two adults and two children. The images revealed that all but one of the participants had made a conscious decision to compose "a family." The importance of the family was also illustrated through the inclusion of pictures of elderly people identified as grandparents by five out of eight group members. This may be a compensatory gesture in lieu of their deprivation. These data bear greater significance since the control group included only one grandparent.

Family Style Myths

The myth that Holocaust family members are in complete agreement with one another seemed to be an important issue to the participants.

Artwork or discussions which pointed to "differences" between participants and their parents were generally seen in a negative light or provoked guilt in group members. For example, during the *fire evacuation* or *packed suitcase technique,* all of the participants, at first, agreed that their parents would fully approve of their selections. However, when a group member ventured to state, "On second thought, my dad would say you should have taken the statues instead of the photograph albums," most of the other participants then admitted their parents would have also suggested changes. Along with these admissions, group members revealed feeling guilty about making these remarks. Several persons expressed being "disloyal" when sharing information about anything other than agreement between themselves and their parents.

Individuation

Due to the losses which Holocaust survivors have experienced, their children hold an extraordinary preciousness for them. The tendency for these parents to infantalize their children is indicated through the participants' childlike appearance in their drawings of the "person" in the House-Tree-Person projective tests (Figure 95). This characteristic was displayed by all of the participants, in contrast to members from the control group. Group discussions also addressed themselves to the overprotective quality which their parents continually displayed, as well as "being too tied to the family." The issue of separation also appeared through the House-Tree-Person projective test when two out of three married participants drew "the person" on a separate page. This phenomenon was not seen in the drawings of the single group members, nor in the drawings of control group single or married persons. In the author's experience, this gesture frequently indicates the need to separate from one's family of origin and difficulty in doing so.

In addition to the childlike appearance, the drawings of the figures are disproportionately oversized (see Figure 95). The person is shown to be as tall or taller than the house. This feature might be an indication of the vast amount of attention which survivors' children receive from their parents—they loom large in their household. This postulation correlates with group members' testimonies that their parents saw them as being very special.

The Holocaust survivors' children are not only extremely close to their nuclear family, but they are also tied to an "extended family" which is made up of other concentration camp survivors. The shared treacherous past makes the survivor peer group an especially supportive, nurturing and protective resource for Holocaust survivors, as well as for their children. Although the extended family brings psychological benefits, it may hamper autonomy for the survivors' children.

Individuation is also made difficult by the "hurt," "sensitive" and "suspicious" characteristics which participants portrayed through the *weaknesses transmitted by parents technique* (Figure 94). To be one's own person, in a world which cannot be trusted, is an extra hurdle which Holocaust survivors' children must overcome to gain their individuation.

Self-Perception in Contrast to Survivor Parents

Although participants drew themselves oversized in view of their family life, a different phenomenon was seen when group members symbolically portrayed themselves in direct contrast to their mothers and fathers. In the *family animal symbol technique* and in the *past-present-future technique,* all of the participants portrayed their parents larger, more detailed, more colorful, and in a more central position on the page than themselves (Figure 91).

It would appear that the Holocaust survivors' past, in spite of its horrors, lent a colorful and often heroic element to the parents. It is symbolic that participants unanimously appeared paled, meager and less interesting than their parents, while the control group exhibited contradictions to all of these dimensions.

Fantasized Coping Mechanisms

Fantasized coping mechanisms were examined through the *avalanche crisis technique*. In this simulated situation, each participant dealt with two adults and two children who were in a cabin in snow when an avalanche occurred. The art task portrayed three out of 16 adults with an action-oriented approach; that is, they helped their families to leave the endangered cabin. The rest of the 13 men and women were immobilized, making no attempt to remove their families; the six illustrated adolescents were equally frozen. The passive orientation to the simulated crisis seemed to stem from an inability to activate a rational or irrational attempt to flee the dangerous environment. This was possibly due to denial, a fatalistic or pessimistic attitude or traumatization.

In the literature on Holocaust survivors, stress is often laid on the maladaptive coping mechanisms which were used during the concentration camp experience and continued on throughout the survivors' lives. Although the avalanche technique responses would seem to affirm this hypothesis, it may not be valid, since the control group's illustrations showed an increase of only two additional action-oriented adults. These five adult responses are still less than a third of the total number of adults. This difference does not represent a significant deviation; therefore, the immobilized response to crisis may not be directly due to their parents' Holocaust experience.

Values

The *packed suitcase technique* revealed objects which were most highly valued. Group members' selection dealt with articles which were irreplaceable. "Monetary" items were included by every participant and mainly viewed as a means for future survival, while the high response for "photographs" indicated the importance of maintaining a record of one's family history. A large percentage of the group members packed sentimental items to demonstrate their attachment to significant others and/or the past. These findings bear greater significance in light of the control group data, which did not deal with survival, family records, or sentiment; their values dealt with attachment to their pets, entertainment equipment and artwork or professional tools.

The importance of relationships was also seen as part of the group members' value system; qualities of "loving warmth," "friendliness," and "caring for others" repeatedly received very high responses for both parents and the participants.

Consciousness-Raising

The consciousness-raising function of the art therapy approach served as the major benefit to the participants. Group members explored their value and communication systems, parental and self-perception, transmitted characteristics and fantasized coping mechanisms. Another dimension of consequence came from participants' engaging their Holocaust survivor parents in discussions about values, perceptions and the past.

Further Investigation

A format for further investigations and research has been laid out here through the art therapy approach. This exploratory pilot study will be extended to persons ages 17 through 32, of middle- through upper-class socioeconomic status, who are not seeking psychological treatment and who can benefit from a consciousness-raising group. The hypotheses presented here must be examined with a larger sampling for valid information on the psychological relationship between Holocaust survivors and their children.

SUMMARY

The art therapy format was used for consciousness-raising and for data collection and assessment. The participants' artwork provided a viable means for self-exploration in regard to: 1) personality traits; 2) value systems; 3) fantasized parental attitudes toward their children's value system; 4) family roles in coping with crisis stress; 5) perception of parents and selves (through a distancing device); 6) characteristics of strengths and weaknesses in parents and self; 7) perceptions of themselves in contrast to their parents; 8) personal aspects which parents and the participants display, versus those which are kept hidden; 9) perception of parents' past, present and future in contrast to respondents'; 10) parental influences on participants' strengths and weaknesses; and 11) personality projective tests. The artwork poignantly portrayed and led to an awareness of family roots and the influences which Holocaust survivors transmit to their children.

CHAPTER 15

Dissolving the Creative Block: Brief Treatment

Michele, 35, was an artist who had suffered a creative block for several years. Deeply disturbed by her inability to paint, she sought art psychotherapy, where she was in treatment for 12 weeks.

DREAM WORK

During her first session, Michele painted her dream from the previous night. It showed a woman shaped as a bottle with her head (painted on a cork) being blown off. Michele interpreted her own artwork as seeing art psychotherapy as a place where she would ventilate "bottled up" thoughts and feelings. She hopefully fantasized "pouring" herself "out on canvas."

INSIGHT

Early in treatment, Michele's first insight was found in an abstract drawing (Figure 96), when she was asked to free associate to the design's forms and colors. She expressed, "I felt the forms were reaching out. I think of myself that way; I'm a giving person in a love relationship." Then Michele added, "Now, all of a sudden, I realize that each form reaches back in. I reach out in love, but I just realized my tendency is to pull back into myself. Perhaps I don't give as much as I think I do. I notice, too, how I carefully controlled and colored everything within the lines. Even that little smudge bothered me. I want everything to appear perfect." After exploring this

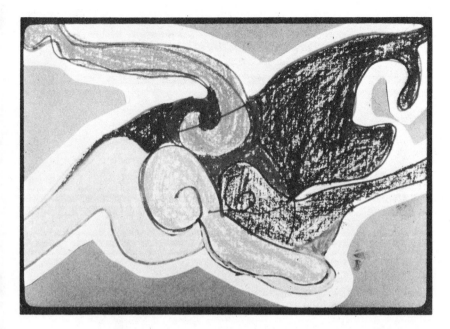

Figure 96.   Abstract design leads to insight

thought further, the client said, "I have not been willing to confront my own little smears, and I certainly don't want anyone else to see any of my imperfections."

CONFLICT REVEALED

At a later time, when Michele painted a person in an abstract manner (Figure 97), she was appalled as she said, "I see a split in the middle of this person. One side says I'm open, I want to give in a relationship; the other side says, stay out. If I really let you in, you'll devour me. These two sides are in conflict. It's hard to let them come together because the separation has a zigzag line; that keeps both sides meshed together, not just next to each other." A large number of paintings and sculptures were devoted to the themes, "I'm open" and "Stay out." Gradually, Michele began to create art which combined her polarities in an attempt to bridge the gap.

CONFRONTING THE UNACCEPTABLE

Shortly after, Michele produced a painting that displayed another part of herself. As she examined the image she stated, "The painting is filled with

Figure 97.   Conflict revealed

shadowed people. The darkness, the unacceptable, is something that I must confront, like the smudge in my abstract painting last month. I tried to wipe it out, but since I couldn't, I had to confront that damn smear and my inner sloppiness.'' As Michele created numerous works of art that were ugly and unpleasing to her, she allowed herself to come face to face with parts of herself which she had denied in the past.

ARTIST BLOCK AS A DEFENSE

In reviewing her artwork, the client was struck by her abstract painting and the accompanying words, "Reaching out and pulling back in." She had connected this with the way she dealt with relationships. A month later, this same picture with its associated statement was tied up to her inability to paint. Michele saw a direct parallel to the time in her career when she was offered a gallery show. She refused to exhibit her paintings for fear of rejection by her critics. Thus, once again "pulling in" was a means of directing fear and rage inward. It was manifested in depression and the drying up of the creative energy.

Michele's overt facade of superiority and covert feelings of unworthiness prevented her from developing deep relationships. Similarly, she unconsciously balked at revealing herself through the art gallery show where inadequacies might be displayed. Therefore, the artist's block as a defense took place.

SUMMARY: ART EQUATES SELF

Towards the termination of her therapy, Michele dashed off a watercolor landscape declaring, "I feel full and green and strong. I am surrounded by color which fills me with warmth. I have looked in those dark places and my fear of looking was greater than the ugliness of what I saw. The sun shines on me and I love its energy, just as I appreciate the coolness of the sky. I feel as though I have come home from a journey." Michele acknowledged the statement as an integral part of herself. She accepted the progress in her development as a person and an artist who had once more tapped into her creative flow.

PART V

Aged Adults

The final and later life stage of development is defined by Erikson as "integrity versus disgust." He postulates that the culmination of healthy self-development is the achievement of "integrity," that is, the acceptance of oneself and one's role in life. If this task is not accomplished, the individual may dedicate this time to unfinished tasks and feelings of despair and disgust.

The developmental tasks designated to later maturity by Havighurst (1952) include: "Adjusting to decreasing physical strength and health, adjusting to retirement and reduced income, adjusting to death of spouse, establishing an explicit affiliation with one's age group, meeting social and civic obligations, establishing satisfactory physical living arrangements."

One of the tasks which is omitted by Havighurst is preparing philosophically for death. Zinberg and Kaufman (1963) claim, "As each developmental phase prepares for the next, so this period before the end of life is under the aegis of what is anticipated."

In working with the geriatric population, the clinical art therapy approach has three purposes: 1) to work with the person's immediate problem; 2) to deal with the issues pertinent to old age; and 3) to help provide the client with a sense of dignity. The major thrust of the therapy is to help the client maintain or reconstruct ego strength and increase self-esteem. For the elderly, this task is often difficult because of either a long history of physical or emotional dysfunctioning or a rapid decline in capabilities. Especially with the confined, a sense of self may have considerably diminished. It is important to help these persons understand and realize the vitality which they still have. This point can be made through the dynamics indigenous to clinical art therapy; the art form serves as concrete evidence of their still existing energy and their continued or reawakened potential for creative self-expression.

Many older people believe their source of identity has been removed. Frequently, this "source" had been grounded in their occupation. Without a job, aged individuals may feel anomalous and useless. For women who understood their roles in terms of being a homemaker, the removal of their function of helping their children or grandchildren is equally devastating. Aiding the old person to redefine his/her identity is a necessary element in treatment. Art psychotherapy offers a special aspect to this focus; it gives the client materials to visually create a new or reconstructed role. A sense of identity is objectified through a collage, graphic or plastic arts.

It is an acknowledged fact that a large number of therapists find it difficult to work with geriatric clients. The sense of hopelessness and impending death implicit in contact with this population can be overwhelming. The art therapist does have an advantage in dealing with the aged because of the dynamics of the creative process, which brings both the client and the therapist a measure of hope. It is the response to something happening—something being formed, communication in motion—which is encouraging. The clinical art therapy experience is a means for preventing the collusion of client and therapist in sinking into feelings of impotence. The artwork is proof of an assertive act which is used for interpretation of the artist's will. Further, it gives the elderly person the opportunity to have a measure of control and opens up possibilities for change.

The author is convinced that in-depth work on lifelong unresolved material is contraindicated for the aged, for it is seldom that these areas can be worked through. Issues of conflict, guilt, rage, separation and loss are dealt with to a therapeutic degree. However, deep investigation tends to activate anxiety and deepen depression. Therefore, the emphasis with geriatric clients should be on *portraying past and current strengths, as well as on creating artwork which increases cognitive skills and maintains or regenerates socialized interaction.*

It is the author's belief that negative transference is of no value in working with the geriatric population. Resistance is too overloading; it drains the client of energy and motivation and often supports the theme of "being punished." In art therapy, positive transference is hastened or strengthened through the art therapist's role as a "provider." The therapist furnishes supplies and is considered as a person who gives something to the client. Although this factor exists with every age population, for geriatric persons its implication may have an even greater effect. "Loss or removal" is a ma-

jor theme in their lives; therefore, something "given" holds special importance. Another element which accelerates the transference is the fact that
the client gains both visual and auditory attention from the art therapist.

A therapeutic alliance is often strengthened by the symbolic contact between client and therapist. For example, at times both persons are engaged
in the artwork and each may create a form which can then be put together,
placed side by side, etc. This connection is often experienced by the client as
a safe or comforting means of contact or closeness and enhances the
trusting relationship.

Another advantage to clinical art therapy is that the client can continue to
create forms away from the art therapy sessions. These forms act as a transitional object, yet simultaneously give the artist a sense of his/her own
power by doing it alone. The client's superego may prevent self-focus;
however, the creative aspect is beneficial for narcissistic indulgence.

The issue of dependency may activate feelings against the persons or
agency with control over the older person's financial and physical being.
Providing the means for expressing these feelings graphically and/or verbally can be of great relief. In addition, the statement of the anger is rewarded
by the message that "This is a socially acceptable way to release rage." At
times it is appropriate for the product to be shown to peers, caretakers,
family or others involved in the client's life.

The reduced sensory stimulation experienced in old age often takes a
psychological toll; therefore, the requirement to use several senses during
the art psychotherapy sessions is beneficial. The client sees, touches and
manipulates a variety of media. Even the sense of smell is utilized and
brought into awareness through the supplies. Although the kinetic aspect
may be limited, it can be enlarged upon through the size of the product,
placement of supplies and management of space.

In spite of a person's role change, at a time of diminishing functional
capacities, self-identity can be strengthened by identifying within the past.
This is recorded graphically in order to gain an understanding of the wealth
of experiences which the client has lived through and collected. The art process itself is also therapeutic from the viewpoint of self-mastery: responsibility, control, choices and decision-making are involved in any creative
work. This involvement helps a person to recognize his/her available
resources. It provides a mechanism for understanding the capacity to activate a plan for change or resolution, portray emotions, communicate symbolically and verbally, and realize they have been seen, heard and respected.

The choice of art media is an important factor in working with the aged.
Since finger dexterity may be limited, materials which are easy to manipu-
late are essential. Media which have proven to be appropriate include: tissue

paper, already cutout collage pictuꞏes, lightweight construction paper, pieces of material with different tactile qualities, wet clay, softer types of plasticene (while, yellow, pink) or slightly heated plasticene (which is hard when cold), long-sized felt pens, oil pastels, glue, light scissors, aluminum foil. In some cases, where the hands are unable to function, it may be necessary or advantageous to have the art therapist create some of the artwork as instructed by the patient.

Art therapy with the geriatric population is presented in the following two chapters. Chapter 16 considers specific issues which are essential to the geriatric person in individual art psychotherapy. Goals, techniques and discussion are included for each directive. Chapter 17 encompasses the theory and application of clinical art therapy for a geriatric group. It is illustrated through the case history of "Mr. Greenberg," a man who initially resisted involvement in the art therapy group. Thematic techniques pertinent to old age and group process are revealed through the record of the participants' group life.

CHAPTER 16

Techniques for
Individual Treatment

Involving Client in Treatment

Directive: *You and I (the therapist) will draw a picture together. Pick your favorite color and give me a color you like. Maybe this picture can be titled "Hello" since this is our first picture together. Your favorite color can stand for you and the other for me.* The therapist produces lines and forms which make contact with the client and are therapeutically responsive. When the pair is finished, the therapist explains how the lines she made were friendly overtures. The patient is encouraged to talk about the shapes which were created.

Drawing together at the beginning of treatment lessens the client's anxiety. The subject "Hello" is a simple and effective way of conveying a message of contact and friendliness.

Build Curiosity

Directive: *The colored xerox paper has the letters G and H on it. Use the oil pastels to create an abstract design out of the letters by connecting lines, filling spaces, putting in squiggles and/or any other means.* Upon completion, the client is encouraged to talk about the various forms which exist in the design. Then the picture as a whole is discussed. Free associations may be elicited from the client. The title may lead to further discussion.

Having something already on the paper is a motivating factor for the client's engagement. The request to put a mark on a blank piece of paper may be overloading for the minimally functioning person.

Acknowledging the Client

Directive: *Symbolize some of the events and attending emotions you have had this week. Select the media of your choice.* The client discusses the events and feelings as they are being drawn. The therapist will decide whether further elaboration or cessation of the subject is therapeutic. This can be handled through conversation or a follow-up directive.

When the therapist pays attention to the daily events artwork, it conveys the respect he/she has for the individual. Simple reporting themes help the client to focus attention and increase self-esteem.

Increase Concentration Span

Each directive is given after the preceding one is completed. *1) Create a feeling through line and color. 2) Identify that feeling to a situation. 3) Add a person to the picture (draw or collage). 4) Draw, paint or use collage to create a background.* First, explore the feelings which were symbolically expressed. Second, talk about the situation which was identified with the feeling. If a negative memory has been evoked, the follow-up directive will deal more fully with the issue or will provide proper closure.

The elderly may have difficulty in staying focused. Therefore, work on increasing the attention span is important. Directives which are done in stages help maintain an interest. By putting it all together, the client will gain a sense of accomplishment and be motivated for increased participation.

Catharsis via Distancing Agent

Directive: *1) From the collage box pick out pictures of objects which represent happiness and anger. 2) In the next step you will sculpt forms which will express happiness and anger. First, pick out a soft piece of colored plasticene for the happy sculpture. Roll it out on the table, then create a smooth form.* After the first step is completed, the second request is: *Select a harder piece of colored plasticene for the angry sculpture: Squeeze it and/or poke it with your fingers or toothpicks, and/or cut it up with the scissors, and/or hammer it with a blunt edge. Create a form which is angular or uneven or rough, or any other form which might be perceived as an angry object.* The client is led into an exploration of emotions, as well as experiencing the process in creating their sculptural forms. The individual is encouraged to discuss the kinetic aspects of the experience and the tactile quality of the medium. The art therapist elicits a verbal description of the form.

Catharsis is experienced through the expression of happy and angry objects. Since the client is not asked to own these emotions, he/she can feel free to display them through the kinetic, tactile and verbal process. It is important to maintain the distancing factor if this directive is used early in treatment.

Positive Lifetime Review

(Note: This technique will take several art therapy sessions). Directive: *Create an album which will show positive aspects of your life experience. They may include incidents from your past, childhood memories, school activities, family happenings, work experiences, situations which offered pleasure, vacations, friends, social affiliations, hobbies, sports activities, etc. Any recall which has a positive association can be shown through a representational or abstract portrayal.* The memories and art are explored as the artwork is being done. The art therapist might need to ask the client questions to help him/her recall the theme in greater detail.

The various memories which are put into concrete form and placed in an album will give the person an opportunity to see the wealth of experiences he/she has lived through and collected. This will strengthen self-identification and will act as a reinforcing agent time and again. Pasting the pictures in an album is an added benefit for the client's self-esteem, for it denotes the importance of one's past life and current creativity. The therapist must review each and every picture and lead the client into discussions which will stimulate further recall. All of the issues mentioned above should be pointed out and positive reinforcement made.

Stimulate Thought Processes Through Reminiscing

Directive: *Create scenes of your past.* The art therapist might suggest a place the patient visited, a job he/she did well, a celebration which he/she attended or made. Encourage memory recall through consciously created images and stimulated free associations. Remind the client of the storehouse of worthwhile experiences he/she has lived through.

Reminiscing activates thought processes. This form of stimulation brings satisfaction to the client. The ego is enhanced by remembering former experiences. The art work also serves as a record which can be mentioned, brought out and viewed at times when the patient needs a pleasant or comforting reminder.

Stimulate Current Recall and Observation

(Note: One of these is selected by the therapist; several can be given in a single session if time permits.) Directive: *Create in pictures or clay or collage: 1) What you ate for breakfast, 2) What you did after lunch, 3) Who you saw yesterday. 4) Draw the clothes you wore yesterday. 5) Draw what I am wearing. 6) Draw the clock on the wall, etc.* The client and therapist talk about the details of the drawing while it is being made. If the client needs help with remembering or observing, the therapist plays an active role in pointing out the necessary information.

Remissive senility requires brain stimulation. Older people have easier access to long past events than current ones. The therapist takes an active part in helping the person with observing and remembering daily routine reality.

Transitional Object

Directive: *The project which you will now start will take several sessions to complete. The theme can be one of your own choice, for example foods I like to prepare, or favorite clothes I used to own, or a garden I planted, or vacation I enjoyed, or clothes I knitted, etc. Select the media of your choice—clay, plasticene, picture collage, drawing, painting or colored construction paper—to portray your chosen theme.* Talk about the personal meaning of the topic. Help the client to remember daily events and to become aware of his/her environment. The project is given to the client to take home or to his/her room. Try to motivate the client to work on it between sessions.

The patient is comforted by having the artwork with him/her as a transitional object. Motivating the client to work independently still maintains the transitional object benefit and adds the dimension of dealing with positive aspects of him/herself autonomously.

Flexibility

Directive: *1) Slightly dampen a large white blotter. 2) Place your brush into the watercolor and shake the brush so the colors sprinkle on the blotter. 3) Either use your scissors to cut out, or tear out the parts of the picture which you like the best. The parts which are unsatisfactory throw away. 4) Paste the part or parts you liked onto a piece of colored paper.* Direct one step at a time to avoid confusion. The therapist talks about the process, then leads the client into discussing the chance to select out what is most satisfying and eliminating what was not desirable. This issue is tied into choices which are available in the client's life.

The focus of the directive and discussion is on taking steps to make changes. The flexibility to see the "parts, rather than the whole" is emphasized. Reinforcement is given to the artist's power to be in control of the situation.

Acknowledgment of Status Change

Directive: *1) Through a picture collage depict your daily life 15 years ago and your daily life now. 2) Form abstract plasticene sculptures which show your feelings about each situation.* The client explains the collage and the feelings regarding the shift in status.

Allow the client to ventilate emotions around the change in status. Recognition of this fact is therapeutic.

Positive Aspects of Leisure Time: Formulate a Plan for Action

Directive: *1) You have some xerox pictures of hands. Place a symbol or symbols into the hands showing the good part about not being busy. 2) Paste magazine pictures which show what you could do with your time.* The client explains the symbols which are placed in the hands. Then the individual is led into formulating a plan. The therapist may need to assist the client by asking about former hobbies. Point out that "time" can be used to an advantage. If the patient has few or no ideas, the therapist can lay out some graphic alternatives.

The therapist helps the patient to focus and begin a specific or group activity. Motivation may be stimulated by laying out ideas and having the art therapist as an interested party.

Curtailed Physical Ability

(Note: This technique is applicable for clients who have physical difficulty in performing some of their daily routine). Directive: The therapist selects one, or possibly two, of the following: *1) Draw the dining room. 2) Use the plasticene to make a symbol for your bed and the bedding. 3) Draw the bathroom. 4) Depict yourself getting dressed.* If the client does not mention the problems which these issues present, then the therapist does. For instance, "The dining room is far away, it takes a long time to get there." "Yes, a number of older people find it difficult to tuck the sheets in." "It takes a lot of strength to brush your hair (shave or put on makeup)." "Getting dressed can be exhausting."

Discussion and acknowledgment lend validation to the relationship of the client's emotions and his/her curtailed physical state.

Stimulate Creativity

Directive: *1) Take a sheet of aluminum foil and paste it on the poster board. 2) Select and tear pieces of colored tissue paper and paste them randomly onto the foil; if they do not paste smoothly that is fine, it will enhance the object. 3) The second step may be repeated several times in overlaying fashion.* Talk about the process, how the client perceived his/her participation in making the collage—what did he/she think of the finished object? Point out the client's ability to be creative.

This art form very often has aesthetic qualities. It is simply made and gives the client pleasure and increased self-esteem. Variations of this technique can be used to motivate the client to participate in creative activity.

Physical Dexterity and Sensory Awareness

Directive (given one step at a time): *Take a piece of plasticene and roll bits of it into balls. Take another colored piece of plasticene, hold it in your hands and squeeze it lightly. Take yet another colored piece, this time pound, pull and poke it. Produce other ways of handling and examining the medium. Finally, place all the pieces on a paper tray and create a plasticene collage or build the piece into a unified sculpture.* Pacing depends on client's finger dexterity and involvement. The therapist asks the client about the experience—what sensations were felt, what experience was liked best or least? Why?

The plasticene has varying degrees of hardness depending on the color. The therapist consciously decides what colors are made available. These depend on the client's hand manipulation power. In addition to the physical dexterity of this exercise, sensation awareness is brought to the client's attention.

Sensory Stimulation

Directive (pace slowly for clear understanding): *Each felt marker has a* *different food odor*. 1) Smell the marker and draw a picture of the food which the odor represents. 2)* Awareness exercise is given by the therapist: *Pick up the plasticene, touch it to your face, notice its temperature, smell it, understand its qualities and pay attention to your reaction. 3) Look over your food drawings. Select out and sculpt one or two of these foods. Use some of the tactile material* (corduroy, dotted-swiss, loose weave drapery fabric) *to press into the plasticene to heighten the imitative quality of the object.* Talk about the smell of the marker and plasticene. Look at the picture of the food. Relate it to the plasticene sculpture. Ask questions: Did you like the smell? How did the plasticene feel? Tell me about the sculptures. What other kind of fruit or vegetable would you like to form? Would you like to make a bowl of fruit in the next session?

The senses of smell, touch and sight are all used to stimulate and/or heighten awareness.

Deal with Unfinished Messages

Directive: *Use the collage to depict family, friends, acquaintances with whom you have left something unsaid. Write or dictate to me (the therapist) What you wish you were able to say to each of these people.* Allow the client to explore the directive at his/her own pace and as fully or minimally as desired. He/she will gauge his/her own tolerance.

All too often, due to their own anxiety, close friends and family refuse to allow the old person, who may be close to death, to give final messages or good-byes. This directive is an attempt to lay out unfinished business and to give some measure of relief and completion to the artist.

---

* Felt markers with food odors can be purchased in toy shops.

CHAPTER 17

Art Psychotherapy
for a Geriatric Group

Vehicle for Gaining Positive Attention

Mr. Greenberg, a widower, lived in a home for the aged. He resisted coming to group. He was a quiet man who indicated that since he stopped working no one cared to hear what he had to say. The first time he came to group he refused to draw. As other group members drew and talked about how they felt about an aide being fired, the therapist pointed out how Mr. Greenberg had left himself out by refusing to participate. When the next request was to *do a mural which contains a plan for voicing your displeasure,* Mr. Greenberg, motivated by the subject, quickly picked up his markers to display a person carrying a "strike banner." The group was impressed and enthusiastic with Mr. Greenberg's suggestion. The thought of a strike appealed to the group; they then discussed the possibilities of putting it into action.

However, when a strike appeared to be unrealistic, Mr. Greenberg said the group could present the mural to the institutional administrators. Everyone agreed with this form of protest, since exposing their feelings and support of the hospital aide was the important factor in their own self-respect.

In group art psychotherapy every person can easily interact and relate with his/her peers.

Encouraging Creativity and Self-expression

The group was told to pair off in teams of two. *Look at your partner and draw his/her portrait. Draw the clothes—pay attention to the color, design, details such as buttons, colors, belts, etc.*

When Mr. Greenberg hesitatingly began the directive, he mentioned that he "couldn't draw so good." However, he became enthused as he became involved in observing the details of his partner's clothes. He decided to reproduce the assignment as representationally as possible (Figure 98). On top of the basic drawing of the dress, he pasted colored tissue paper to illustrate the quality of the fabric. He used plasticene to mold the buttons and belt buckle, which he pressed down on the illustration. Mr. Greenberg rolled out thin lines of plasticene and pressed them down onto the collar to

Figure 98. Mr. Greenberg's portrait of his partner

give the effect of embroidery. At the same time, his partner, Mrs. Freed, was drawing what Mr. Greenberg wore. She used his plasticene idea for representing the design on Mr. Greenberg's sweater.

The next directive was for each person to *draw your own clothing without looking it over.* Most of the group members told their partners that this was not so easy. They began to realize how little attention they paid to what they wore.

The discussion revolved around the fascination of discovering details through the exercise. Mr. Greenberg said it was interesting, "Almost like going on a hike and seeing the things around you." He suggested maybe they could draw the lounge where they met, just to see if they could remember what was on the walls. Most partners talked to each other about their experience, in addition to taking part in the group discussion. The general consensus was that it is easier to draw from observation (partner's clothing) than from memory (their own clothing).

As individuals became more aware of their appearance, better grooming was explored in the context of "paying more attention to ourselves and how we look."

Interaction

The group was asked to *work together to create a structure of a scene.* Plasticene, construction paper, fabrics and wood were available for the project.

At first the group spent time wondering how and if the project was possible. Finally, one of the men said he had been a carpenter so he could set up a house construction by gluing the wood together. Another person suggested that construction paper would be used for the walls. Mr. Greenberg stated it would be best if certain parts, such as furniture, doors, windows, and drapes, were assigned to particular group members. In that way, everyone could make his/her own object and in the end it could all be brought together. A few participants were concerned that they would be unable to contribute anything artistic. The therapist reminded them that she was there to give help to anyone who needed it and mentioned that magazine pictures could fulfill some of their needs. The group agreed to Mr. Greenberg's idea about the assignments. There was a great deal of talking and consulting among the group members. Within a short time, everyone was busy with the project. One woman pasted cloth on cardboard for drapes; another molded plasticene tables and chairs; another drew and colored in the rug. Walls were put up on three sides, leaving one side open in order to place the furniture. Several members agreed that it took on the qualities of a doll house.

Several women reminisced about their past. The carpenter made sure that "Things were sturdy." Mr. Greenberg played the role of the "organizer." One woman assigned herself the task of putting people in the "right place," while another woman, who usually held herself back, received help when she asked group members "what to do." One participant put in the accessories and claimed she liked "to put on the finishing touches." When group members were not physically active, they maintained their interest in the progress of the structure.

The cooperative efforts stimulated group interaction. The less verbal active members found the group projects an easier way for them to participate. The gains included social as well as creative gratification.

Catalyst for Promoting Empathy

When asked to *decorate the outside of a box showing who you are,* Mr. Greenberg left all the sides and top vacant. However, the entire bottom was filled with "a man in the business world." When the group questioned the meaning of the object, Mr. Greenberg explained, "Only the part that can not be seen is interesting. It shows how important I was when I ran a business. The rest is not covered because I'm a nobody now!"

Several other members included parts of their former lives which were related to work or homemaking. However, Mr. Greenberg's box was so poignant that it stimulated all of the participants to talk about the loss of activity, wishes of still being needed, and a diminished connection with their former life-styles.

Concretizing Changing Role and Identity

There was a follow-up to the directive regarding the box showing "who you are" to help people understand that roles may change but an identity exists even without work. Therefore, the group was asked to *open the box and on the inside paste/draw pictures/place objects or clay sculptures which represent what you value, family or friends which are important to you, hobbies, how you spend your time, roles which you have maintained.*

Mr. Greenberg sat for a long time, thinking. He had difficulty with starting. It was suggested that he look through the picture collage box for some ideas (Figure 99). He saw a picture of children. "Yep," he said, "I'm a grandpa and my grandchildren love my stories so I'll draw a book to show I'm still a good storyteller. It's hard for me to read because my eyes are bad, but I'm still a chess player. I belong to the temple; on Saturday my son takes me there and I chant the parts I know by heart. I'll cut out and color a pray-

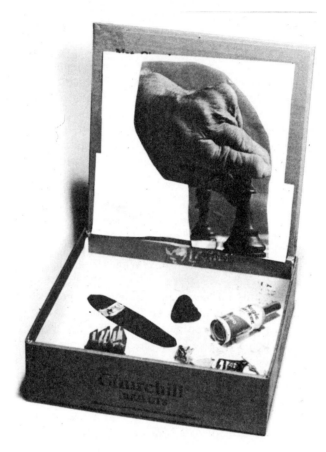

Figure 99.   Concretizing one's identity

er cloth." Mr. Greenberg then went outside for a minute, brought back a
branch which he placed in the box to show he had a number of plants in his
room which he cared for. He pasted a picture of a cigar to represent his "big
shot son" and formed a little ball out of plasticene to stand for his
"daughter who loves sports." For the finishing touches he tucked in a felt
marker to show that he now had a new role, "art therapy participant."
When the box was completed, he closed it only partway because he said he
wanted easy access to seeing the insides. Mr. Greenberg was pleased with
himself as he shared his box. In gaining an understanding of his identity, he
no longer felt he was a "nothing."

The client must be helped to delineate his changing role in order to integrate the shift in identity.

Problem-solving

Colored construction paper, paper trays, paper cups, markers, plasticene, paints, and glue were offered to the group to *create a picnic scene.*
Several people pasted flat pieces of paper on cups for picnic tables. One woman with arthritis rolled some clay for a tree trunk, but her fingers were not nimble enough to make the tree top. She asked for help. The man next to her was delegated to add to her tree, since he couldn't think of anything to do. Someone said, "We must have food on the table." Mr. Greenberg asked if he could draw a chess board on one table. The group was delighted that Mr. Greenberg placed his personal interest in their scene. This gave other members some personal ideas. One lady said she always baked cakes for picnics and proceeded to model one out of plasticene. Another said she remembered a red and green blanket she used to bring to picnics so she could take a nap. She proceeded to make one out of colored construction paper, then laid it down near the tables. The question by the therapist was, "What's missing?" After some thought, they realized their picnic needed people, but they were concerned that they were too difficult to draw. Mr. Greenberg suggested that magazine pictures of people could be pasted on construction paper, then folded on the bottom to form a stand. A sample was made and the group all participated in some phase of the people-making. They were placed at tables, on the blanket, near the chess game, at the food table, under the tree. The group was delighted with the completed product. They were pleased with how innovative they had been, giving each member credit for ideas and the art products which were contributed.

Identifying Universal Problems

The suggestion was to *do a mural which portrays what older people all over the world have in common.* One woman began by drawing eyeglasses, saying "Eyesight isn't so good." A man drew a person making a bed, declaring, "They get tired easier." Another pasted a red oblong, claiming "It's a hot water bottle," as he stated, "We get cold faster than we used to." Mr. Greenberg drew a tombstone, saying matter-of-factly, "We all know the end is not too far off." Someone else offered a book as he said, "We forget a lot we learned, but we remember a lot." A yellow oblong was drawn to illustrate corn and the accompanying statement was, "Our teeth are not so strong," and a band-aid represented physical pain.

When the mural was completed, most people agreed that the pictures applied to themselves as well as the aged the world over. A discussion revolved around the group's mutual problems and the importance of being in an empathic group.

Dealing with Death

When a group member dies, the therapy provides a place for the group members to say goodbye and to deal with their own mortality. The therapist opened the art therapy session by saying, "Everyone knows Mrs. Freed died last night. I will miss her. I know everyone has some feelings about her death." She continued with the request that they *draw an abstract symbol of Mrs. Freed.* In spite of the sadness, the group was eager to begin. Most of the pictures were in pink since that was the color Mrs. Freed most frequently used, and in yellow because she was seen as a warm, friendly person. The group pasted their symbols of Mrs. Freed onto a single page. The therapist next requested: *Make a drawing or picture collage which conveys your personal message to Mrs. Freed.* The pictures showed images of hearts telling how fond they were of the dead group member. Others drew tears, stating they would miss her. Mr. Greenberg drew a dress on one side and a man's clothes on the other. He tore the page down the middle in order to display, "A partner of mine is ripped away, I feel bad."

During the session, the participants themselves decided to do a mural "in memory of Mrs. Freed." They asked the therapist if they could paste up one of Mrs. Freed's art therapy pictures. They then decided that perhaps her "box" should be pasted on a large piece of cardboard since it was so representative of Mrs. Freed. Around it would be a testimonial drawn by all of the group members (Figure 100). The participants were pensive as they created the testimonials, including: gold wrapping paper, which stood for Mrs. Freed's "heart of gold"; aluminum foil which reflected how she would remain in the hearts of the group; a paper doily giving credence to her "sweet delicate nature"; a picture of food expressing her nurturance; a drawing of the sun symbolizing the "warmth" of the missing member; a vase with flowers which was associated with Mrs. Freed as a person of "quality"; and a drawing of an open window showing that "she was open to hear what we had to say."

During the discussion about the way Mrs. Freed died in her sleep, several members told how they wished they, too, would have a peaceful end. As the group was cleaning up, Mr. Greenberg appeared to be the group's voice when he said, "It is hard to have one of us die, but I appreciate having the chance to say goodbye to our friend, Mrs. Freed. If the group still exists

Figure 100.   Memorial to Mrs. Freed

when death comes to me, I only hope that you will give me such a wonderful
and meaningful memorial service.''

SUMMARY

   Individual and interactional group art psychotherapy places a major emphasis on: immediate problems; general issues indigenous to old age;
stimulating thought processes; and providing the client with a sense of
dignity.
   Art tasks and discussion are designed to acknowledge the individual, as
well as the changes old age necessitates; identify universal problems; gain an
awareness of the various senses; increase self-esteem; problem solve; and
deal with death.

PART VI

Psychiatric Hospitals and Day Treatment Settings

This part concerns art therapy as it is practiced in two settings—psychiatric hospitals and day treatment or partial hospitalization programs. It provides information on the similarities and contrasts for patient treatment in each environment.

HOSPITALIZED PATIENTS

Hospitalized psychiatric patients are in an acute stage of dysfunction. They may be in the midst of a psychotic episode, in a state of decompensation and/or in danger of doing harm to themselves or to others. These patients may have a distorted perception of reality and/or lack cognitive skills and emotional control.

Artwork

The patients in an acute psychotic state poignantly reveal their disintegration through their artwork. The product is a statement of their confusion, shown through a lack of organization, meaningless and unrelated images, and disconnected or fragmented forms. Due to these elements, the artwork has an irrational, bizarre appearance. The individual's thought disturbance may be seen in the gross enlargement of the presented symbols. The tortured, insufferable experience which the patient is undergoing is revealed through the distorted and fleeting phantasmagoric images. Incongruities in

271

the form and composition parallel the psychotic person's own incongruent derangement. The primitive quality of the art is due to the blatant stream of primary process. This is expressed through weakened forms and the boldly strengthened use of colors (often at variance with reality).

The lack of thought control makes coping strategies impossible. The hospitalized person may begin the artwork with a particular thought in mind; however, a circuitous process takes place and the final creation often ends up being unrecognizable to the viewer. Confusion around ideas of reference are shown as the symbols in the paintings or sculptures become fused with the meaning and the patient's reality.

A shattered ego is accompanied by cognitive disorganization. Communication systems are disunited and unorganized. The individual's ideas are inchoate, scrambled and fused with unrelated thoughts. The patient's language may contain neologisms, commonly referred to as a "word salad." During the creative process, neologisms are converted to an "art salad." The "art salad" consists of a mixture of parts which are alien to each other, undefined, merged and/or chopped up. The style may be extremely vague or obsessively involved and the meaning of the product is incomprehensible.

Stereotypic, perseverative and bizarre behavior is analogously displayed in the art style. The perservative aspect is shown by a repetitive pattern and/ or motif, and the bizarre element is displayed in a wildness of color, composition and content.

Depersonalization, the psychotic person's loss of self, presents itself in distorted body images. This is illustrated by body parts which are exhibited through detachment, dismemberment, fusion, omission, incongruencies, x-ray vision (display of body insides) and/or labeling of body parts. Human beings may be expressed in abstract or metaphoric forms. Depersonalized paintings and drawings often contain colors which are faint white or light yellow.

Function

The art therapy modality is used to gather clues for initial and ongoing diagnosis. The latter may designate changes as the patient may move in and out of the decompensated state. The artwork often reveals emotions which are in the process of surfacing from a latent to a manifest state. The art products which are created in the art therapy session represent the instant and long-range record of the patient's illness and health, for strengths are recognized as well as pathology. At the end of treatment, artworks offer indications for termination and prognosis. Aside from diagnosis, the major art therapy function is its use as a parallel form of treatment.

The art therapist may initially encourage the dysfunctional person to reveal his/her inner world. This expressive opportunity may offer a cathartic experience for the patient. It also serves as a means for sharing personal conflicts/emotions/fantasies/hallucinations/delusions and/or thoughts with the art therapist. Once this has been accomplished, it is imperative to discontinue work in the area of hallucinations and fantasies. Repeated solicitation of this material only serves to feed into the patient's unreality-oriented system.

Goals

The major art therapy goal is to pull the patient out of a nightmarish, disintegrated, psychotic existence by providing symbolic containment, structure and reality.

As the acute state of psychosis subsides, the art therapist is especially sensitive to the delicate balance of structure and limit-setting versus a less contained art therapy experience. The directives and the media which are offered depend on an assessment of the patient's ego strength and coping mechanisms.

Group Work

The format of the art therapy approach lends itself to the involvement of the patient in group participation. However, many groups are composed of members whose gross dysfunction impedes their interactive ability. Although group process is the ultimate goal, at times it is an unrealistic expectation on the part of the art therapist. In this event, sessions must be redirected to the more viable approach of individual therapy in group. Themes may tempt the participants to interact; however, overwhelming emotions and self-involvement may limit the interactional quality and quantity.

Art therapy directives are selected to give members an opportunity to focus on reality, organized thought, problem-solving, containment and defense retrieval. These aspects are stressed, rather than the pursuit of insight, which is more appropriately applied to patients in the day treatment setting.

DAY TREATMENT

Day treatment or partial hospitalization provides a full day treatment program to dysfunctional individuals while they live at home and in the community. These programs are designed as a hospital deterrent for persons who are in a borderline condition, or as a transitional form of treatment for fragile individuals who have been dismissed from a psychiatric hospital.

DAY TREATMENT PATIENTS

In contrast to the hospitalized person who is totally dysfunctional, the day treatment patient manages to function minimally. There is a more integrated ego and emotional control. The patient may be chronically schizophrenic, borderline or severely depressed. Unlike the hospitalized patient, resistance and defensiveness are heightened and there exists an interactive potential. The day treatment population has impairments which include some of the following: emotional dormancy, apprehension, desperation, extreme vulnerability, impulsive actions, emotional outbursts, concentration difficulties, severe depression, thought disorders and suicidal ideation.

Artwork

Unlike the wild primitive quality of the hospitalized patient's artwork, the day treatment person's artwork often has an overly restricted appearance. The weak functioning ego represents itself through constricted forms, a somewhat integrated composition, subdued or minimal use of color which is congruent with reality, and subject matter which may be appropriate. Although body image perception may be impaired, the artwork leans towards a more complete and realistic illustration than that created by the hospitalized patient.

The stultified style is directly related to the manner in which patients desperately cling to their defenses to maintain control. This is diametrically opposed to the loose style of the decompensated and out-of-control patient, whose defenses have dissolved.

Splits or areas of conflict are revealed through the polarization of forms and/or color and/or content. The sense of isolation is seen by the use of space and the frequent lack of human subjects.

Suicidal ideation may be consciously or unconsciously expressed. Clues to suicidal thoughts may be offered in a metaphoric fashion, for example: a house which is on the edge of a cliff, a tree which is broken and falling over, or a poisoned dog.

Function

In day treatment, the function of the art therapy approach is similar to that of the psychiatric hospital. It is utilized for determining the initial, ongoing and terminating diagnosis and prognosis. Once again, the major art therapy function is that of a parallel form of treatment for individual/conjoint/family/group treatment.

Goals

The hospitalized person's ego is shattered, whereas the day treatment participant is less impaired. In antithesis to the hospitalized patient's uncontrollable mode of functioning, the day treatment patient is often too rigid; emotions and fantasies are suppressed out of the plaguing fear of disintegration. Therefore, the art therapy goals are adjusted to meet the needs of the individual through the assessment of the patient's ego functioning and behavior. The treatment plan in day treatment is directed towards: reality-testing, circumventing obsessional rumination, problem-solving, emotional discharge, slackening of defenses, fantasy exploration, diminishing fearful thoughts and emotions, insight into areas of conflict, clarification of perceptions and attitudes. The task orientation is instituted to effect healthier adaptive responses.

Media

Watercolors, acrylic paints, felt markers, oil pastels, wet clay, plasticene, tissue paper, and magazine collage pictures are the recommended media for use with the day treatment patient.

Group Work

Art therapy directives facilitate group process. Interactions take place, first on a symbolic level, then on a verbal level. Participants are assisted in examining and lowering their defenses, problem-solving, and gaining socialization skills. Primary focus is on interpersonal contact and communication. The group provides a testing ground where participants can take risks in a nonthreatening situation. Members are supportive of each other; where verbal communication is difficult, the artwork may serve to pinpoint problem areas and existing empathy. Verbal and visual feedback offers participants an important means for developing interpersonal communication skills.

The art therapy procedure provides group members with an arena where art is mutually created and cooperative interaction is facilitated. The art tasks include group problem-solving techniques, which are important in generating and integrating resocialization skills.

Chapter 18 addresses itself to the deviations in the treatment approach between psychiatric hospitals and day treatment. For the hospital setting, two sets of illustrations are offered; one presents the history of a group of inpatients who possess sufficient ego strength to engage in group process. The second set of examples deals with a group of severly dysfunctional members who lack the ability to interact. Emphasis is placed on simple art tasks which require mutual involvement. A suggested guide for working with specific disorders is included.

Chapter 19 establishes a procedure for *socialization desensitization*. This method offers the patient opportunities to progressively build up his/her socializing tolerance. Tasks are designed in a specific order which requires a gradual increase in the number of interacting members. The method is illustrated through a case history of an art psychotherapy group in a day treatment setting. Chapter 20 includes three vignettes of individual treatment. Each patient was prescribed art therapy for a specific, yet different, goal: 1) uncovering diagnostic clues to the patient's operational system; 2) facilitating a patient's transition from the inpatient unit to the day treatment setting; 3) diluting of the patient's transference to the primary therapist.

CHAPTER 18

Group Art Psychotherapy in Psychiatric Hospitals

INTRODUCTION

Clinical art therapy provides the therapist with a means for observing the patient's strengths, as well as pathology. These are viewed through the patient's approach, level of involvement, art process, content, and the quality and quantity of interacting ability.

Referrals for group art therapy may be made for numerous reasons. The request may be based on a need for additional information in making a diagnosis, conducting treatment and/or recommending termination. At times it is due to a patient's resistance or impasse in his/her individual psychotherapy. In this event, the art therapy group may act as a catalyst for further exploration or improved adaptive responses, as well as a mechanism for uncovering suicidal ideation. This approach is also used to intrude upon the patient's obsessional system. Art therapy directives deal with this problem by shifting the individual's focus; the artwork gives the patients momentary relief from their ritualistic controls. For the many hospitalized patients who need limit-setting and structure, both directives and media provide a mechanism for defining parameters and containment.

Groups which have the greatest potential for therapeutic interaction are composed of persons from a variety of diagnostic categories. However, when groups are formed with persons who manifest similar symptoms, the art therapist considers themes which deal directly with these symptomatic impairments and avoids issues which are emotionally overloading.

Two sets of art psychotherapy illustrations are presented here. The first demonstrated work with a group of dysfunctional patients who have sufficient ego strength to engage themselves in group process. The second presents directives for patients with a greater degree of dysfunction who have grossly impaired interactional skills.

ILLUSTRATIONS
WITH MODERATELY DYSFUNCTIONAL
GROUP MEMBERS

Warm-up

When beginning a new art therapy group, the commonly used scribble technique is countraindicated. The scribble requires the patient to exercise his/her imagination towards discovered imagery, which is then drawn into the design. This warm-up is inappropriate for the decompensated patient due to the looseness of the scribble itself and the activation of fantasy. It may be valuable for an individual session; however, in group a mass reaction to the surfacing of unconscious material is overwhelming and anxiety-producing. Therefore, a structured type of warm-up, one which will bring about involvement without provoking anxiety, is indicated.

The patients were given magazine photos and instructed to *1) select three photos which appeal to you, then paste them down onto the newsprint paper; 2) write down a few words under each picture.*

The magazine pictures functioned as a distancing device. Choosing pictures is less threatening than creating symbols with crayons or felt markers. The mechanics of trimming pictures and gluing them down provide the group members with a method for becoming involved and contained. The collage gives the patients an opportunity to exercise control over the media and to express themselves. The request for a limited selection of three pictures helps to set forth necessary parameters.

The simple warm-up exercise is completed by the group members' taking turns in showing their collages, with a comment if they wish. Due to the minimal requirements of this technique, all members usually become involved and willingly talk about their pictures. When a group is newly formed, the therapist must assess whether or not it is therapeutic to offer interpretations or comments.

In this newly formed group, the therapist chose not to make any references to the collages, with the exception of one made by Faye, who had been institutionalized the week the group began. This patient pasted three pictures: one of a man who, she said, "was feeling low"; another of two automobiles which "were going around in circles"; and finally a portrait of "a woman who is afraid and tired." When the group commented on their pictures, Faye admitted she was afraid of becoming like the woman in her collage. The therapist responded by pointing out that Faye was already like her pictures. She was "feeling low, going around in circles, afraid and tired" (due to her depression). The clinician pointed out that Faye had helped herself by agreeing to be hospitalized. The patient felt relieved by both the acknowledgment of her mental state and the positive reinforcement about her hospitalization.

Reality Focus

A great deal of the artwork reveals the patients' tendency to deny their hospital existence. Their fantasies place them outside of the institution. They often refuse to work on their separation from home and community. To deal with the reality of their hospitalized existence, the patients were instructed, *draw yourself in the hospital.*

Samantha understood the directive in a literal sense. She drew herself in her room (Figure 101). However, opposing reality, she drew it with striped wallpaper, hanging flower baskets, a rug, chintz curtains, and a fancy

Figure 101.   Focus for reality testing

dresser. During the discussion, the group pointed out that her picture bore no resemblance to the room which she shared with two other patients. To help Samantha deal with her environment, she was asked to use her first picture as "her wish" and to *draw another picture of your hospital room as it really it*. When Samantha finished her second picture, she was able to admit how she refused to see life as it really was.

Faye drew a small x, declaring she felt xed out by her family and society. Jim drew a spider caught in a web as his psychological reaction to being in the hospital (Figure 102). Craig drew "his ambivalent feelings." On one side he made "a prisoner in jail" and on the other side a garden, depicting the hospital as a place of "rest and salvation." During the discussion, the patients empathized with one another. The technique focused their attention on the reality of their situation and the appropriate emotions which accompanied their hospitalization.

Figure 102.   Reaction to hospitalization

Relationships

The theme of the patients' relationships to significant others is introduced through plasticene sculpture. Conscious and unconscious feelings are revealed through the symbols and the placement. The plasticene is used for its tactile quality and the technique requires the patient to imprint his/her hand onto the medium. This procedure facilitates owning the symbol as a part of themselves.

The following directives are given slowly to avoid confusion or overload: *1) Press your hand down on a flattened piece of plasticene, leaving your handprint. 2) Scratch a symbol onto your handprint which represents something friendly about you.*

On her handprint Samantha scratched out lips, which she explained stood for her "friendly smile." Jim's hand portrayed a dog, which represented his "loyalty." Faye's hand had a kitty for her "gentleness." And Craig's symbol was beer, which portrayed his being "a sociable guy."

The follow-up directive requested the group members to: 1) *Model another hand which represents a person you like. 2) Place the two hands in any position.*

Faye placed the two right hands dovetailing each other, giving the sculpture the appearance of a single piece. The artwork seemed to portray Faye's symbiosis with her mother. It was Craig who pointed out Faye's continued dependency on her parents.

Craig created a hand which he claimed belonged to the art therapist. He placed this sculpture inside of his hand. Craig told about his fantasy of becoming good friends with the therapist. Other group members admitted they, too, had similar fantasies.

Samantha made a man's arm with a clenched fist. It had a phallic appearance. Instead of placing it on her handprint, she dropped it down. The fist hit the sculpture so hard the smiling lips were ruined. The patient remarked, "Isn't that just typical of what happens to me—my friendly smile gets smashed."

Craig pointed out how Samantha had "asked for it" by throwing the piece down instead of putting it where it belonged. The art therapist related how Samantha rebelled against the rules by making an arm in addition to the hand. She had also opposed the "friendly theme" of the project. Craig added that Samantha "did not care" and she chose to "let things fall as they may." Although this was typical of Samantha's self-destructive pattern, the concreteness of the incident awakened her self-awareness.

Focus on Need for Hospitalization

Many patients disconnect their personal feelings from environmental situations. The art therapist provides the patients with a vehicle for focusing on themselves in relation to their hospitalization. Patients were given paper trays upon which they were asked to *created two scenes: 1) What the hospital does for you; 2) What it does not do for you.*

Craig (Figure 103) made a figure which was half in a window and half hanging out; he explained that the hospital kept him from killing himself. He also created himself playing his guitar, stating the hospital did not provide him with any solitude where he could practice.

Samantha made a set of wheels, which meant the hospital kept her from spinning her wheels. "What it did not do" was shown in a plasticene model of a man and a woman having intercourse. Samantha complained that the hospital kept a close eye on her and did not allow her to have any sexual outlet. Other patients agreed about the difficulty and frustration which they experienced around the sexual inhibitions which were required of them.

Figure 103. Hospitalization prevents suicide but does not provide solitude

Transference

The patients were encouraged to demonstrate their transference through portraits of the therapist. Patients frequently go through a period of testing the therapist before a therapeutic alliance can be established. The portraits give the patients an opportunity to see the therapist's ego strength. It also dispels omnipotent fantasies of damaging the therapist through their thoughts. This technique serves to display the therapist's strength and her/his ability to accept the patient's feelings without becoming vulnerable or punitive.

The group was asked to *do a portrait of me* (the therapist). This can be a realistic portrayal or an abstract symbol.

Doug (Figure 104) projected his fear of women onto the therapist by drawing Dracula. Faye drew a police force, revealing her reaction to an authority figure. One patient drew a figure running, declaring the therapist

Figure 104.   Art therapist seen as Dracula

was always running things; she was on top of everything. Samantha drew a doctor's uniform and declared that the therapist took care of the group. A paranoid woman drew a person with piercing eyes, declaring the therapist was able to see into the patients' heads. One man made a large heart to portray a caring person. Craig drew the therapist with large hands as a declaration of her nurturance. Finally, Jim drew a scalpel, which may have represented some castration anxiety; however, what he shared was the magical expectation that the therapist would help cut out the bad parts of his personality.

Perception of Art Therapy

It is helpful to the therapist to understand how the patient perceives art therapy. Therefore, the request was made: *Symbolically draw what art therapy means to you.*

Jim drew a bomb which was being defused. He said the picture was self-explanatory—he felt "defused, channeled into a direction." Faye presented a box as she claimed, "a close structure where I can express myself; I don't talk in other groups, here it's easier." Samantha made a web with a flower in the center; she explained, "Art therapy is one of the good things at the hospital. It helped me work through the web I had woven to hide myself." One man drew a zero; he stated, "I could take it or leave it." Craig created people pushing against a wall; he claimed it helped him push away his charm and face up to his sense of hopelessness.

Emotional Responses to a Group Member

Therapists must sometimes make a clinical decision whether or not to deal with the emotional responses which a particular participant elicits in other group members. The patient who evokes the responses must have enough ego strength to tolerate the confrontation. It is also important for the patient to have individual therapy available in order to carry on the work that is started in the group.

Samantha constantly used denial as a defense against her rage. She evidenced a constant, smiling Pollyanna attitude. Her inappropriate affect provoked the rest of the group; however, their feelings toward Samantha were subterfuged.

At a time when the transference to the therapist and the group trust were established, the issue of Samantha's effect on the other participants was dealt with. One day the patient came into group announcing, with a smile, that her privileges were revoked but it was "ok." The group was asked to *draw your feelings when Samantha said it was ok to have her privileges taken away.*

Jim, who had a history of repressing his rage until he became violent, responded to the directive by drawing an explosion which was encapsulated. The therapist interpreted his artwork, relating how Jim kept his anger in until it built up to a point where it destructively erupted. The patient was encouraged to express his emotions at the time they were experienced, to avoid the accumulation of rage and its inappropriate manifestation.

Another response to Samantha was created by depressed, withdrawn Faye, who frequently entertained suicidal thoughts. She painted a red abstract picture which stood for her "blind rage." The patient went on to tell "how very mad" Samantha's actions made her. In fact, she wished she could "strike out and slap Samantha." After this announcement, Faye picked up a black marker to encompass her abstract painting. She said she felt better after expressing her feelings toward Samantha. Faye added how pleased she was with the enclosing black line, which symbolized her self-imposed impulse control.

The therapist, in order to dispel any magical omnipotence, made a point of explaining to the group members that no one could possibly receive any physical pain from angry drawings which portrayed explosions, fights, rage, etc. Attention was brought to Samantha to show how she suffered no punishment from the feedback pictures, yet, at the same time, group members felt relieved after portraying their emotional responses to her actions.

The discussion which ensued dealt with the group members' difficulty in confronting Samantha with her behavior. Several patients also faced their own problems in dealing with the expression of their own rage. Other group members were too threatened by the topic of anger; their denial was seen in the unrelated pictures of flowers, designs or animals. Nevertheless, by dealing with this theme the patients realized the therapist was not threatened by the expression of anger. She could allow and encourage the patients to deal with their emotions in a protective environment.

Self-Identification: Clues for Strengths,
Pathology and Suicide

There are times when it is necessary to understand what patients are thinking and feeling, if their identification is affected by personal, hospital unit, family, and/or societal crises. The issues of identification during this time of crisis is revealed through their artwork. It is essential to evaluate the patient's strengths, pathology, or suicidal potential during the time when therapeutic intervention or watchfulness is necessary. As an example, anxiety, depression, or suicidal ideation may be evoked through a death that is related to the unit or one which receives a great deal of publicity. For example, when Elvis Presley died, the staff was alerted to adversive reactions by the patients who had suicidal tendencies. In order to gain clues as to the patients' emotional state, the following directives were given: 1) *Think of a person with whom you can identify, then write the name on top of the paper.* 2) *Pick out magazine pictures or draw how you identify with that person.*

Doug shared his identification with basketball player Willis Reed. He told how Reed was a man who had been injured, but was able to overcome it. The patient related his identification to the fact that his depression had been precipitated by a serious prolonged physical illness which rendered him incapable of working or participating in physical activities. Doug went on to tell how he became so sorry for himself that he was unable to manage his daily life and had to be hospitalized. Doug's illustrated identification revealed his positive motivation and strength.

Although Faye had admitted suicidal thoughts in the past, in this exercise she identified with her mother. She drew her parent sitting alone, looking out of the window; beside her was a sewing machine. The patient related that she and her mother looked alike; they both enjoyed sewing and were lonely, depressed persons. This information showed that Elvis Presley's death probably did not influence this patient.

Thirty-year-old Craig was a professional guitarist who had made several suicide attempts. As soon as the therapist stated the directive, Craig immediately printed Elvis Presley in large bold print. He drew "reds," claiming he himself had overdosed on reds and he was certain that was how Elvis died. Upon further investigation, Craig admitted that Elvis had been his longtime idol. Considering the patient's identification with Presley, it was necessary to alert the hospital staff to keep a close watch on this patient.

Strength Awareness

When a group member evidences some suicidal ideation in an art therapy session, it is necessary to deal with the patient's strengths. Although the directive was mainly for Craig, all the patients benefited from the following technique: *Draw what you can do to make yourself stronger.*

Jim drew a picture of himself doing exercises (Figure 105); he told the

Figure 105.   Exercise for self help

group he could discipline himself to work on strengthening his muscles. Faye drew herself swimming, dancing and taking art classes; she explained that her psychiatrist wanted her to become more interested in activities. Craig couldn't think of anything, indicating his sense of despair. The therapist encouraged him to look through the collage box to see if the pictures gave him any ideas. Craig rummaged through the photos until he finally selected two images: one was of a garbage can, which meant he could throw his drugs away; the other was of fruit and a glass of milk, which stood for a better diet. These pictures may well have been selected to please the therapist; however, the exercise seemed to give Craig some closure. When the session was over, staff members were informed about Craig's possible suicide attempt.

Emotions Evoked by Holidays

Holiday time often evokes depression for the hospitalized patient. Through the process of externalizing feelings and thoughts, an attempt is made to prevent patients from acting out or withdrawing as a defense against their depression. To provide the patients with structure they are given colored pencils or pens and are requested to *draw an abstract symbol showing feelings about the holidays.*

The holiday was Easter and Passover. Samantha drew several symbols, one of a church, another of a home. When confronted with the fact that these symbols did not show any feelings, the patient took a red pencil and scribbled over the church and home, admitting she was angry that her family would be together enjoying Easter Sunday, while she had to sit and look at all the ''crazies.'' The majority of the group agreed—they, too, felt angry at being institutionalized while family and friends were together.

Faye drew herself very small, crying. She admitted feeling sad. She was worried that her family would get used to having her away; perhaps she would be forgotten altogether. Once again, group members empathized, sharing similar thoughts and emotions.

Craig drew a face with one side of the mouth curved up and the other bent down. He claimed the meaning of the holiday itself meant nothing to him; however, he had to confront the fact that he was institutionalized and not free like the people on the outside.

Jim drew x's all over the page. He stated he was downright angry that he couldn't be with his child to give him Easter bunnies. The therapist pointed out that Jim's anger was very appropriate and that, for him, expressing these feelings and dealing with them immediately was an improvement and beneficial.

Reality-testing

Reality-testing is relevant to the patients' ability to plan a day when they must function independently. Colored pencils are offered as structure since the following directive may stimulate anxiety: *In comic strip fashion, draw what you would do if you could leave the hospital for a few days.*

Samantha drew herself getting all dressed up, having her hair done, buying clothes, rearranging her bedroom and sitting at the phone calling up friends. The group commented that the majority of drawings showed Samantha taking better care of her personal being, which they agreed was good. However, none of the pictures showed her with another person. Samantha defended herself by saying that's what the phone calls were about—she was going to make plans with whomever was available. She voiced concern that most of her friends would be tied up with other plans.

Faye drew herself reading, painting, sitting in the backyard with her dog.

Group members noticed the relaxed atmosphere of the pictures; they were in agreement that Faye seemed less worried recently. It was pointed out that Faye, like Samantha, also depicted herself doing solitary activities. Both women evidently were not ready to socialize.

On the other hand, Craig showed himself, scene after scene, with people: One picture portrayed him with a special girl; another showed him with his family; in other pictures he was with his friends drinking beer, dancing and playing the guitar. The therapist questioned if he was fearful of being alone, since every scene had him busy, doing something with other people. Craig admitted he was not ready to trust himself alone because of his suicidal thoughts.

Jim's artwork was the only one, out of a group of seven, whose images showed his readiness to shift to a day treatment program. He portrayed himself getting up in the morning, getting dressed, eating, doing some isometric exercise, playing in the yard with his son, watching TV, having a friend come over for dinner, fixing a vacuum cleaner, thinking of getting a job such as running an answering service which he could do from his home. The group and the therapist reinforced his practical, well-rounded plans. Jim walked out of the session feeling especially good about himself.

Termination

It is necessary to deal with issues around termination for the patient who is leaving the hospital, as well as for the group members who will remain. Expressing feelings around separation and loss is essential. It is also necessary to provide the group with the model of the patient who has made enough progress to leave the institution and make a reentry into society.

When Craig was preparing to leave the hospital, the group members were asked to *make a plasticene sculpture which represents how you feel about Craig's leaving the hospital.* After the individual sculptures were completed, they were to be placed on a single piece of masonite.

Jim created a ladder which symbolized Craig's reaching the top of his goal. Faye made a champagne goblet to show that the accomplishment deserved a celebration. Samantha molded a cake with "good luck" as a decoration. These sculptures, along with those of the rest of the group, were placed in the center, very close to each other.

Dealing with feelings connecting to Craig's separation were obviously too difficult for the patients. During the discussion several people mentioned they only expressed positive thoughts out of consideration for Craig. They chose not to spoil his departure with their sadness.

Craig modeled himself in the plasticene. He placed the figure away from the group because, he said, a large part of himself was already home. He was sad to leave the group, but was happy to return to a normal environment.

The patients tended to use denial as a defense against the discomfort around separation anxiety. Therefore, work on termination was continued.

To help the group members refocus on their emotional response to Craig's separation, the next directive was given: *Draw a symbol which shows how you feel about remaining in the hospital while Craig is on his way out.*

Jim made the ladder symbol once again, but this time the middle rungs were missing, implying that he himself was not ready to reach the top. Samatha drew a bed covered by a flowered comforter; she said the hospital represented a place that kept her "tucked in safe," adding, "the outside world is a cold place." Another patient drew a number of bills to symbolize the responsibilities and decision-making which were indicative of the outside world; he articulated the importance of the pressureless atmosphere which the hospital offered. Craig was able to handle the group members' responses by creating sublimating drawings.

Chronic schizophrenics frequently make transferences to the institution where their dependency needs are met. The exercise offered a few examples of patients' preferring to remain in the hospital where they were not burdened with coping, problem-solving and responsibilities. Dealing with Craig's termination precipitated the concern about becoming responsible and more independent.

Resistance to Termination

The issue of termination often activates resistance to art therapy. This is evidenced through the patient's lack of ideas or difficulty in initiating a personal symbol. Resistance is overcome by presenting the patient with two copies of a xeroxed hand. The participants were asked to: 1) *Draw a picture onto one hand of what you will hang onto when you leave the hospital.* 2) *On the other draw what you will let go when you leave.*

When the technique was completed, the patients said the xeroxed hands helped get them started. Several patients admitted the blank page was difficult to confront when they were forced to deal with separation.

On one hand, Faye drew a face with the mouth wide open, stating it meant she would still speak up for herself instead of holding things inside. In the other hand, she drew a looney bird for the crazy hallucinations which she had already given up.

Samantha drew the group; she said she would remember the friends she had made and the empathy they had offered her. Although she would keep the memories, she would have to give up the relationships.

Craig put a palette in one hand, claiming he would continue to draw his feelings, since the art therapy approach had been helpful to him. He drew the art therapist because he would probably never see her again.

Jim drew rose-colored glasses as a new outlook and left behind blinders, which stood for his unwillingness to see things as they really were.

ILLUSTRATIONS WITH
SEVERELY DYSFUNCTIONAL GROUP MEMBERS

In groups where the patient's ego strength is non-existent, or minimal, the major emphasis is on simple art tasks with mainly symbolic contact and interaction. A group of four or five persons is ideal—seven or eight is maximum; with more patients, it is difficult for the art therapist to maintain a therapeutic environment.

Warm-up

The object of the warm-up exercise is to get the patient involved without too much strain, fear, or self-consciousness. To alleviate the resistance to beginning an art therapy session, the request is made to *draw a picture or design, into, or around the xeroxed copies of the hands.* The xeroxed hand prints, which are passed out to the patients, give them a foundation upon which they can build. When completed, the patients show their pictures and talk about what they have created (Figure 106).

Following the discussion, the therapist pastes all the hands on a piece of mural paper to give the group a greater sense of accomplishment.

Expressing Needs

Patients may feel respected if they are encouraged to ventilate their needs. Therefore, the directive is to *draw a picture showing what you want from the hospital staff.*

Most members willingly participate in a directive where they can concretely lay out their needs. If they are able to follow the instructions, the discussion period may reveal information which had not been formerly offered to the hospital staff. The therapist can share it with other staff members if this is warranted.

Figure 106.   Xeroxed hand alleviates resistance

Simple Cooperative Tasks

In order to facilitate the awareness in group members of one another, a simple and colorful technique is useful. Divide the group into triads. One person receives colored construction paper, another colored tissue paper, the third colored cellophane. Each person receives some type of stiff paper which will act as a base. Each person is given his/her own bottle of glue. Directive: *1) First person, paste your paper on the base, then pass it to the person next to you. 2) Second person, do the same—you can paste it on top, to the side, or wherever you like, keeping it on the same base. 3) Third person, repeat the same.*

When this is completed, the therapist helps group members talk about the appearance of the art product. The process may be repeated several times, with different colors each time and a different person chosen to begin the project. The effects of the mixed media are usually very interesting and satisfying. Using cool colors on one collage, warm on the second, and mixed on the third provides greater variety and possibility for discussion.

Group Collage

To keep the patients focused into the present and to provide a common theme, group members are given one large sheet of butcher paper for a mural. They are asked to *select two magazine pictures or draw what you did in your activity group today.*

This exercise helps group members to consult or speak with each other. The therapist encourages the patients to ask each other questions and to help one another in picture selection, recall, etc. If the patients can tolerate continued work, they are asked to *make a picture of how you felt about the activity, how the product looks, and whether or not you liked the exercise.* This technique can also be done with magazine pictures, tissue paper, drawings, and/or mixed media.

Group Art Activates Communication

Group participation on a single object brings the members together. If group members have some ego strengths, the exercise can be dealt with on a psychological level. The group is divided into two groups of four (or less). A grocery store carton with the top cut off is the object which is used. If the patients are in need of visual parameters due to their difficulty with control, each side of the box has margins placed on it (this is done by the therapist before the group meets). This can be done by painting a frame or by making one with wide, colored or beige masking tape on each side of the carton. The directive requests each member to: *1) Cut out a pattern from colored construction paper; 2) take turns pasting your pattern onto your side of the box.* Several rounds are made (Figure 107).

If the group members can tolerate or sustain another step, instructions are given for each member to *add a small construction paper pattern onto the other sides of the carton.* Participants are encouraged to talk about the experience.

Involvement

To avoid confusion, directives are kept simple. Beginning with an idea facilitates the patients' interest and sustained involvement.

Figure 107.   Box provides interaction and parameters

A magazine photo of a portrait is xeroxed high on a page. Copies are passed out to the patients as they are asked to *draw the rest of the person, dressing him/her any way you wish.* Discussion follows around the various types of clothes which were created.

Self-expression

Tactile materials help patients gain an awareness of their sense of touch. Therefore, various fabrics are made available (corduroy, velvet, leather, silk, wool, etc.). The patients are given four separate instructions: 1) Select two or three pieces of fabric; 2) cut or tear them into desired shapes; 3) paste them onto the cardboard; 4) use markers to color in between the fabrics, creating an abstract design.

A discussion may be offered around associations which the fabrics evoked.

Limit-setting

The use of a small, stable box, preferably a cigar box, gives the patients a limitation of space. They are asked to: *1) Select three small magazine photos and paste them inside the box.* When this part is finished the participants are told to: *2) Select fabrics which remind you of someone and paste them onto the outside of the box.*

When the group is finished the members are asked to show the inside and the outside of the box. Participants are encouraged to talk about the person with whom they identified the fabric.

Positive Feelings

To educate the patient to express his/her feelings through art, it is helpful to begin with a positive emotion. The directive is to *draw something which you like to look at.*

If the patients are able to follow the directive, a discussion takes place after they have shared the pictures.

Interaction

Interaction is simplified through individual projects which are then put together to form a single piece. Each patient is given a piece of wood, then colored pencils or felt pens (the media depends on the level of regression). The participants are told to *color the piece of wood. When you are finished, the pieces of wood will be glued together to form a single sculpture.*

Upon completion, the group discusses the project—whether or not they enjoyed creating the project, what it looks like, etc.

Nonthreatening Topics

Colored construction paper, felt markers or oil pastels, and paper trays are offered to each patient. They are directed to: *1) Select colors you like. Paste them onto the cardboard tray. 2) Draw a picture of some fruit onto the construction paper.*

When the members complete their artwork they share the content. The therapist asks whether or not the patients like the taste of the fruit they drew. A discussion is encouraged. If the patients can tolerate further interaction, pictures of fruits which are related are placed next to each other, for example, citrus fruits, or similar colored fruits, or fruits with edible skins or non-edible skins, etc. Further discussion can relate to those issues.

GUIDELINES FOR WORKING WITH HOSPITALIZED PATIENTS

Following is a guide for the art therapist's approach to the hospitalized patient and the media. These generalizations should not negate individualized considerations. Frequently encountered behavior patterns for hospitalized patients are cited.

Schizophrenic Patients

In the initial stages of treatment, individual art therapy is appropriate. At a later time, small groups may be introduced. The patient is afraid of failing, of being defeated or hurting others. Therefore, the patient's efforts and products can be praised minimally in an attempt to strengthen the ego. Compliments must be sincere and not overwhelming. Limit-setting is appropriate at first, both in interaction and in the art media, working towards less restricting media. Relationships are slowly established; avoid mutual drawings at first.

Anxiety

Directives toward self expression and positive plans are most appropriate and help develop self-confidence. Avoid subjects which increase or initiate anxiety. Task-oriented art should be something which can be completed in a short time. With an acutely agitated patient, the session might need to be shortened. Self-confidence is the goal and longer periods might be more than the patients can tolerate. Help the patients from ruminating about their fears by using directives which will involve the patients in other aspects of their lives. Aggressive expression through the art is helpful and assurance that this is appropriate should be given.

Apathy

Assign simple projects, easily performed with quick returns of narcissistic gratification (feeling of accomplishment). Use simple media which do not need technical know-how, such as collage or colored tissue paper. Give specific directives, rather than allowing the art suggestions to come from the patient. If the product warrants it, give praise. Involvement with the patient through the actual creative process is beneficial. Color, space which progresses in size, and various media are used to encourage creativity. Make suggestions, while reinforcing any initiative taken by the patient.

Masochism

Offer the patient simple, easily performed art tasks where quick gratification can be realized in order to prevent the patient from becoming overwhelmed, discouraged or defeated. Use directives which are clearly outlined and firmly adhered to. Clay or hard plasticene, wood or plaster are most valuable. If working two-dimensionally, large space and brushes are most appropriate. Art which expresses positive themes and an energetic investment is most productive. Art forms and media which can tolerate heavy handling, banging, etc. as a means of expressing hostility are advisable.

Manic State

Every effort is used to reduce exciting stimuli as much as possible. Face the patient to the wall, or have him/her work alone. Break down tasks to the simplest steps. Select directives which will have a quieting effect. Select quiet colors, simple media, and subjects which will elicit a pleasant memory. The therapist should pick out the media, offering no choices to the patient. The goal is to eliminate anxiety over the art and to help him/her succeed as "quickly" as possible. Offer reinforcement before going onto the next step in the session. When you have built a relationship with the patient, more aggressive directives or free choices may be given.

Passive-Dependency

Begin by working with the patient, pulling back more each time until the patient is working alone on the art forms. Space and forms should be small at the beginning, increasing to larger size as time goes on. Help the patient make his/her own decisions, increasing the number of choices as to color, size, media, etc. Encourage free choices for the subject matter. Be honestly encouraging and complimentary whenever possible. Work which can be continued from one session to another will be most productive when the patient can tolerate long-term gratification.

Hysterical Personality

Simple, easily completed projects and activities are presented at first in order to provide the patient with quick gratification. The therapist should compliment the patients' efforts. Conformity and compliance to group activities should be required with firmness. These patients are to be encouraged in creative expression and given the opportunity for appropriate "showing off." Directives which contain time limits and allow for the expression of unconscious material are valuable.

Aggressive Behavior as a Defense Against Dependency

Creative outlets which instill self-confidence and broaden the patient's interests are important. Display your interest in the patient's artwork and be helpful with the art techniques. However, avoid circumventing the patient's own initiative. Encourage group art therapy which focuses on positive aspects and allows for "joyful" art. Directives should include avenues for new interests. Use a variety of media to facilitate new symbolic explorations. Compliment the patient for his/her use of a variety of art materials. Emphasis should be placed on reinforcing self-expression and self-confidence. Compliments about efforts and the products should be given whenever it is honestly possible.

Obsessive-compulsive Behavior

At first allow for art which will necessitate exactness in work; structured directives are essential. Initially, the choice of media will be limited by the nature of the obsessive fears and the defensive compulsion. Let patients work at their own pace and do not press for completion within a limited time span. After they become more comfortable, allow for art products to be less complicated, planning to continue the product from one session to another. Allow the patients to ventilate feelings regarding the art therapy, time elements, and media. The goal would be towards a loosening of media, space and style.

Guilty Depression

Depressed patients generally have to be given directions. They are usually apathetic and do not readily choose a subject on their own. Tasks should be given with firmness. The art therapist should avoid expressing thanks, praise, solicitousness, or gratification for the accomplished tasks. Use menial drawing tasks, long, tedious, monotonous projects and dull colors. Allow for directives which take a long time, so they become monotonous or boring. Avoid expensive or fine materials that may make the patient feel "this is too good for me." Do not be overly giving, as this will provoke more guilt.

In many instances the first sign of therapeutic response will be the patient's beginning to grumble and complain and express some hostility. It may be appropriate to provide an outlet for aggressive and hostile feelings through clay or plasticene.

CHAPTER 19

Group Art Psychotherapy in Day Treatment

INTRODUCTION

The artwork of day treatment group members reveals weak ego boundaries. In addition, fragmented thinking and/or poor impulse control may be evident. Patients in this setting put a great deal of their energy into shoring up their defenses. This is witnessed mainly in their stilted style and organization, and in the frequent use of dark or dull colors. This is in contrast to the psychiatrically hospitalized patient, whose artwork shows a lack of defenses through the blatant display of primary process. Products in the inpatient unit contain brilliant colors and a looseness in style, composition, and subject matter. The visual difference in the artwork between the day treatment and the hospitalized patient is indicative of the variance in thought processes of dysfunctional versus minimally functional performance.

This chapter on art therapy for day treatment groups will focus on two aspects of a resocialization program. The first is based on an organized method of gradually increasing the number of persons with whom the patient will socialize. A cooperative task orientation is the means for interaction. The second is based on gaining insight, developing an awareness of feelings, and achieving a conscious understanding of cause and effect.

The first aspect helps the patient build up a tolerance for socialization. It is profitable to begin the art therapy sessions by dividing the group into pairs. This provides the patient with a one-to-one relating exercise. After the dyadic work, the patient progresses to a threesome experience, following with foursomes, continuing thusly, until the group is divided in half. The total group may come together towards the end of each session. The rate of progression depends on the readiness of the group members. This method prepares participants to become desensitized to socialization without the instant pressure for interaction.

The theme for the art task may be elicited through the patient's immediate needs, or it may be combined with the directives such as the illustrations which are cited herein.

The second focus of day treatment is not based on the progressive process, although the two methods do complement each other; again the major emphasis is placed on interaction, with the inclusion of expression of emotions and gaining insight.

ILLUSTRATIONS: PROGRESSIVE INTERACTION

Initiating Group Process

The therapist demonstrates to the group how any design can represent meaning. Illustrations are given, such as an upward arrow could represent energy, a book might show that the individual likes to read, a hand may reveal the person's friendliness, etc.

To help group members become immediately involved in group process, a simple direction is given. Participants are asked to *make a symbol which represents something about yourself.*

In one group, after drawing the personal symbols, the artwork was shared. Several members had frantically and compulsively created numerous self-symbols in spite of the request for *a* symbol. The following illustrations concern four members out of a group of 10.

Ann drew several hands to show she was giving; a scribble for her nervousness, an apple for her constant desire to eat; and a sun for her warmth. Ben made: a zero for his tiredness; an aspirin for his headaches; a band-aid for needing medical help; a briefcase because he was a lawyer; and a sun because he liked warm weather. Several members drew their immediate feelings; for instance, Barbara drew a very small x which portrayed her "anxiety." A few people created images which did not reveal anything about themselves; for example, Jim made a sun because it was nice outside and an elaborate question mark, which he explained as "not being sure about this type of group."

The sun symbol was also seen in the art of other participants. Later, as the group progressed, a common symbol would be pointed out by the therapist and explored. However, it was glanced over during the initial encounter, since the emphasis was on establishing individual identity before trying to focus on group identity.

Aside from the cited illustrations, other group members revealed fragmented thoughts through their art and in the discussion. Due to this factor, it was necessary to follow with a directive which would help these participants pull their thoughts together.

Single Focus to Avoid Fragmentation

To avoid the fragmented thinking, the therapist provided a single focus—one which was concrete and immediate. The instructions were: *Draw how you felt about sharing the symbol about yourself.*

The pictures showed the patients' immediate feelings. A zig-zag line equated "nervousness," while a flower stood for an individual's pleasure. Another person drew fingers forming an O for "okay," and one patient drew an F, which portrayed his concerns about being "dumb." A few members drew pictures which represented art therapy itself.

Although the participants had weak ego boundaries, they were able to interact and to contain their fragmented thoughts, staying focused on the issue which was being dealt with.

Dyads: Contact

Initially, group work may be overloading to patients in day treatment who have poor socialization skills and lack motivation for interpersonal contact or communication. Therefore, within the group context some dyadic, triadic and small group work is extremely beneficial.

To diminish anxiety and to build a foundation for resocialization, the therapist divided the group into twosomes. Couples were instructed: *Each partner select a different piece of colored construction paper and cut out a pattern. Then both partners paste your patterns onto the single piece of black construction paper.*

Ben and Jim were a dyad; both men exhibited paranoid symptoms. They took a conservative, separated approach to their artwork. Their piece appeared contained and organized (Figure 108).

This pair had folded the black construction paper in half to create a divisional crease. They worked simultaneously, each person cutting out his pattern and then pasting it on his own side. When the exercise was about to end, each man pasted a tiny cutout in his partner's space.

During the discussion, Ben and Jim voiced their pleasure with the techni-

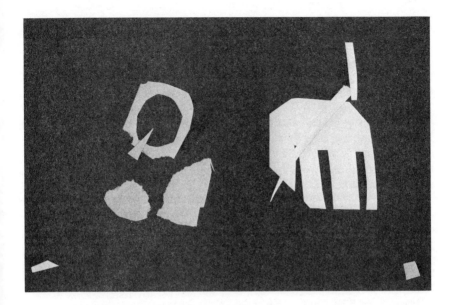

Figure 108.   Dyad comfortable with separate approach

que. They agreed that it had allowed them to work together without any probing or territorial evasion from the partner. They both said they had been pleased with the small patterns which they pasted on their partner's side; it was evidence of the trust which was beginning to be established.

Working in twosomes for the entire session may be a reinforcing therapeutic process. Based on the group outcome, the therapist must assess which is more productive—continued work with matched couples or a larger group project.

When duo drawings are utilized early in group life, the pairs are told to talk about the exercise and the subject matter if one exists. If the dyad appears to have a sense of cohesiveness, the therapist instructs group members to pay attention to their interaction and feelings as they work with their partner. When the art is completed, the patients are instructed to observe: who took up the most space; who connected to their partner; who worked alone, etc. After these points are explored by the partners, the therapist may choose to point out the process and/or contents of the dual artwork.

One pair, Ann and Barbara, interacted with a great deal of spontaneity. Barbara selected dark gray construction paper, cut out a few small patterns, then hesitatingly pasted them into several corners. Ann took several colors—red, pink, and orange. She cut out various sizes and glued them all around Barbara's patterns. Then Ann continued to cover the entire page. The appearance of the final collage was chaotic. Barbara's gray patterns were lost in Ann's excess of color and design.

When the couples were instructed to discuss what happened "on the paper," Ann was informed by her partner that she had "come on too strong." Ann admitted her tendency to "smother people"; however, this was the first time she objectively observed her own behavior. In turn, Barbara became aware of how she had avoided contact by her small, dull-colored patterns, which she pasted in the far corners of the page. Both patients showed the artwork to their primary therapist in individual sessions, where it was fully explored.

Triads: Tasks Initiate Interaction

Work in triads helps the day treatment patients to continue to build tolerance and trust for larger group work. The following directive is divided into three parts: first, individual work; second, artwork which is created by a threesome; third, total group project.

Part 1: Individual Work

Due to the day treatment patient's rigid defenses, a small risk-taking experience is offered through the following directive: *Connect your feelings to colors—use the colored tissue paper to make a collage representing these feelings.*

The colored tissue paper collage medium allows the product to be completed in a short span of time. The results are interesting and very often have an aesthetic quality. The simple and effective procedure in creating a tissue paper collage is nonthreatening to patients who function weakly, have a harsh superego and/or have difficulty with small motor coordination.

The entire group utilized the medium effectively and creatively. Participants interacted verbally with enthusiasm as they created their collages. There was a great deal of interchange and sharing of the sheets of colored tissue paper; comments were made on the color and dimensional effects which took place when the papers were overlaid or glued down.

Barbara usually did artwork which displayed her morbidity. She ordinarily used red and black colors. Perhaps due to the large array of the attractive tissue paper colors, or the enthusiasm which permeated the room, Barbara, for the first time, used cheerful oranges, greens, and pinks (Figure 109). During the verbal sharing time she excitedly reported, "I finally got in touch with some good feelings."

Figure 109.   Tissue paper collage encourages minor risk-taking experience

Part 2: Triads

Threesomes were formed to perform a task which would be cooperatively created. Each group of three was given a single piece of paper large enough to contain the three individual tissue paper collages which had just been completed. The triads were instructed to *paste the three individual tissue paper collages onto the one piece of paper; discuss the placement if you wish.*

Barbara, as part of a triad, waited until her partners pasted down their artwork. Their collages overlapped each other on the right side of the page. Then, on the far left side, Barbara pasted her cheery collage. During the small group discussion, she explained she had not been ready to place her collage near the other two people in her triad, although she felt fine about her partners' proximity to each other. The partners were delighted to be close to each other. One person was disappointed about the division in the artwork; the other individual did not offer an opinion.

Barbara was unique in stating the reason for her collage placement. Most group members seemed to think that feelings "just happened to be expressed." This attitude is common in the beginning stages of group life. As the patients in art therapy witness a continuity of the emotional component, they become educated to its function and goals.

The groups of three were encouraged to talk about their personal experience in making three separate products into a single piece of art. They were also asked if they liked the final project and its apearance.

After the small group discussion, the total group was brought together for discussion. Everyone agreed they liked the idea of combining their collage with two other people. Some patients were surprised how nicely their own product blended with the others. Other patients felt their pieces were especially enhanced when they were combined with their partners' artwork.

Part 3: Total Group Work

Working towards large group work in stages lessens group anxiety and assists group cohesiveness. If the therapist believes the group participants can handle the transition from triad to the total group, then the therapist connects all of the triadic murals by pasting them together. A discussion follows concerning the thoughts about the process and the visual aspect of the final total group project.

Most of the participants voiced pleasure in the appearance of their monumental mural. This process always creates an impressive piece of artwork due to the larger size and the multicolored effect of the superimposed tissue paper. Regardless of participants' feelings about their individual contribution, the majority felt their own triadic artwork was the best part of the total mural. Only Barbara was still self-involved. Unable to make the shift to the group, she related her continued pleasure with her individual collage. However, her increased self-esteem served an important purpose. To quote Barbara, "My part is really different because of the way I bunched it up; it is the most three-dimensional part of the mural. I don't even mind that our piece was placed in between the other two groups; I'm no longer on the edge, but I feel I can handle being close to the other group members—on paper anyway!"

Foursome: Promoting Resocialization

Artwork done on a carton provides a vehicle for four persons to work in close proximity to each other. Each person may work on his/her own side, yet group interaction is a necessity. The group is divided into foursomes. The carton is placed before each group of four persons, along with acrylic paints, construction paper, glue, and felt pens. The patients are told to *create four aspects of your day treatment. Each person is responsible for one part which will be displayed on one side of the carton.*

One foursome, composed of Barbara, Ann, Ben and Jim, decided to portray their complaints about the day treatment unit. Ann's request for tranquilizers had been refused. Barbara had missed her bus, receiving only part of her individual therapy session. Ben was moving to a new apartment and Jim wanted to play ping-pong, but the net was torn.

Ann urged everyone to illustrate his/her unhappiness. Ben insisted on uniformity. He suggested each side be covered with acrylic paint, then they could paint or draw the scene with felt pens or oil pastels. Barbara, concerned about her ability to portray her shortened session, asked if she could include magazine collage. Jim said he wanted to work in between Ben and Barbara.

Everyone agreed to work within the boundaries of their side of the box. Ann had difficulty keeping the paint within her boundaries. To help her out, Ben made masking tape margins for her so that she could maintain herself within the given space. After giving her side a pink acrylic background, she drew her wish that the nurses station was manned by her psychiatrist, who would willingly give out the medication (Figure 110).

Figure 110.   Foursome works on carton to portray aspects of day treatment

Barbara tried to duplicate her psychiatrist's office. She used a magazine photo of a uniformed doctor (although her therapist did not wear a uniform) and on the wall where a clock exists she painted a picture. Barbara complained about not getting her full session when coming late was beyond her control; she felt inappropriately punished.

Ben was unable to maintain his thought of day treatment; instead he made a picture of his new apartment. He tied it in with day treatment by saying he was moving closer to the hospital.

Jim created an elaborate activities room, filled with all types of equipment, as a way of protesting against the broken ping-pong net. He was feeling deprived and angry, displacing his emotions onto the ping-pong situation.

During the activity, all the sets of four spoke to each other; they shared materials and talked about procedures; some asked for advice, others offered it. Most people found the carton exercise a good experience. The withdrawn people were surprised that their "space" was equal to others. They found it easy to be in group when individual art was made while small group interaction was going on.

Small Group Construction: Motivation for Socialization

Continuing to build up the tolerance for group work, members were divided into two groups. Various media were at the disposal of the members; wood pieces, colored construction paper, plasticene, felt markers, acrylic paints and large sheets of masonite which could be used as a base. The directive was to plan and *create an outdoor day treatment activity*.

Ann and Jim joined a group with three other people. Ann vied for leadership power. Although she pushed her idea that day treatment patients attend a concert, the other patients vetoed this idea. Jim suggested that they go to a sports event. The majority of themes coincided with the individual's personal area of interest. Finally, the group decided to work together on going on an outing.

Ann created plasticene food. Jim used pipe cleaners to make a place where they could play ball. One man made a checker set out of paper and plasticene; another person painted a bus on a piece of wood, while the patient next to him was busy cutting out photos of people which she glued on to the windows of the bus. There was discussion about the size of the constructs and where they should be placed and general talk about their activities during the outing.

The other group had created a trip to the beach where the patients were swimming, looking for seashells, playing ball, and eating sandwiches. Both art therapy groups were brought together as each person explained his/her contribution to the scene. This was followed by a general discussion on the way patients responded to day treatment outings in the past. They were encouraged to show their constructs to the activities director as evidence of their interests and planning ability.

ILLUSTRATIONS: GROUP PROCESS AND SELF-EXPLORATION

Expression of Positive Feeling Stimulates Socialization

A safe antidepressing subject for day treatment patients deals with positive emotions. Instructions were given for the group to *create a colored construction paper collage around a topic dealing with positive feelings. You may draw onto the collage if you wish.* A large sheet of brown butcher paper was tacked up on the wall to serve as a base for the collage.

Ann, in an attempt to control the group, immediately took over (despite her objections to the project) by initiating the theme of "sharing good feelings which the participants feel towards each other." She quickly passed around the bright-colored paper as she informed everyone to cut out symbolic forms. Jim objected to Ann's imposing dominance. He suggested the "good feelings" revolved around the day treatment program. The other patients agreed to Jim's idea. They cut out shapes, which they then pasted onto the butcher paper in a random fashion.

Ann started the discussion period by telling the group her form was similar to the ashtray she had just completed in occupational therapy; she was pleased with its result and planned on giving it to a friend for her birthday. Jim made a group of circles, representing his favored "verbal group," which was led by a social worker. Barbara formed a colorful palette, signifying her good feelings about art therapy since it gave her a chance to feel hopeful. Ben, instead of reporting a good feeling, scribbled over his construction paper to portray his fear of not getting better.

Expressing Fearful Material

Patients who withhold the expression of fearful material were given permission to reveal those thoughts. The therapist felt it was important to deal with Ben's collage regarding his worry about "not getting better," especially since this was a concern which most patients held in common. Therefore, the group members were given pieces of plasticene and were then instructed to *portray your concerns about not getting better.*

Everyone molded an abstract or representational symbol which revealed his/her fear of remaining a minimally functioning person. Ann rolled several colors together, which meant, "I'll always be scrambled." Ben formed a skull; he said "I'll die before I get it together." Jim made a·cube which represented " Control over myself may be only temporary." Julie made a turtle which portrayed "I'm afraid I'll never be able to stick my neck out. I'll always stay in my shell," and Barbara made a red arrow to show "It's hard to believe I'll ever finish up with my depression and anger."

Expression of Rageful and Impotent Emotions

Barbara's response, which dealt with her working through her anger and depression, elicited a group discussion. Group members bordered on revealing their own similar feelings. To facilitate the patient's expression of suppressed emotions, the group members were given gray wet clay (less regressive than red clay). This medium helps patients to ventilate their anger through tactile manipulation. The directive was to *sculpt a symbol which represents your anger behind the thought of not getting better.*

Several members made spirals which they began from the outside and whirled inwards. Although this gesture was made unconsciously, it indicated anger which is turned inwards. Patients who withdraw tend to make spirals which go from the outer to the inner space. One patient who had poor impulse control placed his string-like plasticene in an opposite manner. This is often indicative of anger which is handled through outward aggression. Another participant formed a pair of boxing gloves; he stated, "I'm so mad, I feel like punching Dr. X." One man formed a thunderbolt; it portrayed the patient's fear of admitting anger (although, uninterpreted, it may have represented his concerns about being struck by God if anger was expressed). Finally, a passive-aggressive patient created an appointment slip, symbolizing the fact that she tried to get out of going to her appointment when she was angry at her doctor. These mutually shared feelings gave the patients an opportunity to understand that they were not unique, that other group members could understand and relate to their feelings of rage and impotence.

Planning and Role-playing

Making plans for the weekend while in art therapy group is productive and practical for the patients. It encourages the participants to set goals, to rehearse and to receive feedback from other members. Acrylics are purposely used in case the patients want to make changes. This medium dries quickly and can be covered over with little effort. The participants are requested to *paint your plans for the weekend.*

Ann covered the entire page with pictures of shops, food, liquor, a movie marquee, dancing, running, knitting needles and several other images which were lost in the vast array of symbols. The group told Ann that she was impractical and that her plans were typical of her usual way of overloading herself. The therapist suggested that Ann decide which three items had priority, cut those illustrations out and paste them down on a separate piece of paper. This approach gave Ann a way of simplifying her plans.

Barbara drew herself sleeping and watching television. The group confronted Barbara with her continued withdrawal. They suggested that she add some things which could be done outside of the house. Ben created a garden scene to show he planned on planting flowers and pruning shrubs and a lamp which was something he was making in his workshop. Jim showed himself on a bus. He planned to visit a friend up in the mountains.

The planning project is helpful for the patients who need structure to manage through the weekend. Follow-up drawings may be done after the weekend to explore how the patients attained their goals, or why they were not fulfilled.

Anger Appropriately Expressed

Day treatment patients tend to withhold angry feelings. They are often concerned with the thought that the art may trigger a loss of control. Therefore, initially, themes which allow a "safe" expression of anger are utilized. The patient must be shown that the appropriate expression of anger need not be destructive. The scratchboard technique is symbolically useful since it entails scratching the surface to allow what is underneath to come through. A "safe" theme is provided for the patients in an attempt to educate them to ventilate their anger through art or verbally.

One week the occupational therapy room was closed due to reconstruction. Most of the patients were upset since they were in the process of making Christmas presents. Taking advantage of this incident, the art therapist gave the patients stiff pieces of paper. They were instructed to *use felt markers to color the whole piece of paper, then cover that entire surface with a dark-colored oil pastel or crayon.* Each patient was then given a toothpick and instructed to *use the toothpick to scratch the surface and create a design which expresses your feelings about having the occupational therapy room closed.*

Ann colored the paper with many colors, and then made a green overlay; she scratched loops, circles, and wavy lines, then crosshatched over the entire page until the green overlay was almost completely gone. She said her art conveyed her fury with the administration for not having the O.T. room fixed at night when it was not used by the patients. Barbara used green and red on the bottom with a blue covering (Figure 111); she scratched a butterfly design to portray the ceramic plaque she was making in occupational therapy. Barbara said she was disappointed, but realized it couldn't be helped. Ben placed red on the bottom with a black overlay; he scratched out the picture of an octopus, relating that he was furious since things were always being taken away from him. Jim used dark blue over light blue, scratching out a tic-tac-toe game. He claimed it made little difference to him, since he disliked the childish things which were made in O.T.

Ann and Ben received positive reinforcement for expressing anger in a

Figure 111.   Scratch board technique illustrates what is under the surface

socially accepted way. Barbara was asked to draw another picture which showed how she felt when she was disappointed.

Symbolic and Verbal Interaction

The "pass around picture" requires participation from all of the group members. Patients may initially be fearful of adding onto another member's drawing; however, with full permission from the therapist it is fun for most patients, with interaction as a mutual part of the process. Each person is given a piece of white newsprint or colored construction paper, and is offered one oil pastel or felt marker. They are informed of the procedure: *Each person will draw until the therapist calls time, then he or she passes the picture on to the person to his or her right, who will then proceed to draw on the page which is placed in front of him/her.* The procedure will continue until the original picture has made the entire round.

Functioning persons can tolerate the pass around technique without a topic. In fact, it lends to the excitement of its creation. The hospital patients find this confusing and respond more favorably to a given theme. In both situations, the art therapist has used the topic of *having fun*.

Groups in day treatment, as well as those in the hospital, have enjoyed the project. They say it is like a game. The mutual pictures reveal many people swimming, dancing, drinking beer, running in the rain, and hearts for loving. The discussion may end up dealing with the joy of the experience and the fact that everyone has made a positive contribution.

Introspection: Value Systems

It is important for the patients to be conscious of their set of values and the fact that it still remains as a part of themselves. Frequently, individuals identify totally with their patient-self. They unrealistically feel stripped of healthier aspects of themselves.

Each member is given a number of sheets of white paper and a choice of drawing or painting supplies. The patients are required to: 1) *Draw or paint an abstract symbol which represents your values—each one on a separate page. Write its meaning on the bottom of the page.* When the members have completed the pictures, the art therapist gives each person a plain paper bag, telling the group: 2) *Look over your pictures, the values which you always have as a patient or nonpatient are to be placed in the bag. The rest are to be cut out and pasted on the outside of the bag.*

The patients began this directive by discussing the meaning of values. Several members gave explanations and stated examples. When the subject was clarified, everyone created his/her own symbols. Several members watched other people gather ideas which pertained to themselves. The verbal interaction acted as a catalyst to stimulate the weaker members to become involved. Many of the bags displayed: hands and hearts to depict friendship and people helping each other; books representing education; dagger, handcuffs and guns, which meant crime should be punished; and pictures of lakes, skies and freeways, referring to the necessity of removing smog. Several people drew money and purses, stating that money was important—with the exception of Ben, who stated, "It isn't as important as one's health." Then there were individual value symbols, which included: a scale stating the need for women to be equal; a mother and her child, which related that mothers must take good care of their children; a red cross, which stood for the need of the government to provide fine quality hospital care; a picture of a trim-looking person proclaiming good grooming was essential; and gym weights which emphasized keeping one's body in good condition.

Most group members found all their pictures belonged inside the bag. A few people pasted pictures on the outside; these appropriately applied to the day treatment specifically, such as a clock which portrayed the need to keep up with the day treatment program, a doctor's uniform which meant the need to stay in therapy, and a paintbrush that symbolized art therapy treatment.

Motivation for Social Change

The patients need to perceive themselves as social beings in order to be motivated towards change. Group members are given various painting and drawing media and a large plain paper bag. They are instructed to representationally or abstractly *create the face you present to new people you meet on one side of the bag. Then on the other side create the face you would like to present.*

One patient drew the same portrait on both sides of the paper, taking the directive literally. Ann also repeated the picture; however, she wanted to maintain a cheery face because she thought that was appropriate for new acquaintances. Barbara used her red and black abstract design on one side to show her gloom; on the other side she painted a free-flowing watercolor picture in soft shades of blue and pink to represent pleasantness. Ben cut out the shape of a face which he left vacant. He said it was indicative of the group's comments about his lack of affect. For the face he would like to present, Ben cut out another facial pattern, but this time he filled in the features to express his desire to show himself as a real person. Jim drew a sad face to relate his depressed facial expression on one side; on the other he drew a smile. Most of the other group members also symbolized a shift towards a desired change.

Understanding Patients' Concerns

It is important for the art therapist to understand what is affecting the group. On occasion, the entire group may appear moody or lethargic. At a time when this occurred the therapist asked the group to use the more malleable plasticene colors of yellow, white or pink to express what you are concerned about.

Jim made a child; it related how much he missed his son. Ben created forms which were lopsided to reveal his free-floating anxiety. Barbara sculpted a book, which represented her wish to return to school. Ann hyperventilated as she squeezed and twisted her plasticene, expressing her fear of going out of control and becoming violent. She was so upset that she left the room.

The group began to talk about what had happened. They reported that Ann was angry with one of her primary therapists from an earlier session.

Response to a Member's Behavior

It is important to deal with the emotions which a patient stirs up in other people in the group. Therefore, after Ann fled the session, watercolors were handed out to facilitate expression. The directive was given to paint how Ann's actions affected you.

Ben painted a wall, which meant he isolated himself from anger and desertion. He continued on to illustrate himself as an icebox, explaining he became frozen around angry feelings and outbursts. As a rule, Ben chose colors which were bold and stood out; this time he selected grayed tones. Barbara painted herself boxed in; she labeled it "helpless." In sharing her picture, she told how she wanted to reach out to Ann but was frozen. She compared herself to Ben as the "icebox." Other group members whose pictures were less expressive agreed with similar ways of denying desertion, anger and the possibility of losing control. Jim was able to draw a picture which he crumpled up, saying that he resented Ann's lack of control and felt she should have stayed in the group even "if she couldn't hang on to herself." Participants found that they could relate to both sets of references—feeling frozen and impotent by their lack of action, yet resentful and angry with Ann for leaving the group.

When Ann returned to the next session, the group shared their artwork with her. She was able to understand how provocative her behavior had been. It was important to give Ann an opportunity to express herself without being placed in a defensive position. With this in mind, the next directive was focused on self-perceptions.

Self-perceptions

To give Ann and the rest of the group a chance to reveal how they perceived themselves, group members were asked to use the photo collage material to *select a picture which shows how you see yourself.*

Ann's picture depicted herself as a child. She said it meant she was "dependent on the hospital." Not knowing what to do with these emotions, she expressed the need to "run away and take a vacation." Ann became aware of the fact that when she allowed herself to be dependent, she would panic and seek flight.

Barbara selected a picture of a mother cat with her kittens. One kitten had strayed from the rest of the litter. The stray was circled by Barbara to depict her sense of isolation and vulnerability.

Jim's photo was of a large hand holding a piece of sludge. He related the picture to seeing himself as worthless.

Ben's image showed a man with children crawling all over him. He added the words, "But who is there to take care of me?"

Other group members also expressed their dependency needs. Apparently, Ann's abandonment in the previous session evoked feelings of helplessness. It was therefore necessary to continue to deal with these emotions through follow-up artwork.

Exploring Dependency Needs

To validate central issues which are mutually felt and to maintain group interaction, two large trays were placed in the center of the table. The group was asked to create in plasticene two symbols: one which represented *how you feel when your needs are met* (all of these objects to be placed on a single tray), then one which stood for *how you feel when your needs are unmet* (placed on the other tray).

On the tray which portrayed "met needs," Ann placed a "pacifier," Barbara a "comforter," Jim a "contained box," and Ben a "complete person." Other participants placed a warm sun, a relaxed kitten and a smiling face. On the tray for "unmet needs," Ann placed a figure with the head missing, Barbara put down a fetus, Jim a figure bent over in pain, and Ben portrayed a "half a person." All of the other participants created images of people drowning, falling and crushed.

In dealing with dependency, the issue of identity continued to be explored. The clustering of figures on a single tray decreased the anxiety level, leaving the patients free enough to share information with each other.

Self-evaluation

Introspection provides group members with material which can be worked upon in groups and brought into their individual treatment. Vicarious insights may also be made. The group was divided into halves. Each team was given a very large piece of butcher paper and felt pens. Members were instructed to *make a mural by creating symbols which represent how you can gain more self-acceptance.*

The group interacted during the entire process. Members kept track of each other's pictures, asking for meanings and comparing their thoughts. The group decided not to repeat symbols which other participants had already drawn on the paper. During the discussion period they could claim anyone's symbol as also a part of themselves.

Barbara had drawn figures which stood for being less scared, sane, artistic, and autonomous. Ann's abstract drawings portrayed calm, nice, feminine, and organized characteristics. Ben's designs represented his need to be free (not a worrier) and more trusting of other people. Jim's realistic pictures were of dumbbells for becoming stronger, dynamite which was xed out to illustrate an ability not to explode, and money which meant earning a good living.

The participants offered each other reinforcement when they thought a patient had made some gains towards their conception of gaining greater self-acceptance. The patients decided on a follow-up directive, in which they selected a single symbol as a goal, then proceeded to depict a plan which showed how that attribute might be attained.

Problem-solving

Periodically, techniques may be offered to assess the patient's ability for problem-solving. Pictorial fantasies which are not threatening allow the patient to reveal attitudes towards crisis situations and the capacity to be innovative in order to survive.

The participants were asked *to imagine you were on a trip driving through an isolated area when your car got stuck. In comic strip fashion create a series of scenes or abstract symbols which relate what you would do.*

Ann's series showed her checking over her food supply, eating slowly while thinking of a car coming by to rescue her. Then a series of pictures showed her knitting, cleaning out the car and rearranging things in her trunk. Group members could see Ann's positive attitude about being rescued. She used the waiting productively; her compulsivity was used to an advantage, warding off the fear of not being rescued. The participants enjoyed Ann's portrayal, giving her credit "for turning a bad scene into something positive." Ben commented that, for Ann, being in a situation which was limiting was good for her. It kept her from trying to do too much.

Barbara's series was brief. It showed her relaxed, reading and sleeping, in spite of the fact that she had drawn her hair standing on end out of fear. Barbara was confronted by the group for using her usual defense of withdrawal; they suggested other ways in which she might have handled the situation.

Ben's drawings had him in the car with two other men. It portrayed the three men taking the car apart and repairing it. The other group members were delighted that he had included the two other people; they realized the therapist did not limit the patient to being alone on the trip. The group verbally applauded Ben for his positive imagination.

Jim's series (Figure 112) showed his car being stuck in a sandy pit. He used his shaving foam to write "help" on the auto's roof. Pictures showed him breaking off tree branches to place under the tires. The remaining pictures were dark, depicting nighttime. Jim's pictorial attitude showed some ingenuity; however, his negative attitude kept him from working through his rescue fantasy. Ben suggested perhaps a helicopter could sight Jim's shaving foam sign for help. Jim agreed to the idea, and proceeded to draw the helicopter into the last picture. Barbara pointed out that it was interesting he didn't place it before the night picture instead of after, indicating he, like herself, had to suffer.

Group Problem-solving

As a follow-up to the individual problem-solving exercise, a group project was offered. Some patients had been unable to make plans or to carry them through their crisis fantasy. Group planning gave these patients a chance to benefit from the ideas which other members put forth.

Figure 112.   An individual problem-solving task

The group was divided into two. Each smaller group was given a plastic tray, plasticene, pieces of wood, pipe cleaners, construction paper, cardboard cartons, acrylic paints, felt markers, scissors and glue. They were informed to *imagine yourselves as a group marooned on an island. Create the situation and the part which each person will play.*

The interaction which was necessary to figure out the most productive solution took up most of the session. Therefore, the plans were formulated and participants had just enough time to begin to create their individual props. The completion of the project was delayed until the next art therapy session. The therapist observed the patients' ability to delay the gratification of completing their plans. In the following session most patients resumed the project with interest and enthusiasm.

Barbara and Ben were on a team with three other people. The group, remembering Ben's solution to the auto fantasy, looked to him for guidance. However, Ben said he wanted their ideas first. One man suggested dividing the laborers into food hunters, food preparers and hut builders. Another man claimed it was hopeless because they would never be rescued. Barbara voiced her idea of building their own community, which would function by itself in case they weren't rescued. The other woman on the team was delighted with the arrangement of three men and two women, but voiced concern that they would get on each others' nerves, suggesting each person have his or her own hut to live in. Ben agreed with the ideas; however, he felt it would be important to set up a place for smoke signals. He also claimed that when they were marooned it was due to their ship's being destroyed; however, this team escaped on a lifeboat and they should consider charting a trip to another island where transportation home could be arranged. The group found Ben's contribution comforting and plans were laid out designating what each person would make for the project (Figure 113).

Ben made the boat out of construction paper, Barbara created food out of plasticene and the other female painted the island with water around it. One man used the carton to make a hut and the fifth person formed each member of the group out of construction paper.

Barbara began to reminisce about Robinson Crusoe; other members chimed in, recalling how he had survived. Many of the ideas from the book were used regarding the issues of food and clothing. The issue of sex was discussed. The group decided the men would take turns having intercourse with both women. Barbara became anxious during this aspect of the discussion. Ben recognized Barbara's concern and reminded her that the whole project was only an uunrealistic fantasy. She was able to dismiss (or bury) her problem relating to intimacy with men and continued planning how they would make a calendar on the tree to keep track of the dates.

Figure 113.   Problem-solving through a group project

After both groups shared their artwork and plans, they were each given the opportunity to make any changes they desired. Several alterations were made due to new ideas which were gained from the other team.

Termination

When a member is leaving the day treatment program, termination is dealt with over a number of sessions. Ann announced her doctor's permission to discontinue day treatment in the near future. The group was given felt pens and asked to *draw how you feel about Ann's leaving.*

Ben's picture portrayed Ann reaching her goal by standing on top of a mountain. However, he did not convey his feeling about Ann's leaving. The rest of the group members approached this directive in a similar manner—by saying goodbye or congratulations to Ann. No real feelings about her discharge were expressed. Ann had been asked to *draw how you feel about leaving the group.* In her picture she separated herself from the group with a heavy black line. She said, "I'm separated, but thinking about the group. I'm telling them to take care." Her picture pointed out her need to separate herself as quickly as possible; she, too, was unable to explore her feelings in leaving the members of the group and the day treatment program. The therapist pointed out to the group members how their pictures and the discussion conveyed a great deal about their thoughts and wishes; however, it was difficult for them to reveal their emotions about Ann's leaving.

Separation

Dealing with separation evokes the issue of loss—both unworked-through previous losses and the loss of the person who is leaving. In addition, it serves as a confrontation to the patients' own separation from day treatment. This is often especially difficult to face due to their strong dependency needs.

To help the group members to deal more directly with Ann's termination, the issue of "separation" stayed in focus. A large piece of butcher paper was placed on the wall, oil pastels were laid out, and the therapist told the patients they were all to work on a mural which would *express feelings about separation.*

Ben's picture showed him "feeling stuck." He said he was caught in the circle and could not find a way out. He was upset with the thought of being unable to reach his own goal. The group pointed out a small opening which

Ben hadn't noticed, showing him there was a way out. Jim also portrayed similar feelings of "being stuck." He drew himself with a ball and chain attached to his leg. Barbara's worries around the thought of leaving the program were exhibited by a picture of a person with a seeing-eye dog.

Ann's picture, placed in the middle, showed herself waving goodbye. She put a frame around her picture as an assurance that she would remain separated and her space would be barred from contact. During the discussion, the therapist interpreted Ann's picture. She referred to the noncommittal expression as a possible way of hiding ambivalent feelings—perhaps sadness, but also joy in the disaffiliation of people with obvious emotional problems. The interpretation gave relief to Ann, as well as to several other group members who were also getting close to termination.

It is frequently noted that patients separate themselves out in the artwork when they are preparing to leave. Confronting and verbally revealing these feelings in group are often too threatening due not only to the relief but also to the guilt of disengaging themselves from those who are left behind.

CHAPTER 20

Individual Art
Psychotherapy

INTRODUCTION

Referrals to art therapy are routinely made by staff psychiatrists who request diagnostic clues and/or a corrective emotional experience for the patient. Some assignments are also made with a specific focus. Three case history examples are presented to explore the goals and techniques. The first illustration concerns Ann, a patient with manic-depressive mood swings who was referred to art therapy by the staff psychiatrist. He designated a single session with a request for clues into Ann's operational system. The second case history involves William, a young man who was withdrawn and seldom spoke. He needed help to facilitate his transition from the inpatient unit to the day treatment program. The last patient presented is Ellie, whose transference to her psychiatrist needed dilution.

ANN: DIAGNOSTIC CLUES TO OPERATIONAL SYSTEM

Ann*, 30, had been diagnosed manic-depressive, manic type. She was an attractive, anorexic woman who had been married eight years. The patient had voluntarily committed herself into the hospital. She had shown signs of hyperactive behavior, rapid pressured speech, insomnia, and malnutrition (due to irregular and bizarre eating habits). The acute precipitant of the pa-

---

*For more about Ann, see Chapter 19.

tient's decompensation was unclear. When Ann was hospitalized, she was extremely agitated and disorganized. She exhibited atypical psychotic signs and symptoms, vacillating between conveying an infantile, dependent personality and an omnipotent, obsessive-compulsive personality.

A week before the patient was being transferred from the hospital to the day treatment program, the staff psychiatrist requested one art therapy session to gain clues to Ann's operational system. The questions that needed clarification included: the type of coping mechanisms Ann used, her approach to problem-solving, and the elements that exacerbated her manic defense.

Diagnostic Clues

During the art therapy session, Ann appeared withdrawn, made no eye contact and inadvertently giggled. She talked a great deal in an attempt to resist the art therapy experience. To deal with the patient's avoidance, the art therapist utilized the collage medium, since it is the least threatening art material and it tends to help the patient get involved easily. Ann was asked to *pick out three to five pictures which make a statement about you.*

The patient displayed a guarded distance. She attempted to control the session by verbalizing at great length and by taking time to look through a great many pictures, often pausing to read the print on the back. Ann handled the photographs with grabbing, clutching gestures. Many of the images were wrinkled or torn in the process. Although the therapist requested a small number of pictures, the patient selected 13 images to paste down. She began to put dots of glue down on specific areas, but before long it was smeared all over the page, her hands, and the table. Pictures and printed words were haphazardly placed. Some overlapped; others hung off the page. There appeared to be no order or sense of boundaries.

Ann's art task approach and process were seen as analogous to her problem-solving life-style. She began with a brief quality of control which quickly turned into a frantic effort, with difficulty in maintaining limits and a tendency to regress. The content of the artwork offered further diagnostic clues. Dependency needs were possibly revealed through the large number of pictures showing children, dolls, and women serving food or breastfeeding a child. Indications of depersonalization appeared through an image which she claimed was very important; it was a vague, veiled picture of a woman (the patient's age) who, Ann said, "viewed the world through a window pane." At one point the patient lapsed into the first person.

During the discussion period, after most of the pictures were explained, Ann began to cry and shouted, "Enough!" The therapist inquired if a particular part of the collage had upset her. Unable to answer, she expressed her desire to end the session. The patient's obvious vulnerability showed that dealing with unresolved emotional conflicts was too overloading. The therapist saw the patient's attempt to control the session as an effort to contain herself and keep her thoughts in check.

As the assessment continued, the therapist shifted to the more structured media of colored pencils and a small sheet of paper. The patient was asked to *draw whatever you wish.*

At first, Ann carefully drew a number of lines. Her pace increased as she seemed compelled to fill the entire page. The anxiety started to build up as she colored in all of the negative spaces. Ann tried desperately to avoid overlapping the colors. At that point, although the artwork was congested, it still appeared organized. The patient then used her eraser and fingers to blend the colors together. The original design, so painstakingly drawn, became more and more smeared, until finally it was completely obliterated. Ann tried to reestablish her design, but it was impossible to retrieve. She then became confused and depressed. This was in contradiction to her explanation of the warm colors being expressive of her positive feelings.

To help the patient understand her own dynamics, the therapist reviewed the manner in which the artwork was created. She reminded Ann how the design was initially very organized; then, in her attempt to fill the page and the spaces, she became more and more agitated until she ended up smearing the composition until it became unrecognizable.

The therapist ventured to ask if Ann behaved in a similar way at home. Perhaps she started things in an organized manner, then became overly involved, overwhelmed, disordered, and depressed. The patient admitted the connection between her approach to the art task and her dysfunctional coping mechanisms. She validated the interpretation as she cited an example: "Just before I got into the hospital, I took on all kinds of responsibilities. I wanted to do everything on my own. I started to get upset because everything was piling up on me. There were all kinds of projects which I had promised to do. I got more and more nervous as everything seemed to be going wrong. Nothing in my life seemed to come out the way I wanted it."

WILLIAM: FACILITATION IN TRANSITION

William was a 25-year-old, tall, attractive, physically strong young man. After two years of marriage he divorced his wife. At the time of hospitalization, his five-year-old son was being raised by the patient's married sister. Raised by extremely religious, strict parents, William had been disowned at the age of 17 for smoking marijuana.

The patient resided in a board and care facility. He had a history of numerous psychiatric hospitalizations. Precipitating factors which led to the last hospitalization were complaints of auditory and visual hallucinations, paranoid delusions, and suicidal and homicidal thoughts.

William was on the inpatient unit for a period of three months; group art therapy had been a part of his treatment. He was being transferred to a day treatment program. The patient's behavior was withdrawn and mainly nonverbal. The staff psychiatrist recommended William for individual art therapy to help him with his transition to the day treatment program and to give him a means for expression.

Clarification

During the first art therapy meeting, the art therapist focused on clarifying the reason for William's individual art therapy treatment. He was given a set of watercolors and asked to paint *why you are being seen by yourself in art therapy.*

William cooperated, as he painted a picture (Figure 114) of a hooded head. The image was familiar to the art therapist, who in the past had seen the patient draw this figure to portray his delusions. However, this time William marked an X over the painting. The patient explained the X meant he had "wiped out seeing the ghost." He realized day treatment meant he was improving, since he no longer hallucinated. The art therapist agreed with William's perception; she complimented him on his ability to communicate so vividly through the art. She added that he was assigned to art therapy since he responded so well to this modality.

Mutual Drawings: Symbolic Support

Mutual drawings were done by the patient and therapist together. This technique helped the patient to establish trust in the therapist. It is especially beneficial to the withdrawn and/or paranoid patient, who finds it a nonthreatening type of contact. It also gives the therapist a chance to observe the patient's spatial needs, style of communication, and ability to make or accept connections to the therapist and take risks.

William was asked to *draw a picture with me* (the therapist). He drew himself as a small stick figure. The therapist responded with a figure of herself next to the patient. William followed with a tree, saying, "Anything connected to nature is free"; then he drew clouds, lightning bolts, and rain. Although the therapist saw the patient's "freedom" as something which was tenuous, in danger of being damaged by the elements, she offered no

Figure 114.   Improved condition symbolized by xing out hallucinations

interpretations. Instead, she implied her protective role by drawing an umbrella. The therapist later identified the umbrella to the patient as her symbol for the help she was offering William through art therapy.

Responsibility for Setting Goals

To encourage the patient to take responsibility for his own treatment goals, William was asked to *create something which shows the goals you want to work on in and out of day treatment.*

For his day treatment goals, William used drawing and collage to focus on "getting along with people." Although this was a positive thought, worthy of reinforcement, the pictures showed only a few people with heads turned away, and in desolate surroundings. This seemed indicative of William's paranoia and sense of isolation.

For goals outside of day treatment, a picture of a female serving foods was pasted half off the page (it was placed near the therapist). William identified this picture with his desire "to find a girlfriend." This goal revealed the functioning aspect of the patient's ego, with an appropriate wish to find a person with whom he hoped to have a relationship. In addition to William's conscious desire to find a girlfriend, the therapist wondered if he was subconsciously dealing with his positive transference to her.

Building a Therapeutic Alliance

In an attempt to increase William's self-esteem, the simple medium of collage was used. The patient was asked to *pick out three to five pictures that will tell me something about yourself—something you feel comfortable sharing.*

William said that the four colored photographs which he selected all related to his love of the outdoors and his worry about man destroying the environment. At this point in the treatment, he placed his fears onto the outside world, although the environment represented his own concern for survival.

Images of butterflies triggered off a discussion around the habits of "migration." The therapist pointed out the similarity to William's past history, since he had been placed in various homes and facilities. She empathized with the patient, acknowledging the difficulties and hardships of being shifted around and rootless.

The clinician went on to question William about a picture of a small boy and girl. William said it represented his love of children. He explained how comfortable he felt in the presence of youngsters, claiming they did not hold any judgments against him. These comments brought about an admission of the immense pain William had suffered in his childhood. The patient spoke of the lack of communication, guilt which was heaped upon him by his parents through their strong superego influence, and their physical and emotional child abuse.

William was positively touched by his ability to share himself and by the therapist's empathic response. He was comforted by the thought of having the artwork as a transitional object.

ELLIE: DILUTE TRANSFERENCE TO PRIMARY THERAPIST

Ellie was a 16-year-old female who had been diagnosed with an "over-anxious reaction of adolescence." She was an exceptionally bright, verbal, warm, and angry young person. The patient had a history of school phobia and a symbiotic relationship with her mother. Her parents were divorced. She lived with her mother and had romantic fantasies about her father, whom she saw once a month. Ellie was furious with him for having another daughter with his second wife.

The patient was rebellious in school and towards society. Her school attendance was irregular. She was agitated, anxious, and depressed, frightened of her disorientation and delusions. The referral to art therapy was made by her primary therapist, who wanted to split Ellie's transference, in an attempt to dilute it.

Assessment Clues

Initially, Ellie combined watercolors and collage materials. Her artwork showed her interest in the outdoors and adventurous activities. In general, her pictures reflected the patient's feelings of isolation, lack of relationships and uncertainty around her sexual identity (it was consistently impossible to identify the gender of the people she painted or selected).

Patient's Perception of Family

Ellie repeatedly complained that her artwork was not "good enough." She conveyed a poor self-image and a need for approval as she continued to criticize her creations. In order to gain an understanding of the patient's perception of her family in relation to herself, Ellie was asked to *draw your family* (Figure 115).

Ellie used the red marker to draw her mother as extremely feminine and sexy. Close by she drew herself, small in size, with no hands, feet or breasts. She wore pants, shirt, and a tie-like scarf similar to the one worn by her father in the picture. He was also drawn small, his eyes were blank, and he wore blue clothes like herself. However, he was placed at a distance from Ellie. Her half-sister was eliminated. The facial expression on the mother was angry, but Ellie commented it was one of depression and boredom. This may have indicated the mixed messages she received from her mother, or possibly a projection of her own feelings.

Although Ellie's self-drawing had unconsciously showed her ineffectiveness, by a lack of hands or feet, she said she saw herself as "carefree." The patient did not offer any other comments. The therapist wondered if the father's blank eyes were indicative of his "being blind to her" and the outstretched hands as a compensatory wish for Ellie to be held by him. The elimination of the half-sister was probably her intense desire to have her literally "out of the picture." The suggestion of a possible sexual identity problem needed further observation for confirmation.

Figure 115.   Family perceptions revealed

Identity Fantasies

For follow-up information on the issue of Ellie's identification, the therapist asked the patient to *draw a picture of how you wish you could be.*

Ellie painted a childlike figure, ineffectual and asexual. Her wish to be a child stemmed from her fear of growing up, oedipal fantasies, a wish to replace the newborn half-sister and a desire to regress to the time when her mother and father were still married.

Sexual Models

The issue of sexual models was brought up through instructions to *use collage material to select pictures of women you admire or would like to model yourself after.*

Ellie's collage represented two women. One was abstractly symbolic with an eye under a layer of water. It may have expressed Ellie's depression, or possibly a wish to return to the womb. The patient did not speak to the issue—she said she wished for an older man, "one who will take care of me." The patient's longing for her father was veiled and no interpretation was made. The other picture was of a woman at a desk, which showed how she would like to feel; it represented "competency as a career woman." The therapist encouraged Ellie to specifically identify career women whom she knew or admired. A discussion ensued about the type of positions they held, where they worked, their goals in life, etc.

Aiding Autonomy: Free Choice Artwork

As the treatment phase began, the accent was on giving Ellie a greater sense of independence. Therefore, media choices were often given over to the patient; *free choice* directives were encouraged. With the patient who has a tendency towards fusion, a delicate balance must be maintained between emotional nourishment/support and self-responsibility.

Ellie was offered several large sheets of paper to paint *whatever you wish*. On the first sheet of paper (Figure 116) she painted two houses—one in gray on the edge of some rocks, the other in the snow. She titled the picture "the good and bad houses." The patient refused to talk about the bad house, offering, "The good house is a house where I would be happy; it's in the

Figure 116. Free choice artwork

mountains.'' Ellie's father lived in the mountains; although she did not identify the house specifically, it is assumed that her fantasies still dealt with her wish to be united with this parent.

In the second picture, Ellie once again divided the picture into two parts and again the conflict of good and bad was observed. On one side there were two cartoon pictures of men. One man was reaching to put a letter into the mailbox slot; the other was throwing something into the trashcan. The patient pointed to the picture containing the letter, stating that she, as the letter, usually feels small. Her low self-esteem and the feelings of being controlled were pointed out. However, her ego strength was shown by pictures of a woman, tennis racket and canoe. Ellie expressed her desire to play tennis and to go camping. The patient was encouraged to become involved in these activities on weekends.

In the months that followed, Ellie continued to lay out goals. Often the art was used as a role-playing device to help her carry through her plans.

Art Therapy Benefit

To explore the transference, Ellie was instructed to *create a sculpture which shows how it feels to be in individual art therapy.* Ellie rolled out and scrambled the plasticene to describe her ''scrambled idea of being disconnected from herself.'' She told how confused she felt. Then she molded a band-aid which represented her ''relief.'' Ellie said the art therapy approach enabled her to express some of this confusion on the paper.

Dilution of Transference

After several months of art therapy, the psychiatrist reported Ellie's transference had leveled to a point where this issue could be dealt with productively. For an ongoing diagnosis of Ellie's transference to staff members, she was periodically requested to *portray the staff members doing something.*

In the beginning, the patient's artwork which portrayed her psychiatrist took up most of the space. Ellie consistently placed herself next to him, whether he was in a session with her or walking down the hall to his office. The other staff members were either individualized or together, but Ellie was never in their space. As time went on, the art therapist grew in size and was later accompanied by the patient. The art therapist never attained the stature of the psychiatrist, nor was she ever as close to Ellie as he was. However, the psychiatrist began to shrink in size and, although still oversized, he took on a more normal appearance. Sometimes Ellie showed him on the telephone or apart from her as he sat alone in his office.

Ellie's transference to the staff psychiatrist had been therapeutically diluted. She had made good progress, although her socialization skills needed improvement. She was transferred from individual treatment to group art therapy.

PART VII

Rehabilitation and Treatment of Chronic Pain

REHABILITATION

Physical rehabilitation includes the total person—both psychic and somatic healing are wedded during the rehabilitation period. The patient is the recipient of team treatment from medical doctors, nurses, clinical art therapists and physical therapists. The psychological art therapy goals for the patient are to initiate and/or maintain a motivation for self-acceptance and adjustment.

Patients who undergo critical physical changes often suffer a loss of self-esteem. It is essential to deal with the change in body image and to help the patient institute a compensatory means of accommodation. The process for working through the trauma includes: eliminating the defense of denial; ventilation of fear (related to the patient's prognosis, physical impairment, and sense of isolation and/or abandonment); release of rage against the bodily assault; and mourning (where loss is involved). Dealing with these issues makes the reintegration of the self possible.

Expressive and goal-oriented art therapy within the dynamic approach pursues insight, catharsis, and resolution. The focus of treatment is on helping the individual gain maximum autonomy within the boundaries of his/her disability.

At the beginning of treatment, the art therapist must assess the patient's physical and cognitive capacities. The manner in which the media are handled and the artwork itself help reveal the patient's manipulative abilities and self-image; these factors give clues for diagnosis and prognosis. The art therapy approach gives the patient the means for recording overt thoughts and emotions, as well as the unconscious covert mechanisms at work. Art therapy is dramatically beneficial for persons whose speech is temporarily or permanently impaired. The nonverbal, visual aspects of this modality gives the patient an opportunity for communication, self-expression and interpersonal exchange which otherwise might not be possible.

In part, the pessimism which invades rehabilitation patients is due to their disability and to the regressive nature of hospitalization. The necessary dependency is often demoralizing. Yet, at the same time, the patients must take responsibility for their recovery. It is essential to their well-being that the patients experience some measure of success and be in a situation where they are in control. In the art therapy session, the patients, active participants, are in full charge of their own decision-making and can gain awareness about their ability to still be productive and to problem-solve. It is this small measure of accomplishment which serves as the foundation for patients to build future trust in themselves and hope.

To help the patient with psychological recovery, positive transference is necessary in the treatment of the rehabilitation patient. This is hastened through the art therapy approach. The art therapist brings materials which help the patients make their emotional statements through a simple scribble, shaky line, picture collage, or an imprint on clay. Moreover, the clinician is an empathic person who sees, hears, and acknowledges the patients' feelings during this crucial and painful time of their lives.

Symbolically, the art therapy session proves to the patient that dependency (regression due to the need to be taken care of) and independency (taking responsibility) can coexist during the period of rehabilitation.

CHRONIC PAIN PATIENTS

Chronic pain patients are treated in a number of pain clinics and centers and in private holistic group practices. The chronic pain patient exhibits a constellation of behavioral and emotional symptoms. Black (1975) defines the chronic pain syndrome as a characteristic cluster of symptoms, including intractable pain, multiple pain complaints (usually not proportionate to existing somatogenic problems), preoccupation with pain, and multiple diagnostic medical examinations. Black found chronic pain patients with components of neurosis, depression, anxiety and a lack of realistic plans for the future. In later stages, patients used excessive dosages of medication. Where surgery (often multiple) had been performed, no organic pathology was found.

Treatment for the chronic pain patient is performed by a team of medically and psychologically trained professionals, whose emphasis is on the total person. The multidisciplinary staff may consist of a combination, or all, of the following: orthopedists, neurologists, neurosurgeons, art therapists, social workers, psychologists, physical therapists and recreational theapists, and psychiatrists. In addition to the traditional types of interventions, a combination of innovative approaches may include biofeedback, auto-hypnosis, relaxation techniques, meditation, guided fantasy, transentaneous nerve stimulation, acupuncture, acupressure and bioenergetics.

The goal of therapy is self-management. The patient is an active participant in learning to minimize or dissolve the pain and to change his/her attitude towards it. The art therapy modality, as part of the multidisciplinary team approach, is utilized for diagnosis, treatment, and prognosis for self-management. This approach is always in accord and complementary to the other forms of treatment which the patient receives.

Clues to personality and psychological style of functioning are discovered through the art format. The data are collected through the patient's approach to the situation, use of the media, content of art forms, and verbal comments. During treatment, art therapy functions as: 1) communication vehicle for describing pain; 2) means for confrontation of behavior related to pain; 3) documentation of emotions and attitude towards pain during treatment; 4) tool for insight into attitude towards pain; 5) symptom substitution; 6) relaxation technique; 7) imagery recruitment for mind-controlled analgesia; 8) catalyst for expanding verbal information regarding the pain; 9) instrument for graphing gains during treatment.

*****

Rehabilitation and treatment of chronic pain are described in the following four chapters. Chapter 21 describes the case history of Mrs. Day, a foot amputee victim. Short-term art psychotherapy encouraged communication, dealt with the reality of her disability, provided a means for understanding alternatives and stimulated the motivation for reentry into her home life. Treatment procedures and interpretations are portrayed. The basic issues related to rehabilitation are dealt with through art psychotherapy. Although the sessions are individualized to suit Mrs. Day's needs, the underlying aspects are related to a great many rehabilitation patients, regardless of their particular disability or personal history.

Chapter 22 relates individual art psychotherapy for Mr. Hughes, a chronic pain patient. The record presents the case from the assessment stage through termination. Concretizing the pain, assessing the intervention, autogenic training, and reinforcement of painless moments are a part of the treatment plan. Chapter 23 contains vignettes of chronic pain patients at the beginning and the end of their pain center treatment. The art therapy format is utilized as a tool for assessing gains and prognosis for self-management.

Chapter 24 relates conjoint marital art therapy for Mr. Tate, a stroke victim, and his wife. The case history includes the goal of helping the patient experience himself as a person of worth and as an important part of the marital unit. Treatment included the facilitation of the spouse's appropriate need to individuate. Intrapsychic as well as interpersonal aspects are explored in the long-term treatment of Mr. and Mrs. Tate.

CHAPTER 21

Individual Art Psychotherapy on a Rehabilitation Unit

Mrs. Day was a 35-year-old, married woman with a 10-year-old child. She was in an automobile accident which necessitated the removal of one foot. The patient became severely depressed and refused to talk about the pain or condition with any of the staff members or with her family. The doctors felt her physical condition had progressed to the point where being fitted with an artificial limb was important. However, Mrs. Day was unapproachable regarding this matter, engaging in phantom limb fantasies. Her denial as a defense against experiencing her loss was so great that the prognosis for her emotional recovery was a concern.

Rapid Positive Transference

The rapid positive transference is crucial to the treatment of persons undergoing rehabilitation. Patients in this setting are often not psychologically oriented. They wonder how art therapy can help their recovery. The therapist must present him/herself as a person who will deal with the patients' concerns and feelings which are elicited through their physical impairment. It is important for the art therapist to explain how emotional elements have an effect on restoring their health. The patients are notified that simple art tasks and discussion will help them through their difficult time. The therapist demonstrates how easily expressive symbols can be created.

To engage the patient, the therapist invited Mrs. Day to join her in drawing an abstract design. Together they drew lines, filled in spaces, and elaborated upon basic forms. The patient liked what had taken place and another picture was drawn. However, this time the therapist encouraged Mrs. Day to produce the major part of the picture. Another, final picture was created by the patient herself.

Self-expression

In the following session, after a brief warm-up exercise, Mrs. Day was asked to *select and mount collage pictures which express feelings about people or places*. The patient willingly cooperated by looking over the images in the collage box. As she pasted the pictures, she commented that this procedure was a pleasant change from the hospital routine. Mrs. Day was then asked to *write below the pictures any free association which comes to mind*. When asked to talk about the artwork and the association, the patient willingly began with the picture of a "little girl," which she related to her "lonesomeness for her daughter." Then she pointed to a "group of musicians," which she said stood for her "love of music." Mrs. Day added that she was a capable pianist. "A meadow scene" symbolized a love of nature. However, it was the last picture, of two pedestals, which held Mrs. Day's attention. She claimed she was unaware of why it held her fascination; she was unable to free associate to this image. Although the therapist felt it represented her wish to have two feet, this went unmentioned due to improper timing. What was discussed was the pleasantness of the musicians and meadow scenes. Then, referring to the child's picture, the therapist empathized with the hardship of being away from her child.

Reality Confrontation

The next suggestion was to *create in an abstract manner symbols which represent the advantage and disadvantage of visiting hours*. Without hesitation, Mrs. Day drew the disadvantage first by making an x with a jagged border around it, saying she wished she could see her husband more often; yet, for the advantage, she drew a "smiling face," stating she always had to be cheerful when her family was around and it was a strain. The art therapist acknowledged Mrs. Day's ambivalence with some encouragement to allow herself to be more sincere with her family.

Mrs. Day had to be taken away for x-rays; therefore, complete closure to the session was impossible. However, the patient asked the art therapist when she would be returning. It was evident that she looked forward to the next session.

Concretizing the Disability

After several sessions, Mrs. Day was asked to *draw your family going somewhere*. She drew herself, her husband and child all skiing. The therapist pointed out that without a prosthesis this sport would be impossible; she asked the patient if she had been considering a fitting for the artificial limb. The patient became irritated and angry with the therapist for making her disability a reality. To help her deal with this issue, she was asked to *draw or use collage showing how you were before and after your accident*. Showing her resistance, the patient claimed she didn't feel like drawing. She reached out for the plasticene. Mrs. Day went on to change the subject by speaking about her lunch being late. As she spoke, she quite unconsciously began shaping blocks out of the plasticene, then proceeded to build a wall out of the brick-like shapes. The therapist interpreted this to the patient as a desire to block out the reality of the loss of her foot. Then she continued to urge Mrs. Day to *make a before and after the accident portrait*.

The patient drew herself dancing on one side of the page; on the other side, she drew the accident scene with herself moaning and her blood streaming down the street. Mrs. Day became very anxious. To help her express and deal with the horror of the accident, the therapist said to *create a quick abstract symbol showing how you feel right now*. The patient took black and red markers to literally attack the page with x's, arrows, and scribbles. Then she picked up a blue crayon and added tear drops (patient's interpretation) all over the page. Holding back tears, her body began to shake. The therapist told her it was all right to cry. Mrs. Day burst into tears; her body rocked as she moaned, "No one has let me talk about the accident. Anytime I wanted to mention it, I was told to forget about it, everything is going to be all right."

It was important for Mrs. Day to ventilate her experience; therefore she was asked to *draw the accident in full detail*. Mrs. Day reviewed the accident, both pictorially and verbally. The session was extended to allow her to complete the experience.

Expression of Rage

An assault to one's body produces rageful feelings. It is essential for these emotions to have an outlet, or the repressed rage may be manifested in depression. In addition, the fury of being an "innocent victim" elicits the question "Why me?" The patient must be given an opportunity to state these thoughts and the accompanying anger. For the exploration of overwhelming emotions, plasticene is used for its tactile flexibility. The patient can ventilate her feelings by pushing the medium as well as by making forms which communicate a message.

Mrs. Day was asked to *use the plasticene to depict how you feel about your foot being amputated* (Figure 117). She pushed, pulled and cut the plasticene, claiming that was the only way she could make the medium pliable. At first she rolled out two columns, one tall and the other short, with a disc on top of each. The patient related that the forms stood for a scale and it showed "there is no justice!!!" This was followed by a figure of a red devil which told the therapist she was "mad as hell." Her third sculpture was a finger pointing up, with a question mark carved on it. She said the finger was an obvious symbol and the question mark was something which perpetually plagued her: "Why me???"

Guilt and Punishment Fantasies

It is not unusual for persons who undergo physical disabilities to have unrealistic guilt and punishment fantasies. Creating and discussing these fantasies help to diminish the self-torturing, self-destructive search to understand the cause and effect of their impairment. Following Mrs. Day's

Figure 117.   Amputee depicts her feelings

last sculpture which stood for "Why me?", the directive was: *When you ask the question "Why me?" express some of your answers in a medium of your choice* (Figure 118). Using the crayons, Mrs. Day drew a little girl; then she took her finger and smeared the child's dress. She questioned if she was being punished for not being a good enough mother. Then she drew a portrait of a man, which she explained represented feeling guilty about not being giving enough in her sexual relationship with her husband. For the last item she drew a foot, as she ironically stated, "Maybe I didn't put my best foot forward."

With everything so clearly laid out in front of her, Mrs. Day realized her reasons for "being punished" seemed foolish and without substance. The

Figure 118.   Guilt and punishment fantasies

patient decided to stick to the reality factors: The automobile in front of her went out of control and she was the innocent victim. Mrs. Day decided to stop plaguing herself with the "why" of her circumstance and to begin to deal with the "now." The therapist asked if the "now" involved being fitted with the prosthesis. The patient nodded her head in affirmation.

Expression of Fear

Patients often suppress their fearful thoughts from their families and doctors. At times this is due to fantasies of abandonment. At other times, friends and relatives are unable to tolerate the patients' feelings and subterfuge dealing with emotions. It is extremely important for the therapist to precipitate the expression of fears and worries which plague the patient. Mrs. Day was given a paper bag with the suggestion: *On the outside of the bag draw the best things that can happen to you.* Without hesitation, the patient drew: herself in the kitchen; running with her child; hugging her husband; eating at a picnic. These were explained as she drew the pictures on the outside of the bag.

The next request was to *select collage pictures which reveal your fears and worries. Paste each emotion on a separate page.* When this was done, Mrs. Day was encouraged to *throw these fears and worry pictures inside of the bag.* Then the patient was told she would have the opportunity to reveal the contents of the bag. Mrs. Day seemed eager to share her images and thoughts. She looked inside to make a conscious decision about the order in which the pictures would be shown.

First she chose the picture of a woman; Mrs. Day removed one of her feet. She related that she worried that she would "never feel like a whole person again." Next, she pulled out a picture of skis; she said she was sad because she would never again participate in her favorite sport. The following picture was of a woman over whom she had scribbled. She voiced her concern that her daughter would see her as defective and be ashamed of her. Next came an image of a bed; she was afraid that her sex life would be drastically affected, since she feared her husband would find her physically repulsive. The last picture was of a house, depicting her worry about being incapable of taking proper care of her family.

Alternatives for Adaptation

Laying out fears and fantasies is essential in the course of treatment for rehabilitation patients. However, it is very important to help the patient understand that alternatives are available for adaptation. For this goal, Mrs. Day was asked to *place a symbol which represented a way of dealing with each particular problem which had just been stated.*

On the picture of "not feeling like a whole person," Mrs. Day loosely sketched a prosthesis. She said if she got the artificial limb, dressed herself up, and began wearing makeup again, she would probably begin to feel better about herself. Next to the skis, she drew a zero. During the discussion, the therapist encouraged her to ask the doctor what her future chances were of participating in this sport. The patient agreed to ask questions about her physical mobility with the use of an artificial foot. In regard to Mrs. Day's fear that her child would be ashamed of her, she drew arms, hands, and a heart, saying perhaps their love will compensate for the physical impairment. The next picture revolved around her concern about her sex life; Mrs. Day became so nervous she was unable to think of a symbol. The therapist suggested that Mrs. Day discuss this with her husband. If it was too difficult, then conjoint art therapy sessions could be arranged for her and her husband. The sessions would deal with the various adjustments which would be necessary for Mr. and Mrs. Day, including the issue of their sex life. Mrs. Day welcomed the suggestion and drew in a palette designating the conjoint art therapy sessions. Lastly, concerning the problem of being capable of taking care of the household, the patient used the picture of a woman with a maid's uniform. She said they could afford more help than she had formerly received. Perhaps the chores which took a lot of walking could be handled by a helper. Mrs. Day also realized that some duties could be done while she sat. She added she could still sew and do other things which depended on the use of her hands, not her feet. The therapist agreed and, in order to establish realistic goals, again encouraged the patient to find out the prognosis for future mobility, pain factors, etc.

For closure, the patient was asked to decide which pictures she wished to put back in the bag and which were to be kept out. Mrs. Day dropped into the bag the pictures of "not being whole again" and the one referring to her sex life. As she did so, she explained she was not ready to deal with those issues at that moment. However, she felt good that she could face up to her other problems.

Regain Sense of Identity and Increase Self-esteem

A change in body image is usually devastating to the ego, and patients often need to work on regaining their sense of identity. With this goal in mind, Mrs. Day was handed a box with the request to *decorate the outside of the box to show what roles you played before your accident. Then on the inside create attributes you still have.* The patient used magazine pictures on the outside of the box to depict former roles; they displayed a smiling person, a family, a woman playing the piano (all self-explanatory). The inside of the box, which contained her attributes, was explained as she developed it. Mrs. Day dropped pink velvet on the bottom and sides, declaring she was basically a soft, gentle person; then she plucked a flower from her bedside, threw it inside as she stated she was feminine; Mrs. Day added a stone which represented her involvements where she "never left a stone unturned"; a piece of leather stood for her "durability" and a feather meant "people get tickled" by her sense of humor.

Citing and reinforcing former coping mechanisms are important in rehabilitation. The patient is helped to regain some self-esteem by pointing out positive attributes still a part of the person. The box lent affirmation to Mrs. Day's strength and determination. It showed her to be a person who had the capabilities to overcome her devastating physical and emotional trauma. It also reminded her that much of her former life could be resumed. The therapist left the box with the patient, suggesting it was "a gift you made for yourself."

The following week the patient reported that she showed the box to her husband. The therapist mentioned that, if the patient felt ready, perhaps her artwork revealing "her fears" could also be shared with her spouse, adding that perhaps consideration could be given to showing her husband something other than the "smiling face."

Rehearsal for Home Return

Discharge elicits anxiety in the patient. Concerns over "not being taken care of" are exacerbated and worries over having too much responsibility at home loom large in the patient's thoughts. Dischargees may fret about their homes' physical structure, which is so different from the hospital. Rehearsal through art and role-playing facilitates the move back home. In preparation, Mrs. Day was asked to *use the plasticene to create the rooms in your house. Use trays for bases.* The therapist explained this was being done to help the patient with her transition to home. Mrs. Day was also told the project was a large one and encouraged to complete the artwork on her own time (then the discussion would take place during the next art therapy session). Mrs. Day began the project and agreed with the suggestion to complete it while she was alone. She became very involved in the artwork, working on it steadily for almost a week. Each room was created on a separate tray. They were completed with furniture (telephone and all), figures of her family, her dog, housekeeper, etc. The patient reported that she had shown it to her husband and they did their own rehearsal, finding that the telephone, kitchen utensils and bathroom accessories could be rearranged for greater convenience. Mr. and Mrs. Day used the artwork to deal with the practical aspects of the patient's return home. The therapist voiced her delight with Mrs. Day for taking charge.

Mrs. Day was offered colored construction paper, markers, paints, glues, scissors and two trays. She was asked to use the media to *make a construction around the theme of going home* (Figure 119). Mrs. Day took both trays—on one she built the hospital, on the other, her home. She created herself with two heads. She placed the figure in between the trays, setting one foot on each tray. Each head was facing in the opposite direction—one towards the hospital, the other towards the house. As she spoke about her ambivalence, she claimed, "I'm afraid to leave the hospital in order to go home, yet I love going home and ridding myself of this place. I'll miss the therapy sessions and the doctors and nurses, but now I miss my family. I'm happy but I'm scared to go home. Staying here was safe." Then Mrs. Day noticed that she had made her house much larger than the hospital and realized that her home held the biggest place in her life and she was ready to leave. The following week the patient took off one of the heads, put both feet of the figure on the house tray as she declared, "I guess it's time that I went home."

Figure 119.   Ambivalence about leaving the hospital

Termination

Saying good-bye is always an important part of any therapy. All too often in life people are not given the opportunity to verbally and emotionally put some closure on an experience or a relationship. It is of special importance to the person in a rehabilitation setting, since the end of therapy and hospitalization is a step before returning to a more normal life. It is a good-bye to a part of the physical recovery and hello to a homecoming and continued emotional adjustment.

Mrs. Day and the therapist dealt with the feelings around goodbye for several sessions. However, at their final art therapy meeting the patient and the therapist both engaged themselves in creating sculptures which showed the negative and positive aspects of termination.

The therapist made a portrait of herself; one side of the face was smiling, the other, tearful. She showed it to Mrs. Day, saying she felt good to have been involved with a person who worked so hard at self-exploration and who had great strength and courage to overcome the major trauma of being an amputee; the sad part was saying "good-bye."

The patient formed a heart out of red plasticene; removing a segment from the side she said, "I'll miss you, you are the first person with whom I shared what was in my heart." Then, for the positive aspect of termination, she made three figures forming a circle. She said, "This is my husband, my child and myself—it stands for being united as a family once again."

SUMMARY

Art therapy goals and treatment in rehabilitation encompass the following: gain a rapid positive transference; work on denial as a defense by having the patient concretize her disability; expression of rage and impotence; reveal guilt or punishment fantasies; clarify the prognosis; work through perceptual inaccuracies; mastery and catharsis; acknowledge former strengths; activate motivation for recovery; regain sense of identity; increase self-esteem; accept limitations along with the new body image; delineate new modes of adaptation; deal with discharge anxiety; rehearsal for termination and home reentry.

CHAPTER 22

Individual Art Psychotherapy for a Chronic Pain Patient

In this case history, directives and details of the art therapy sessions are not fully stated. Detailed information is eliminated to avoid redundancy and to present a generalized focus which would be applicable to all chronic pain patients.

CASE HISTORY

Mr. Hughes was an unmarried, 45-year-old man. Due to his insufferable pain, the patient quit his job eight months before applying for self-management training. Mr. Hughes moved into his widowed mother's home, where he had lived for the past three months. The patient suffered from severe chronic head pains located in the frontal lobe. Mr. Hughes had numerous medical examinations, including exploratory brain surgery, the results of which lacked evidence of organic abnormalities. Medication gave the patient either brief or no relief.

Assessment Information

When the patient entered the pain center, he was given a battery of psychological tests. In addition, the art therapist offered the House-Tree-Person test (Buck, 1970; Jolles, 1971; Machover, 1949). During the initial

349

art therapy meeting, Mr. Hughes was asked to use color for three pictures of 1) a House, 2) a Tree, 3) a Person, each of which was to be presented on a separate page. The house was methodically drawn; its most prominent aspect was the detailed brickwork. The door's peephole was heavily drawn and the darkly draped windows were given a great deal of attention. His free association about the house was: "An artist lives there alone with his girlfriend." The tree, rapidly done, leaned to one side with leafless branches. Mr. Hughes said, "It is a middle-aged tree who lost its leaves because it was winter and the branches were kinda weak." The drawing of the person displayed a child dressed in short pants, a buttoned-up shirt with a tie and a belt with an elaborately designed buckle. The hands were very small, the head large; both feet and nose were omitted. When the art therapist asked for information about the person, Mr. Hughes said, "It's just a dumb kid." The House-Tree-Person was drawn again at the end of treatment as a means for assessing changes in body image, self-esteem and attitude toward pain.

Concretizing the Pain

In order to record the patient's perception of his pain and to begin to deal with the pain and his attitude toward it, Mr. Hughes was asked to *draw yourself and your pain*. The patient drew himself full length, in a side view. The head, which drooped forward, was disproportionately large, with emphasis on the frontal lobe. There was an angry expression on the face. He delineated his pain with a red marker by outlining the forehead drawing of the exposed frontal lobe of the brain, convoluted, tied in knots with heavy black marks. Mr. Hughes explained the drawing, "It feels like lead bullets are stuck in my brain. It's so painful I can't keep my head up."

Describing the Pain: An Ongoing Record

To maintain a record of the pain, specific directives are repeated at various intervals. This offers the patient a source of comparison and the therapist a tool for ongoing diagnosis. Mr. Hughes was frequently asked to *make a plasticene symbol showing your pain today.*

The first time he showed his pain he molded a head, then placed ten toothpicks into the forehead (Figure 120). He said his head had a "piercing, jabbing ache, with intermittent heavy, thud-like pounding." (Follow-up sculptures on this subject are recorded later in the chapter.)

Figure 120.   Symbol portraying pain

Assessing Pain Intervention

The extent of the patient's preoccupation with pain is revealed by the request to *paint a picture of your own choice.* Mr. Hughes showed himself holding his head between his hands. He talked about the awful headache he had the previous day. A second *free choice* picture showed a wet cloth on his forehead, and a third revealed the patient in bed, incapacitated. All three pictures related to Mr. Hughes' pain, evidence of his obsession about headaches. If the self-management program is successful, the free choice illustrations change in subject matter, as an indication of interest outside the physical discomfort.

Self-awareness of Attitude Towards Pain

Chronic pain patients frequently see themselves as passive victims with no control. They often experience their pain as an impingement from the environment. Therefore, it is essential for the patient to realize how his/her perception inhibits self-management. To help the patient understand his attitude towards pain, the session was divided into three parts. First, Mr. Hughes was instructed to *create a plasticene abstract symbol of your pain today*.

The patient chose the colors red and brown. He squeezed the plasticene time and again, leaving an imprint of each finger, with the clay forcing itself up between the fingers. This, he said, represented his "brain." Mr. Hughes then stuck toothpicks into the form to show how much it hurt.

For the second part of the directive, the request was made to *create an abstract form which stands for yourself*. The patient quickly broke off a lump of pink plasticene, as he stated, "That's me."

The third step was a role-playing technique. The patient was asked to *give a voice to each art form—one for the pain, the other for yourself. Then carry on a dialogue between the two forms*.

Pain: I'm busy pounding away.
Mr. Hughes: I know you are, you keep me from working and from having a social life.
Pain: Why don't those doctors do something for me?
Mr. Hughes: Yeah, I'm at my wits' end.

The dialogue continued in that vein until the art therapist interpreted the patient's view of the pain as something which functions by itself and waits to be alleviated by an outside medical source. A discussion followed around the issue of self-management.

Autogenic Training

The art therapy autogenic training is composed of a four-part technique. It is offered routinely in conjunction with other types of therapies. The art therapy aspect of treatment would be of limited value if it were not a part of a broader program.

The autogenic training is composed of: Part I, a relaxation exercise; Part II, imagery induction; Part III, reinforcement of pleasant, painless feelings; Part IV, comparative assessment. This technique was frequently given to aid Mr. Hughes in developing his ability to relieve his pain.

Part I—Relaxation Exercise

The patient was given Japanese watercolor brush, sponge, watercolors, a carton of felt pens and paper. To begin, he was slowly paced through a body relaxation exercise (see page 217). This followed with instructions to *leisurely paint broad horizontal bands of color with varying tones of greens, blues and purples.* Mr. Hughes was slowly paced through the instructions to allow him to concentrate on each color, its tone and intensity, and to be aware of the way the paint spread across the page. As one page was completed, another painting was begun, repeating the same procedures. When Mr. Hughes appeared to be in a relaxed or meditative state, he was given the next directive.

Part II—Imagery Induction

Mr. Hughes was instructed to keep his eyes closed and to visualize a pleasant experience. He was encouraged to verbally share his imagery. The patient described the details of a boat, the warm breeze, the way it made him feel, and the movement of the boat. He vividly imagined the colors of the sky and the water. As his visualization continued, he described a seaport where the ship was about to land. When Mr. Hughes opened his eyes, he was asked to *record your active imagination through a painting.*

Part III—Reinforcement of Pleasant, Painless Feelings

In order to reinforce the positive feelings behind the sailing event, Mr. Hughes was asked to *use the plasticene to form abstact symbols of how you felt during the trip.* He rolled out soft, colored balls as he spoke about his feelings of "wholeness and peace."

Part IV—Comparative Assessment

Comparative artwork gives the patient a chance to see his gains through self-management techniques. Therefore, after the active imagination sculpture, Mr. Hughes was again asked to *sculpt your pain.* The "before" art form was created in plasticene. It was a bumpy mass with a number of toothpicks in it (less than the first pain sculpture). In the "after" sculpture Mr. Hughes, to show only a little pain, broke a toothpick in half and placed it into the plasticene. As the patient talked about his feelings during the fantasy exercise, he realized he had experienced practically no pain. Mr. Hughes became optimistic about expanding his capacity for self-controlled pain reduction.

Awareness of Pain Benefits

The art therapist helped Mr. Hughes minimize the pain through his insight, as well as through self-management reinforcement. It is important to explore the "payoffs" or secondary gains of pain, since minimizing or eliminating it may also mean giving up the benefits. Therefore, Mr. Hughes was asked to *make a picture collage of the benefits of having pain.* Mr. Hughes slowly looked over the pictures, pausing when some image caught his attention (Figure 121). He explained the pictures as follows. "A nurse" meant he was being "cared for"; "a man in an office" represented his "lack of financial responsibility"; "the automobile" signified his "abdication" of attending to his "mother's social needs"; a telephone reminded him how he used his "illness to get out of numerous activities." Mr. Hughes was surprised by the content of his pictorial statement. He claimed he was shocked to find his illness had "benefits." The issues of his dependency and resentment were dealt with at a later stage in therapy.

Observing Progress Through Artwork

As treatment progressed, "pained self-sculptures" were repeatedly made. Changes were seen in the diminishing size of the face and forehead, until

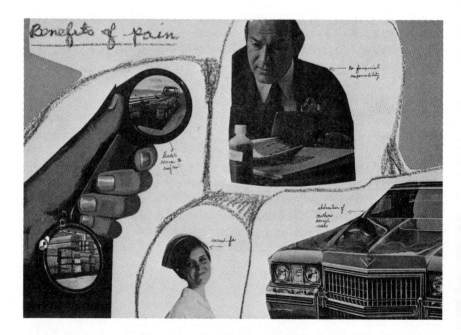

Figure 121.   Awareness of pain benefits

these features were finally realistically proportioned. In addition, the head no longer drooped forward and the facial expression lacked the look of anguish and pain. Eventually, the figure became upright and the hands changed to normal size, although the feet remained ineffectively small. Although most of the changes were not consciously made, Mr. Hughes purposefully decreased the number of toothpicks (representing pain) as he advanced in his self-management.

The free choice pictures began to change in topic. They revealed a lessening in obsessional thoughts about his illness. In the middle of treatment, Mr. Hughes sometimes left out a pain-related subject. He would paint pictures of a spectator sport, portrait of a friend, or a still-life. Towards the end of treatment, he painted mainly landscapes, seascapes, fantasies and plans about his future.

In one of the terminating sessions, Mr. Hughes was asked to *draw a House, Tree and Person.* The final comparative drawing of a tree revealed a thicker trunk than in his first picture, as well as firmer branches with a number of new green leaves. He said, "The tree is strong and beginning to grow leaves because it is spring and the weather is warm." The tree, which is an indication of one's self-image, grew in size as the pain decreased and the body image improved.

The second house picture appeared similar to Mr. Hughes' initial picture. However, the free association differed. This time he said, "The house is empty. The owners went away." Psychologically, the house often displays the family situation. The patient's chronic pain treatment did not include reference to his family life; therefore, the meaning of the house picture would be merely conjecture on the part of the author.

The final drawing of the person showed a teenage boy wearing jeans, a shirt with no buttons, and a belt with a large buckle. The hands were placed in the pockets. The head was normal size with a smile on the face. All the necessary features were included, with a special emphasis on the hair. Mr. Hughes' free association about the person was, "He's just graduated school; he's glad he passed his exam with flying colors." The drawing seemed to imply that Mr. Hughes was feeling positive about his accomplishment of diminishing pain.

All the artwork was reviewed with the patient as he was getting ready to terminate. Mr. Hughes was able to interpret for himself the obvious physical and psychological gains which he had made in the pain center. The artwork poignantly mirrored his pain reduction and a renewed interest in his environment.

CHAPTER 23

Art Therapy as an Assessment Tool for Self-Management

The following vignettes describe drawings created by chronic pain patients at the beginning and end of their pain center treatment. Any gains which were shown were indicative of the total program, not art therapy alone. All drawings were on standard 12" x 18" sheets of paper with felt pens in answer to the request *draw your pain*. The pictures were used for the assessment of the individual's treatment gains and prognosis for future self-management. Whenever appropriate, they were interpreted and discussed.

ILLUSTRATIONS

Mr. Hosemann

Initial picture (4" high, placed on far left side of page). Mr. Hosemann drew only the top half of a figure. He developed a pain chart, showing how different colors stood for difference types of pain—orange for prickling sensations; blue for dull, nagging hurts; black for continuous sharp pains. Compulsively and in a lively tone of voice, the patient talked about his medical problems and his chronic pain.

Final picture (6" high, placed on right on center of page). Only the upper part of the body was again created. However, the detail was omitted and it was vaguely drawn. Mr. Hosemann stated he had improved, then went on to describe his pain. He resisted drawing as he told the therapist it was easier to discuss his pain verbally. Mr. Hosemann said he knew the would regress when he returned to his job, claiming it was the rest in the hospital which improved his health.

Comments

Mr. Hosemann's minimal drawings depicted his lack of both involvement in the art therapy and commitment to regulation of pain. His prognosis indicated a doubtful maintenance of decreased pain.

Miss Dunn

Initial picture (5" high, placed on bottom center of page). Miss Dunn drew a person turned to the side with an arrow stuck in its back (Figure 122). The person is passively standing in the fireplace. The patient explained that the person is roasted and on fire. Her back felt like it had been hit with an arrow.

Figure 122.   Passive approach to pain

Final picture (12" high, covers entire page). There is a fire at the bottom of a mountain. The person is halfway up the mountain. Miss Dunn explained she was partway there. The patient related how she was taken by surprise when she saw her first picture and realized that she had depicted herself as "passively standing by while being tortured."

Comments

The contrast in the content of the drawings displayed Miss Dunn's optimism toward conquering pain. Her passivity motivated a determination for self-management. Miss Dunn's prognosis indicated continued progress for pain reduction techniques.

Mr. Fujita

Initial picture (figure 6" high placed in upper left corner of page). Mr. Fujita drew the back view of a full length figure. It was drawn in a blue outline with mottled brown blotches all along the left side of head, neck, back, leg and arm. The patient described his pain as knotty, similar to an outer nerve which was in spasm.

Final picture (figure 10" high placed in the center). Mr. Fujita drew the front view, full length, clothed figure of a young person drawn in blue. A thin, smooth, brown line is next to the blue. Next to it is a large symbol of a warm sun and the words below it, "Made it." The patient explained the figure was looking at the warm sun which represented his pain-free days and his goal of many more. He was delighted with his self-portrait stating, "This person is nice looking. He can handle things. I can see that I've really changed."

Comments

The patient's picture portrayed an attitude of confidence in reaching his goal. Mr. Fujita's positive change in self-perception indicated a prognosis of continued use and progress in pain reductive techniques.

CHAPTER 24

Art as a Voice: Marital Conjoint Treatment

INTRODUCTION

The Patient

Mr. Tate, 58, was a stroke victim. He was diagnosed with sensory apraxia with marked retirement of kinesthetic feedback which affected his tongue placement. This dysfunction affected his speech, which was impossible or, at best, extremely difficult to understand. In addition, he suffered from limited paralysis of the right arm and leg. Mr. Tate, stripped of his former means of communication, was in a severely depressed state. It was essential to provide him with a vehicle for self-expression.

Artwork: A Language

Initially, Mr. Tate was seen in individual art therapy. He was soon able to graphically express his rage and impotence as he repeatedly created phallic symbols which were xed out, bound up and boxed in (Figure 123A). Mr. Tate demonstrated his feelings of being "meshed in" by exhibiting a person encapsulated and with a wired grid over his mouth (Figure 123B). On one occasion he titled a picture "Frustration" as he drew two sides of himself: 1) "My Psychosis" which was exemplified by a phallic symbol with a zigzag line across it; and 2) "My Happy One" depicted through a profile of his face (Figure 123C). The fear of being mentally deranged was exposed

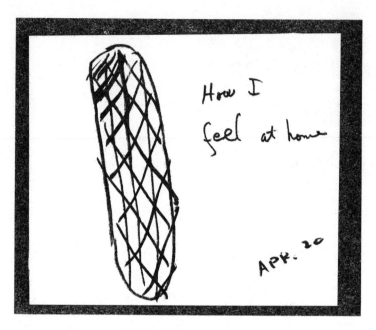

Figure 123A.   Impotence

Figure 123B.   Blocked

Figure 123C.   Fear of brain damage

through the split personality pictures; the client had never before revealed this concern to anyone. The art therapist explored this issue and in all honesty assured Mr. Tate he was not psychotic.

Over and over again, Mr. Tate drew himself as a "zero," a "non-person," a "no-thing," a "minus." For example, one picture displayed a face with a blank square over it, hiding the features; he wrote the man was "An Abstract: Forsaken" (Figure 123D). He later admitted, "The man represented me." All of the images poignantly revealed Mr. Tate's totally depleted sense of worth.

On one occasion the client created a collage which showed a man hanging up a sign which stated, "Closed due to illness" (Figure 123E). Upon the art therapist's investigation, the patient's unrealistic concerns were exposed. Mr. Tate feared the doctors were hiding a negative prognosis about his physical condition. The author, in touch with the patient's medical doctors, was able to convince Mr. Tate that information was not being withheld. The

Figure 123D.   Demeaned

patient verified his relief, as he smoothed out a piece of plasticene, with a note saying, "My mind is easier."

The client continued to use the art to ventilate and explore daily experiences, frustrations evoked by organic dysfunction, demeaned social and economic position, and a change in family interactions. The nonverbal element in the art therapy was particularly crucial, for it brought life to Mr. Tate's thoughts and emotions, which otherwise would have been buried in a grave of noncommunication.

MARITAL THERAPY: INTERACTIONAL COMMUNICATION

Mr. Tate's dramatic use of the art therapy approach made it a viable modality for marital treatment. His need to share pent-up feelings with his wife was a primary consideration. Mr. Tate's treatment had a two fold goal:

Figure 123E.   Prognosis questioned

first, to validate him as a person by dissipating his conviction of being worthless; and secondly, to validate him as a spouse.

Mrs. Tate, 60, was an attractive person who appeared far younger than her years. Her determination and boundless energy drove her to ceaseless efforts towards her husband's recovery. She was a bright, verbal woman who relied on intellectualization as a defense. At first she refused to voice her vulnerabilities, believing this would convey an inappropriate form of weakness. Her husband reacted to her façade of "super strength" by refusing to confess his own fears and feelings of impotence. The couple colluded to suppress genuine feelings and communication.

Due to her anxiety, Mrs. Tate tried to "protect" her spouse. She made a point of "taking over for him" and, more frequently than not, literally spoke for him.

In the first marital art therapy session, in contrast to his involvement in individual treatment, Mr. Tate was quiet and affectless. He appeared to be a submissive, helpless person. On the other hand, his wife's assertiveness and vebosity gave the impression that she held the psychological power in the marriage.

Mutual Drawing: Diagnostic Mechanism

In the second session, Mr. and Mrs. Tate were asked to *draw a picture together*. The subject was a Christmas tree (Figure 124). Mrs. Tate began with a green crayon by establishing the left side of the tree. Her husband followed by completing the other half of the image in red. Although Mrs. Tate awaited her turn, her husband went on to draw tinsel swinging from one side of the tree to the other; he continued to place objects on the branches. Finally, Mr. Tate stopped and handed his wife the crayon. Although she appeared disappointed, she dismissed her feelings to draw presents under the Christmas tree. The final gesture was made by Mr. Tate as he placed a star on the top of the Christmas tree.

The underlying dynamics displayed in this exercise were diametrically opposed to the impression of "passive Mr. Tate" with his "active wife." In this situation, the myth of "Mrs. Tate being boss" was destroyed, for her husband was now very much the leader, almost to the point of taking over the whole session. He was confident, autonomous, strong and not at all dependent on his wife. In turn, the change in Mrs. Tate's voice and affect was obvious; she abandoned her brisk and forthright dominance and subsided into the role of a much weaker, subordinate, and reactive follower. The author used the art product to interpret the couple's interactional mode of functioning. She suggested that Mr. Tate, in spite of his impairments, still controlled the marital relationship to a large extent.

Futility Expressed and a Response

In the following weeks, concerns, anger, sadness, and joys were expressed. For example, on one occasion, Mr. Tate drew a hot dog shape which had a criss-cross design on it; he claimed it showed how he felt at home. The castrated symbol related to an incident where Mrs. Tate took the phone away from her husband to simplify the telephone communication. Upon request, Mrs. Tate drew a picture of the telephone situation. In response, her husband drew a picture, under which he wrote, "My feelings are not important, she acts as if I were gone." When the therapist asked about the meaning of the word "gone," he wrote, "dead." Then he added

Figure 124.   Conjoint drawing

his hopelessness by writing, "Things are pretty futile." Mrs. Tate, over-come by her husband's pictorial statement, drew a woman crying (Figure 125). Next to it she printed, "Sorry if I made Jim feel inadequate." It was the first time Mrs. Tate allowed herself to be empathic and show her tender side to her husband.

The art therapy approach was gratifying, for it provided Mr. Tate with a voice equal to that of his wife.

Denial Confronted

When conjoint art therapy treatment began, Mrs. Tate's denial system was all pervasive. She maintained an optimistic facade. For instance, when Mr. Tate drew a picture of his "depression" and "low feelings," his wife answered with, "How can you feel low when you are working so hard to get better?" The therapist encouraged this woman to allow her husband his emotions. As time went on it became increasingly difficult for Mrs. Tate to criticize her husband's depression, since concrete evidence of his emotions evolved in front of her eyes. She learned to pay attention to her spouse and to respect him and his feelings.

Figure 125.   Awareness and an apology

Honesty and Catharsis

It was the collage medium which helped Mrs. Tate to lay out some genuine answers to the art therapist's questions, "How do you feel at the present time?" "How do you wish you could feel?" Through images, Mrs. Tate revealed current feelings which she had suppressed verbally (Figure 126). She pasted a nut and bolt to indicate she felt bolted down, or, as she put it, "In a vise," and a workhorse, which was labeled "overburdened." In answer to the question of how she wished to be, Mrs. Tate chose a robot to express her desire to be "feelingless." A butterfly represented a "freedom to fly away from problems" and a newly hatched chick stood for her wish to be "just born." This collage was a monumental first step for

Figure 126.   Suppressed message expressed

Mrs. Tate in giving herself permission to express her fantasies without the burden of guilt. Allowing these thoughts to be conveyed was therapeutic as a catharsis and as a step towards dealing with her appropriate vulnerability.

Imagery Exposes Fears

The art therapist suspected Mr. Tate's compliance was a reaction to the fear of abandonment. With this in mind, the author asked the Tate couple to *draw what would happen if you were not "good."*
Mrs. Tate made a plasticene sculpture which symbolized "I'm good because it's important that I respect myself." Her husband drew two pictures on one sheet of paper (Figure 127): The first was described as "A man on a mountain, he tries suicide"; the other was a man seated in a wheelchair in a "convalescent home." The picture was obviously Mr. Tate's worry that his wife would have him "placed" if he did not concede to her ideas. Mrs. Tate was asked if the convalescent placement was a possible alternative.

Figure 127.   Fearful fantasies alleviated

Aghast by her husband's fantasies, she declared that a nursing home would *never* be considered.

Mr. Tate's suicidal ideation was dealt with in terms of having so little control over many areas of his life. However, it was essential to work on the patient's positive attributes. Therefore, the art directives which followed required pictorial statements delineating two topics: *Mr. Tate's strengths and available resources.*

Artwork as a Tool of Support

While focusing on autonomy, the couple was asked to *select photos which show what your spouse can do for his/herself.* Mr. Tate responded with humor as he selected several comical pictures. The first (Figure 128) was of a woman under a hair-dryer with huge rollers in her hair and a cha-grined look on her face; next to it he wrote, "Why, oh why, do you not go to the beauty shop?" Another image displayed a heavy woman in leotards doing exercises with an expression of disgust; Mr. Tate wrote what he "im-agines this woman is thinking—'wish I could do a group of exercise tricks.' " The third photo showed two women at lunch having a friendly conversa-tion. The last picture was of a young girl near school carrying books; he wrote, "You always wanted to finish school—go ahead."

During the discussion time, Mr. Tate expressed his wish for his wife to en-joy herself and to get away from home. He told his wife he was capable of

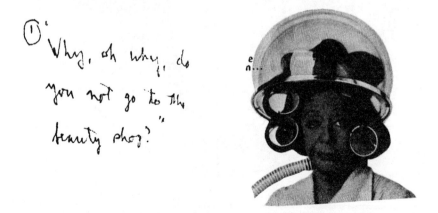

Figure 128.   Encourages wife to do something for herself

being left alone for several hours at a time. The therapist supported Mr. Tate's opinion and encouraged his wife to get out of the house, reasoning that the benefits would apply to her husband as well as to Mrs. Tate, for Mr. Tate desperately needed confirmation of his ability to fend for himself.

Ongoing Diagnosis

Comparative pictures were used for ongoing diagnosis. As in the beginning of marital therapy, eight months later the couple was asked to *draw together*. Unlike the first Christmas tree picture, the second drawing was simultaneously created (Figure 129). Each person drew one-half of a complete circle; each stayed in his/her own space. Each design differed, yet was com-

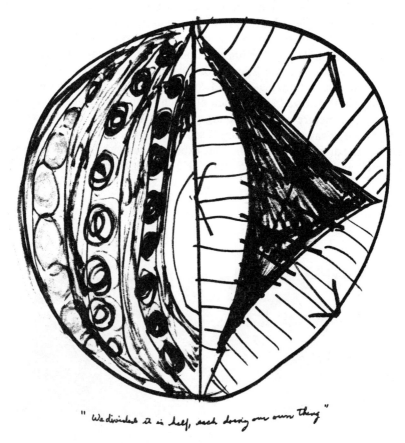

" We divided it in half, each doing our own thing "

Figure 129.   Increase in autonomy

plementary to the other side. The finished product was indicative of greater sense of autonomy within a limited space. It provided a realistic assessment of the couple's gains. Through treatment, Mrs. Tate learned to give her husband more psychological space and responsibility. Yet because of practical needs they remained continuously involved.

Two years later, Mrs. Tate had graduated from college and was a volunteer doing psychological research. Mr. Tate drove the car, attended a class at school, did some photographic work, and volunteered his services in a hospital. Nearing termination, the couple was asked for a third time to *create a product together* (Figure 130).

Figure 130.   Final sculpture reveals improved marital dynamics

Mrs. Tate, using plasticene, construction paper, and some play props, created a scene of an island surrounded by calm waters. She made two people relaxing under a palm tree. She declared it was "an isle of refuge." The sculpture indicated her feelings about art therapy. Her husband also chose to create his own sculpture; it was a car which he said gave him some "freedom." In this last mutual project, *artwork together* meant sharing the media and placing the sculptures side by side after they were completed. Interpretations regarding the comparative mutual artwork were offered by the art therapist as evidence towards their increased autonomy.

SUMMARY

Together Mr. and Mrs. Tate used the art therapy approach to express themselves as individuals and as a couple. Their former defense mechanisms of denial and intellectualization were dissolved through the visual confrontative aspects of treatment.

For Mr. Tate, the art format was a salient factor, for initially it freed him of the excruciating labor of producing speech. His innate creative ability enabled him to validate his existence as a man who could express and share his inner life.

Mrs. Tate used the artwork as a mechanism to stay focused on painful and confrontative problem areas and as a means for understanding and working towards separation and individuation.

REFERENCES

Ackerman, N.W. *Psychodynamics of Family Life: Diagnosis and Treatment of Family Relationships.* New York: Basic Books, 1958.

Aleksandrowicz, D. Children of concentration camp survivors. *Yearbook of the International Association for Child Psychiatry and Allied Professions,* 1973, *2,* 385-394.

Axelrod, S., Schnipper, O.L. & Rau, J.H. *Hospitalized off-spring of holocaust survivors; problems and dynamics.* Paper presented at the Annual Meeting of the American Psychiatric Association, Atlanta, May 1978. In press, Menninger Clinic.

Axline, V.H. *Play Therapy.* Boston: Houghton Mifflin, 1947.

Barocas, H. & Barocas, C. Manifestations of concentration camp affects on the second generation. *American Journal of Psychiatry,* 1973, *130,* 830-821.

Bateson, G., Jackson, D., Haley, J. & Weakland, J. Toward a theory of schizophrenia. *Behavioral Science,* 1956, *I,* 251-264.

Bell, J.E. Family group therapy: A new treatment method for children. *American Psychol.,* 1953, *8,* 515 (7).

Bell, J.E. The family group therapist: An agent of change. *International Journal of Group Psychotherapy,* 1964, 14.

Bell, J.E. *Family Therapy.* New York: Jason Aronson, 1975.

Betensky, M. *Self-Discovery Through Self-Expression.* Springfield: Charles C. Thomas, 1973.

Black, R.G. The Chronic Pain Syndrome. *Surgical Clinics of North America,* 1975, *55,* 999-1011.

Blos, P. *On Adolescence.* New York: Free Press, 1962.

Bowen, M. A family concept of schizophrenia. In *The Etiology of Schizophrenia,* ed. D.D. Jackson, pp. 346-372. New York: Basic Books, 1960.

Bowen, M. Family psychotherapy with schizophrenia in the hospital and in private practice. In *Intensive Family Therapy,* eds. I. Boszormenyi-Nagy and J.L. Framo, pp. 213-243. New York: Harper, 1965.

Brown, S. Family therapy. *Manual of Child Psychopathology,* ed. B. Wolman. New York: McGraw-Hill, 1972.

Browne, E., Laybourne, P.C. & Wilson, V. Diagnosis and treatment of elective mutism in children. *Journal of the American Academy of Child Psychiatry,* 1963, *2,* pp. 605-617.

373

Buck, J. *The House-Tree Person Technique,* revised manual. Los Angeles: Western Psychological Services, 1970.

Caplan, G. *Principles of Preventative Psychiatry.* New York: Basic Books, 1964.

DeGraaf, T. Pathological patterns of identification in families of survivors of the holocaust. *Israel Annals of Psychiatry,* 1975, 335-363.

Erikson, E.H. *Childhood and Society.* New York: Norton, 1950.

Erikson, E.H. *Identity and the Life Cycle.* New York: International Universities Press, 1959.

Flesh, J.O. Children of Holocaust Survivors: An Exploratory Study Utilizing the Art Therapy Modality. Unpublished Research Paper, 1979.

Freud, A. *The Ego Mechanisms of Defense.* New York: International Universities Press, 1936.

Gardner, R.A. *Therapeutic Communication with Children.* New York: Science House, Inc., 1971.

Gondor, E.I. *Art and Play Therapy.* New York: Doubleday, 1954.

Greenblatt, S. The influence of survival guilt on chronic family crisis. *Journal of Psychology and Judaism,* 1978, *2,* 19-28.

Hammer, E.F. *The Clinical Application of Projective Drawings.* Springfield: Charles C. Thomas, 1971.

Havighurst, R.S. *Developmental Tasks and Education.* New York: Longmans, Green, 1952.

Hoppe, K. Psychotherapy with survivors of Nazi persecution. In *Massive Psychic Trauma,* eds. H. Krystal & W.C. Niederland. New York: International Universities Press, 1968, 204-248.

Jackson, D.D. Family interaction, family homeostasis, and some implications for conjoint family psychotherapy. In *Individual and Family Dynamics,* ed. J. Masserman. New York: Grune & Stratton, 1959.

Jessner, L. Some observations of children hospitalized during latency. In *Dynamic Psychopathology in Childhood,* eds. L. Jessner & E. Pavenstedt. New York: Grune & Stratton, 1959.

Jolles, I. A catalog for the qualitative interpretation of the House-Tree-Person (H-T-P-). Los Angeles: Western Psychological Services, 1971.

Karr, S. *Second Generation Effects of the Nazi Holocaust.* San Francisco: California School of Professional Psychology, 1973.

Kestenberg, J. Psychoanalytic contributions to the problem of children of survivors from Nazi persecution. *The Israel Annals of Psychiatry and Related Disciplines,* 1972, *10,* 311-325.

Kestenberg, J. Introductory remarks to symposium: children of the holocaust. *Yearbook of the International Association for Child Psychiatry and Allied Professions,* 1973, *2,* 359-362.

Klein, H. Families of holocaust survivors in the kibbutz: psychological studies. *International Psychiatry Clinics,* 1971, *8,* 67-92.

Klein, H. Children of the holocaust: mourning and bereavement. *International Yearbook of the Association for Child Psychiatry and Allied Professions,* 1973, *2,* 393-410.

Klein, H. & Last, U. Some characteristic psychological reactions of children of holocaust survivors as reflected in their attitudes towards the persecutor representation. *Yearbook of Adolescence Psychiatry,* 1978.

Klein, H. & Reinharz, S. Adaptation in the kibbutz of holocaust survivors and their children. In *Mental Health in Rapid Social Change,* ed. L. Miller. Jerusalem Academic Press, 1972.

Kramer, E. *Art as Therapy with Children.* New York: Schocken, 1971.

Kwiatkowska, H.Y. *Family Therapy and Evaluation Through Art.* Springfield: Charles C. Thomas, 1978.

Lidz, T., Cornelison, A.R., Fleck, S., and Terry, D. The intrafamilial environment of schizophrenic patients. 1. The father. *Psychiatry,* 1957, *20,* 329-342.

Lipkowitz, M.H. The child of two survivors: A report of an unsuccessful therapy. *The Israel Annals of Psychiatry and Related Disciplines,* 1973, *II,* 141-155.

Machover, K. *Personality Projection in the Drawing of the Human Figure.* Springfield: Charles C. Thomas, 1949.

Mora, G., DeVault, S. & Schopler, E. Dynamics and psychotherapy of identical twins with elective mutism. *Journal of Child Psychology and Psychiatry,* 1962, *3,* 41-52.

Morris, J.V. Cases of elective mutism. *American Journal of Mental Deficiency*, 1953, *57*, 661-668, #4.

Moustakas, C. *The Child's Discovery of Himself*. New York: Ballantine Books, Inc. 1966.

Naumburg, M. *Dynamically Oriented Art Therapy: Its Principles and Practices*. New York: Grune & Stratton, 1966.

Newman, L. Emotional disturbance in children of holocaust survivors. *Social Casework: The Journal of Contemporary Social Work*, 1979, 43-50.

Peller, L.E. Models of Children's Play. In *Child's Play*, eds. R.E. Herron & Brian Sutton-Smith. New York: John Wiley and Sons, Inc., 1971.

Plank, E.N. *Working with Children in Hospitals*. Chicago: Press of Case Western Reserve University, 1971.

Putstrom, E. & Speers, R.W. Elective mutism in children. *Journal of the American Academy of Child Psychiatry*, 1964, *3*, 287-297.

Rakoff, V. Children and families of concentration camp survivors. *Canada's Mental Health*, 1969, *14*, 24-26.

Rakoff, V., Sigal, J.J. & Epstein, N.B. Children and families of concentration camp survivors. *Canada's Mental Health*, 1966, *14*, 24-26.

Rosenberger, L. Children of survivors. *Yearbook of the International Association for Child Psychiatry and Allied Professions*, 1973, *2*, 375-378.

Russell, A. Late psychological consequences in concentration camp survivor families. *American Journal of Orthopsychiatry*, 1974, *44*, 611-619.

Satir, V. *Conjoint Family Therapy* (Rev. ed.) Palo Alto: Science and Behavior Books, 1967.

Shore, M.F. *Red is the Color of Hurting*. Rockville, Md.: U.S. Department of Health, Education and Welfare, 1971.

Sigal, J. Second generation effects of massive trauma. *International Psychiatry Clinics*, 1971, *8*, 55-65.

Sigal, J. & Rakoff, V. Concentration camp survival: A pilot study of effects on the second generation. *Canadian Psychiatric Association Journal*, 1971, *16*, 393-397.

Sigal, J., Silver, D., Rakoff, V. & Ellin, B. Some second generation effects of survival of the Nazi persecution. *American Journal of Orthopsychiatry*, 1973, *43*, 320-327.

Stone, L.J. & Church, J. *Childhood and Adolescence*. New York: Random House, 1957.

Tracktenberg, M. & Davis, M. Breaking silence: Serving children of holocaust survivors. *Journal of Jewish Communal Service*, 1978, *54*, 294-302.

Trossman, B. Adolescent children of concentration camp survivors. *Canadian Psychiatric Association Journal*, 1968, *12*, 121-123.

Wanderman, E. Children and families of holocaust survivors: a psychological overview. In *Living After the Holocaust: Reflections by the Post-War Generation in America*, eds. Y. Steinitz with D.M. Szonyi. New York: Bloch Publishing Company, 1976.

Wynne, L.C., Ryckoff, I.M., Day, J. & Hirsch, S.E. Pseudomutuality in the family relations of schizophrenia. *Psychiatry*, 1958, *21*, 205-220.

Zinberg, N.E. & Kaufman, I. Cultural and personality factors associated with aging: An introduction. In *Normal Psychology of the Aging Process*, eds. N.E. Zinberg, I. Kaufman. New York: International Universities Press, 1963.

BIBLIOGRAPHY

Abel, T.M. Figure drawing and facial disfigurement, *American Journal of Orthopsychiatry,* *23,* 253-264, 1953.

Adler, G. *The Living Symbol: A Case Study in the Process of Individuation.* New York: Pantheon Books, 1961.

Albee, G.W., and Hamlin, R.M. An investigation of the reliability and validity of judgments of adjustment inferred from drawings. *Journal of Clinical Psychology, 5,* 389-392, 1949.

Alexander, F. *Psychosomatic Medicine: Its Principles and Application.* New York: Norton, 1950.

Alexander, F. The psychoanalyst looks at contemporary art. In *Explorations in Psychoanalysis,* ed. R. Lindner. New York: Julian Press, 1955.

Alexander, F. A contribution to the theory of play. *Psychoanalytic Quarterly, 27,* 175-193, 1958.

Allen, F.H. *Psychotherapy with Children.* London: Kegan Paul, 1947.

Allen, G. *The Colour-Sense.* Boston: Houghton, 1879.

Allport, G. *Pattern and Growth in Personality.* New York: Reinhart and Winston, 1961.

Alschuler, R., and Hattwick, L.W. *Painting and Personality.* Chicago: University of Chicago Press, *1 & 2,* 1947 (rev. ed. 1969).

Altman, C. *The Dream in Psychoanalysis.* New York: International Universities Press, 1969.

Ames, L.B., Metraux, R.W., Rodell, J.L., and Walker, R.N. *Child Rorschach Responses.* New York: Brunner/Mazel, 1974.

Ames, L.B., Metraux, R.W., and Walker, R.N. *Adolescent Rorschach Responses.* New York: Brunner/Mazel, 1971.

Anastasi, A., and Foley, J.P. An analysis of spontaneous drawings by children in different cultures. *Journal of Applied Psychology, 20,* 689-726, 1936.

Anastasi, A., and Foley, J.P. A survey of the literature on artistic behavior in the abnormal: Historical and theoretical background. *Journal of General Psychology, 25,* 111-142, 1941.

Anastasi, A., and Foley, J.P. An experimental study of the drawing behavior of adult psychotics in comparison with that of a normal control group. *Journal of Experimental Psychology, 34,* 169-194, 1944.

Arieti, S. *The Intrapsychic Self.* New York: Basic Books, 1967.

Arnheim, R. *Art and Visual Perception.* Berkeley: University of California Press, 1967.

377

Arnheim, R. *Toward a Psychology of Art.* Berkeley: University of California Press, 1967.
Arnheim, R. *Visual Thinking.* Berkeley: University of California Press, 1969.
Auerbach, J.G. Psychological observations on "doodling" in neurotics. *Journal of Nervous and Mental Disorders, 111,* 304-332, 1950.
Axline, V.M. *Dibs in Search of Self.* Boston: Houghton Mifflin, 1966.

Bandura, A., and Walter, R.H. *Adolescent Aggression: A Study of the Influence of Child-Training Practices and Family Interrelationships.* New York: Ronald, 1959.
Barker, A.J., Mathis, J.K., and Powers, C.A. Drawings characteristic of male homosexuals. *Journal of Clinical Psychology, 9,* 185-188, 1953.
Barnes, M., and Berke, J. *Mary Barnes.* New York: Ballantine Books, 1971.
Barron, F.M. Creativity in children. In *Child Art: The Beginnings of Self-Affirmation,* ed. H.P. Lewis. Berkeley: Diablo Press, 1973.
Barten, H., and Barten, S. *Children and their Parents in Brief Therapy.* New York: Behavioral Publications, 1973.
Beck, H.S. A study of the applicability of the H-T-P to children with respect to the drawn house. *Journal of Clinical Psychology, 11,* 60-63, 1955.
Bell, J.E. *Family Group Therapy.* Public Health Monograph 64. United States Dept. of Health, Education and Welfare, Washington, D.C., 1961.
Bell, J.E. *The family in the hospital: Lessons from developing countries.* Washington, D.C.: U.S. Government Printing Office, 1970.
Bell, J.E. Impact of emphasis on family units. In *Perspectives in Child Psychopathology,* ed. H.E. Rie. Chicago: Aldine-Atherton, 1971.
Bell, J.E., and Bell, E.A. Family participation in hospital care for children. *Children, 17,* 154-157, 1970.
Bender, L. (ed.) *Child Psychiatric Techniques.* Springfield, Illinois: Charles C. Thomas, 1952.
Bender, L., and Lipkowitz, H.H. Hallucinations in children. *American Journal of Orthopsychiatry, 10,* 471-490, 1940.
Bender, L., and Rapoport, J. Animal drawings of children. *American Journal of Orthopsychiatry, 14,* 512-527, 1944.
Benedek, T. The emotional structure of the family. In *The Family: Its Functions and Destiny,* ed. R.N. Anshen, 202-225. New York: Harper, 1949.
Benedek, T. *Studies in Psychosomatic Medicine, Psychosexual Functions in Women.* New York: Ronald, 1952.
Berensohn, P. *Finding One's Way with.Clay.* New York: Simon and Schuster, 1968.
Berger, M. *Videotape Techniques in Psychiatric Training and Treatment.* New York, Brunner/Mazel, 1970.
Bergman, T. *Children in the Hospital.* New York: International Universities Press, 1965.
Berkowitz, I.H. (ed.) *Adolescents Grow in Groups.* New York: Brunner/Mazel, 1972.
Bettelheim, B. *Love is not Enough.* Glencoe, Illinois: The Free Press, 1950.
Bettelheim, B. *Symbolic Wounds.* Glencoe, Illinois: The Free Press, 1954.
Bettelheim, B. *The Empty Fortress.* New York: The Free Press, 1967.
Bettelheim, R. *Symbolic Wounds: Puberty Rights and the Envious Male.* New York: Collier Books, 1967.
Biber, B. *Children's Drawings: From Lines to Pictures.* New York: Bureau of Educational Experiments, 1934.
Biller, H.B. Father absence and the personality development of the male child. *Developmental Psychology, 2,* 181-201, 1970.
Birren, F. *Functional Color.* New York: Crimson Press, 1937.
Birren, F. *Color in Your World.* New York: Collier Books, 1966.
Blos, P. *The Adolescent Personality.* New York: Appleton-Century-Crofts, 1941.
Boszormenyi-Nagy, I., and Spark, G.M. *Invisible Loyalites: Reciprocity in Intergenerational Family Therapy.* New York: Harper and Row, 1973.

Bowlby, J. *Child Care and Growth of Love*. Harmondsworth: Penguin, 1953.
Bowlby, J. *Attachment and Loss: Separation*. London: Hogarth Press, *2,* 1973.
Burns, R.C., and Kaufman, S.H. *Kinetic Family Drawings*. New York: Brunner/Mazel, 1970.
Burns, R.C., and Kaufman, S.H. *Actions, Styles and Symbols in Kinetic Family Drawings*. New York: Brunner/Mazel, 1972.
Bychowski, G. Struggle against the introjects. *International Journal of Psychoanalysis, 2,* 83-91, 1958.

Cane, F. *The Artist in Each of Us*. New York: Pantheon, 1951.
Caplan, F., and Caplan, T. *The Power of Play*. Garden City, New York: Anchor Press/Doubleday, 1974.
Cappell, M.D. Games and the Mastery of Helplessness. In *Motivations in Play, Games and Sports*. eds. R. Slovenko and J.A. Knight. Springfield, Illinois: Charles C. Thomas, pp. 39-55, 1967.
Cole, N.R. *The Arts in the Classroom*. New York: John Day, 1940.
Coleman, J.S. *The Adolescent Society*. New York: The Free Press, 1961.
Coleman, J.S. *Adolescents and the Schools*. New York: Basic Books, 1965.

D'Ambrosio, R. *No Language but a Cry*. New York: Dell, 1970.
Davis, J.E. *Play and Mental Health: Principles and Practices for Teachers*. New York: Barnes, 1938.
Dax, E.C. *Experimental Studies in Psychiatric Art*. London: Faber & Faber Ltd., 1953.
Dennis, W. *Group Values through Children's Drawings*. New York: John Wiley and Sons, 1966.
Despert, J.L. Technical approaches used in the study and treatment of emotional problems in children. *The Psychiatric Quarterly, 12,* 176-194, 1938.
Despert, J.L. *The Inner Voices of Children*. New York: Brunner/Mazel, 1975.
Di Leo, J.H. *Young Children and Their Drawings*. New York: Brunner/Mazel, 1970.
Di Leo, J.H. *Children's Drawings as Diagnostic Aids*. New York: Brunner/Mazel, 1973.
Downey, J.E. *Creative Imagination*. New York: Harcourt, Brace and Co., 1929.
Dragastin, S., and Elder, G.H., Jr. *Adolescence in the Life Cycle*. New York: Halstead Press, 1975.
Dreikurs, R. *The Challenge of Parenthood*. New York: Duell, Sloan and Pearce, 1948.
Ducasse, C.J. *The Philosophy of Art*. New York: Dover, 1966.
Dudek, S.Z. The artist as person. Generalizations based on Rorschach records of writers and painters. *Journal of Nervous and Mental Disease, 150,* March, 1970.

Ehrenzweig, A. *The Hidden Order of Art: A Study in the Psychology of Artistic Imagination*. Berkeley: University of California Press, 1967.
Ehrenzweig, A. *The Psycho-Analysis of Artistic Vision and Hearing*. New York: George Braziller, 1967.
Erikson, E.H. Clinical studies in childhood play. In *Child Behavior and Development*. eds. R.G. Barker et al. New York: McGraw-Hill, 1943, 411-428.
Erikson, E.H. *Insight and Responsibility*. New York: W.W. Norton, 1964.
Erikson, E.H. *Identity: Youth and Crisis*. New York: W.W. Norton, 1968.

Fagin, C.M. *The Effects of Maternal Attendance During Hospitalization on the Post-Hospital Behavior of Young Children: A Comparative Study*. Philadelphia: F.A. Davis, 1966.
Ferber, A., Mendelsohn, M., and Napier, A. (eds.). *The Book of Family Therapy*. New York: Science House, 1972.
Fischer, C., Hull C., and Holtz, P. Past experience and perception: Memory color. *American Journal of Psychology, 69,* 546-560, 1956.
Fischer, R. Art interpretation and art therapy. In *Psychiatry and Art*. ed. I. Jakab. Basel: Karger, 1969, 33.

Foulkes, S.H., and Anthony, E.J. *Group Psychotherapy* (2nd. ed). Harmondsworth: Pelican, 1966.
Fraiberg, S. *The Magic Years.* New York: Charles Scribner Sons, 1959.
Frank, A. *The Diary of a Young Girl.* New York: Doubleday and Co., Inc., 1952.
Frankl, V.E. *Man's Search for Meaning* (rev. ed). Boston: Beacon Press, 1963.
Freud, A. Role of bodily illness in the mental life of children. *Psychoanalytical Study of Children, 7,* 69, 1952.
Freud, A. *The Psychoanalytical Treatment of Children.* New York: Schocken, 1964.
Freud, S. *On Narcissism: An Introduction.* (1914), *14,* 69-102. Standard Edition.
Freud, S. *Beyond the Pleasure Principle.* London and Vienna: International Psychoanalytical Press, 1922.
Freud, S. *A Phobia in a Five Year Old Boy* (1909), *10,* Standard Edition. London: Hogarth, 1955, 52, 85.
Freud, S. *The Interpretation of Dreams,* New York: Basic Books, 1958.
Fromm, E. *The Forgotten Language.* New York: Grove Press, 1951.

Haley, J. *Strategies of Psychotherapy.* New York: Grune and Stratton, 1963.
Haley, J. *Problem-Solving Therapy.* San Francisco: Jossey-Bass, 1976.
Haley, J. and Hoffman, L. *Techniques of Family Therapy.* New York: Basic Books, 1967.
Haller, J.A. (ed). *The Hospitalized Child and His Family.* Baltimore: Johns Hopkins Press 1967.
Hammer, E.F., and Piotrowski, Z. Hostility as a factor in the clinician's personality as it affects his interpretation of projective drawings. *Journal of Projective Techniques, 17,* 210-216, 1953.
Hardgrove, C.B., and Dawson, R.B. *Parents and Children in the Hospital.* Boston: Little, Brown, 1972.
Harms, E. *Essentials of Abnormal Child Psychiatry.* New York: Julian Press, 1953.
Harris, D.B. *Children's Drawings as Measures of Intellectual Maturity.* New York: Harcourt, Brace & World, 1963.
Hartley, R.E. *The Complete Book of Children's Play.* Thomas C. Crowell, 1957.
Hartley, R.E., Frank, L.K., and Goldenson, R.M. *Understanding Children's Play.* New York: Columbia, 1952.
Hatterer, L.J. *The Artist in Society: Problems and Treatment of the Creative Personality.* New York: Grove Press, 1965.
Herron, R.E., and Sutton-Smith, B. *Child's Play.* New York: John Wiley and Sons, 1971.
Hill, A. *Art versus Illness.* London: George Allen and Unwin, 1945.
Hill, A. *Painting Out Illness.* London: George Allen and Unwin, 1951.
Horowitz, M.J. *Image Formation and Cognition.* New York: Appleton-Century Crofts, 1970.
Horrocks, J.E. *The Psychology of Adolescence.* Boston: Houghton Mifflin Co., 1962.
Howells, J.G. (ed). *Theory and Practice of Family Psychiatry.* London: Oliver & Boyd, 1968.
Howells, J.G. (ed). *Modern Perspectives in Child Psychiatry.* New York: Brunner/Mazel, 1971.
Howells, J.G. (ed). *Modern Perspectives in Adolescent Psychology.* New York: Brunner/ Mazel, 1971.
Howells, J.G. (ed). *Modern Perspectives in International Child Psychiatry.* New York: Brunner/Mazel, 1971.
Hulse, W.C. Childhood conflict expressed through family drawings. *Journal of Projective Techniques,* 1952, *16,* 66-79.

Jackson, D.D. The question of family homeostasis. *The Psychiatric Quarterly Supplement,* 1957, *31,* Part I, 79-90.
Jackson, D. *The Etiology of Schizophrenia.* New York: Basic Books, 1960.
Jackson, D. The martial quid pro quo. In *Family Therapy for Disturbed Families.* eds. G. Zuk and I. Boszormenyi-Nagy. Palo Alto: Science and Behavior Books, 1966.
Jackson, D.D. (ed). *Communication, Family and Marriage.* Palo Alto: Science and Behavior Books, 1968.

Jackson, D.D. (ed). *Therapy, Communication and Change.* Palo Alto: Science and Behavior Books, 1968.

Jacobi, J. Pictures from the unconscious. *Journal of Projective Techniques, 19,* 264-270, 1955.

Jakab, I. (ed). *Psychiatry and Art.* New York: S. Karger, *I* (1968), *II & III* (1971), *IV* (1975).

Jolles, I. A study of the validity of some hypotheses for the qualitative interpretation of the H-T-P for children of elementary school age. Sexual identification, *Journal of Clinical Psychology, 8,* 113-119, 1952.

Jung, C.G. *Memories, Dreams, Reflections,* recorded and edited by Aniela Jaffe. New York: Pantheon Books, 1963.

Jung, C.G. *Man and His Symbols.* New York: Doubleday, 1964.

Jung, C.G. *The Portable Jung,* ed. J. Campbell, trans. R.F.C. Hull. New York: The Viking Press, 1971.

Kahana, R.J., and Levin, S. Aging and the conflict of generations. *Journal of Geriatric Psychiatry,* 1971, *4,* 115-135.

Kalff, D.M. *Sandplay.* San Francisco: Browser Press, 1971.

Kellog, R. *The Psychology of Children's Art.* New York: Random House, 1967.

Kinget, G.M. *The Drawing Completion Test, A Projective Technique for the Investigation of Personality.* New York: Grune & Stratton, 1952,

Klein, M. *The Psychoanalysis of Children.* London: Hogarth Press, 1932.

Koestler, A. *The Art of Creation.* New York: Macmillan, 1964.

Kramer, E. *Art Therapy in a Children's Community.* Springfield: Charles C. Thomas, 1958.

Kris, E. *Psychoanalytic Explorations in Art.* New York: International Universities Press, 1952.

Kubie, L. *Neurotic Distortion of the Creative Process.* Lawrence, Kansas: University of Kansas Press, 1959.

Kubler-Ross, E. *On Death and Dying.* New York: Macmillan, 1969.

Landgarten, H. Lori: Art Therapy and Self Discovery. 16 mm. sound film in color. Los Angeles: Art Therapy Film Distributors, P.O. Box 1289, 90272.

Landgarten, H. Mutual task oriented family art therapy. *Proceedings of the American Art Therapy Association,* 1974, 24.

Landgarten, H. Group art therapy for mothers and their daughters. *American Journal of Art Therapy, 14,* 1975, #2.

Landgarten, H. Changing status of art therapy in Los Angeles. *American Journal of Art Therapy, 15,* 1976, #4.

Landgarten, H. My struggle with maintaining a dual professional identity: artist and art psychotherapist. *Proceedings of the American Art Therapy Association,* 1977, 38-39.

Langer, S. *Feeling and Form.* New York: Charles Scribner Sons, 1953.

Langer, S.K. *Philosophy in a New Key.* Cambridge, Mass.: Harvard University Press, 1957.

Lansing, K.M. *Art, Artists, and Art Education.* New York: McGraw-Hill, 1969.

Laqueur, H.P. LaBurt, H.A., and Morong, E. Multiple family therapy. In *Current Psychiatric Therapies,* ed. J. Masserman. *4,* 150-154, New York: Grune and Stratton.

Levy, S. Figure drawing as a projective test. In *Projective Psychology,* eds. L.E., and L. Bellak. New York: Knopf, 257-297, 1950.

Levine, M., and Galenter, E. A note on the tree and trauma interpretation in the H-T-P. *Journal Consult. Clin. Psychol., 17,* 74-75, 1953.

Lewis, H.P. (ed). *Child Art: The Beginnings of Self-Affirmation.* Berkeley: Diablo Press, 1973.

Linderman, E.W., and Herberholz, D.W. *Developing Artistic and Perceptual Awareness: Art Practice in the Elementary Classroom,* (2nd ed). Dubuque, Iowa: W.C. Brown, 1969.

Lindsay, Z. *Art and the Handicapped Child.* New York: Van Nostrand Reinhold, 1972.

Lidz, R.W., and Lidz, T. The family environment of schizophrenic patients. *American Journal of Psychiatry, 106,* 332-345, 1949.

Lidz, R., and Lidz. T. Therapeutic considerations arising from the intense symbiotic needs of

schizophrenic patients. *Psychotherapy with Schizophrenics,* eds. E.B. Brody & F.C. Redlich. 168-178. New York: International Universities Press, 1952.
Lidz, T. Schizophrenia and the family. Psychiatry, *21,* 21-27, 1958.
Lidz, T. and Fleck, S. Schizophrenia, human integration and the role of the family. In *The Etiology of Schizophrenia,* ed. D. Jackson. 323-345. New York: Basic Books, 1960.
Love, H., Henderson, S., and Stewart, M. *Your Child Goes to the Hospital.* Springfield: Charles C. Thomas, 1972.
Lowenfield, M. *Play in Childhood.* New York: John Wiley and Sons, 1967.
Lowenfeld, V. *The Nature of Creative Activity* (2nd ed). London: Routledge and Kegan Paul, 1952.
Lowenfeld, V. *Your Child and His Art.* New York: Macmillan, 1954.
Lowenfeld, V. *Creative and Mental Growth* (3rd ed.). New York: Macmillan, 1957.
Lowenfeld, V., and Brittain, W.L. *Creative and Mental Growth* (6th ed.). New York: Macmillan, 1975.
Luscher, M. *The Luscher Color Test.* New York: Random House, 1969.

Macgregor, R., Richie, A., Serrano, A., and Schuster, F. *Multiple Impact Therapy with Families.* New York: McGraw-Hill, 1964.
Maclay, D. *Treatment for Children.* New York: Science House, 1970.
Mahler, M.S. On child psychosis and schizophrenia: Autistic and symbiotic infantile psychoses. *Psychoanalytic Study of the Child, 7,* 286-305, New York: International Universities Press, 1952.
Maritain, J. *Creative Intuition in Art and Poetry.* New York: Pantheon Books, 1953.
McHugh, A.F. Children's figure drawings in neurotic and conduct disturbances. *Journal of Clinical Psychology, 22,* 219-221, 1966.
McKeller, P. *Imagination and Thinking.* London: Cohen and West, 1957.
Meares, A. *Hypnography.* Springfield, Illinois: Charles C. Thomas, 1957.
Meares, A. *The Door of Serenity.* London: Faber and Faber, 1958.
Meares, A. *Shapes of Sanity.* Springfield, Illinois: Charles C. Thomas, 1960.
Messeldine, H.W. *Your Inner Child of the Past.* New York: Simon and Schuster, 1963.
Millar, S. *The Psychology of Play.* Baltimore: Penguin Books, 1968.
Milner, M. *On Not Being Able to Paint.* New York: International Universities Press, 1967.
Milner, M. *The Hands of the Living God.* New York: International Universities Press, 1969.
Minuchin, S. *Families and Family Therapy.* Cambridge: Harvard University Press, 1974.
Minuchin, S. Montalvo, B., Guerney, B., Rosman, B., and Shumer, F. *Families of the Slums: An Exploration of their Structure and Treatment.* New York: Basic Books, 1967.
Moustakas, C.E. *Children in Play Therapy.* New York: McGraw-Hill, 1953.
Moustakas, C.E. *Psychotherapy with Children.* New York: Ballantine Books, 1959.
Moustakas, C.E. *Creativity and Conformity.* New York: Van Nostrand Reinhold, 1967.

Naumburg, M. *Studies of the "Free" Art Expression of Behavior Problem Children and Adolescents as a Means of Diagnosis and Therapy.* New York: Coolidge Foundation, 1947.
Naumburg, M. *Psychoneurotic Art: Its Function in Psychotherapy.* New York: Grune & Stratton, 1953.
Naumburg, M. *Schizophrenic Art: Its Meaning in Psychotherapy.* New York: Grune & Stratton, 1953.
Naumburg, M. *Dynamically Oriented Art Therapy: Its Principles and Practices.* New York: Grune & Stratton, 1966.
Neumann, E. *Art and the Creative Unconscious: Four Essays.* New York: Princeton University Press, 1969.
Noble, E. *Play and the Sick Child.* London: Faber and Faber, 1967.

Oakley, C. A. Drawings of a man by adolescents. *British Journal of Psychology, 31,* 37-60. 1940.

Peterson, J. A. Marital and family therapy involving the aged. *Gerontologist, 13,* 27-31, 1973.

Petrillo, M., and Sanger, S. *Emotional Care of Hospitalized Children.* Philadelphia: Lippincott, 1972.

Pfister, O. R. *Expressionism in Art, Its Psychological and Biological Basis.* London: Kegan Paul, Trench, Trubner and Co., 1922.

Phillips, W. (ed). *Art and Psychoanalysis.* Cleveland: World Publishing Co., 1963.

Pickford, R. W. *Studies in Psychiatric Art: Its Psychodynamics, Therapeutic Value and Relationship to Modern Art.* Springfield, Illinois: Charles C. Thomas, 1967.

Plank, E. *Working with Children in Hospitals: A Guide for the Professional Team.* Cleveland: Western Reserve University Press, 1962.

Prinzhorn, H. *Bildnerei der Geisteskranken.* Berlin and New York: Springer-Verlag, 1968.

Prinzhorn, H. *Artistry of the Mentally Ill: A Contributuon to the Psychology and Psychopathology of Configuration.* New York: Springer-Verlag, 1972.

Progoff, I. *The Symbolic and the Real.* New York: Julian Press, 1963.

Prugh, D. G., Staub, E. M., Sands, H. H., Kirschbaum, H. M., and Lenihan, E. A. A Study of the emotional reactions of children and families to hospitalization and illness. *American Journal of Orthopsychiatry, 23,* 70-106, 1953.

Rabin, A. I., and Haworth, M. R. (eds). *Projective Techniques with Children.* New York: Grune and Stratton, 1960.

Rainwater, C. E. *The Meaning of Play.* Chicago: University of Chicago Press, 1915.

Rank, O. *Art and the Artist.* New York: Knopf, 1932.

Rank, O. *Art and the Artist: Creative Urge and Personality Development.* New York: Agathon Press, 1968.

Read, H. *The Meaning of Art.* London: Faber and Faber, 1936.

Redl, F., and Wineman, D. *Children Who Hate: The Disorganization and Breakdown of Behavior Controls.* Glencoe: Free Press, 1951.

Redl, F., and Wineman, D. *The Aggressive Child.* Glencoe: Free Press, 1957.

Rees, H. E. *A Psychology of Artistic Creation.* New York: Bureau of Publications, Teachers College, Columbia University, 1942.

Reitman, F. *Psychotic Art.* London: Routledge and Kegan Paul, 1950.

Reusch, J. *Therapeutic Communication.* New York: W. W. Norton, 1961.

Reusch, J., and Bateson, G. *Communication.* New York: W. W. Norton, 1951.

Rhyne, J. *The Gestalt Art Experience.* Palo Alto: Science and Behavior Books, 1962.

Rie, H. E. (ed). *Perspectives in Child Psychopathology.* Chicago, New York: Aldine-Atherton, 1971.

Robbins, A., and Sibley, L. B. *Creative Art Therapy.* New York: Brunner/Mazel, 1976.

Robertson, J. *Young Children in Hospital.* New York: Basic Books, 1958.

Rogerson, C. H. *Play Therapy in Childhood,* London: Oxford University Press, 1939.

Rubin, J. A. *Child Art Therapy.* New York: Van Nostrand, Reinhold, 1978.

Sachs, H. *The Creative Unconscious: Studies in the Psychoanalysis of Art.* (2nd ed.). Cambridge, Mass.: Sci-Art Publishers, 1951.

Salk, L. *What Every Child Would Like His Parents to Know.* New York: McKay, 1972.

Satir, V. *Conjoint Family Therapy.* (rev. ed.). Palo Alto: Science and Behavior Books, 1967.

Saunders, R. J. *Art for the Mentally Retarded in Connecticut.* Hartford, Conn.: Connecticut State Department of Education, 1967.

Schachtel, E. G. On Color and Affect. *Psychiatry, 6,* 393-409, 1943.

Schachtel, E. G. Projection and its relation to character attitudes and creativity in the kinesthetic response. *Psychiatry, 13,* 69-100, 1950.

Schachtel, E. G. *Metamorphosis.* New York: Basic Books, 1959.

Schaefer-Simmern, H. *The Unfolding of Artistic Activity.* Berkeley: University of California Press, 1948.

Schildkrout, M. S., Shenker, I. R., and Sonnenblick, M. *Human Figure Drawings in Adolescence.* New York: Brunner/Mazel, 1972.

Schmidl-Washner, T. Formal criteria for the analysis of children's drawings. *American Journal of Orthopsychiatry, 2,* 95-103, 1942.

Schneider, D. E. *The Psychoanalyst and the Artist.* New York: Farrar, Straus and Co., 1950.

Schorsch, R. *The Psychology of Play.* Notre Dame: University of Notre Dame, 1942.

Schrut, A. Fantasy games aid children's emotional growth. *Science News, 90,* 83, 1966.

Sears, R. R., Maccoby, E. E., and Levin, H. *Patterns of Child Rearing.* Evanson, Illinois: Row, Peterson & Co., 1957.

Sechehaye, M. A. *Symbolic Realization.* New York: International Universities Press, 1960.

Shore, M. F. (ed). *Red is the Color of Hurting.* Bethesda, Md.: N.I.H.M., 1967.

Spark, G. M., and Brody, E. M. The aged are family members. *Family Process, 9,* 195-210, 1970.

Speers, R. W., and Lansing, C. *Group Therapy in Childhood Psychosis.* Chapel Hill: University of North Carolina Press, 1965.

Spiegel, J. P., and Bell, N. W. The family of the psychiatric patient. In *American Handbook of Psychiatry,* (ed). S. Arieti. *1,* 114-149. New York: Basic Books, 1959.

Stern, M. Free painting as an auxiliary technique in psychoanalysis. In *Specialized Techniques in Psychotherapy,* (eds). G. Pychowski and J. Despert. New York: Basic Books, 1952.

Sugar, M. (ed). *The Adolescent in Group and Family Therapy.* New York: Brunner/Mazel, 1975.

Sullivan, H. S. *The Interpersonal Theory of Psychiatry.* (1st ed). New York: W.W. Norton, 1953.

Ulman, E., and Dachinger, P. (eds). *Art Therapy in Theory and Practice.* New York: Science Books, 1975.

Ulman E., and Levy, B. L. Judging Psychopathology from Paintings. *Journal of Abnormal Psychology, 72,* 1967.

Vogel, E. F., and Bell. N. W. The emotionally disturbed child as a family scapegoat. *Psychoanalytic Review, 47,* (2), 21-42, 1960.

Washner, T. S. Interpretations of spontaneous drawings and paintings. *Genetic Psychol. Monogr., 33,* 70, 1946.

Waelder, R. *Psychoanalytic Avenues to Art.* New York: International Universities Press, 1965.

Watzlawick, P., Beavin, J. H., and Jackson, D. D. *Pragmatics of Human Communication.* New York: Norton, 1967.

Weakland, J. The double bind hypothesis of schizophrenia and three-party interaction. In *Studies in Schizophrenia,* (ed). D.D. Jackson. New York: Basic Books, 1960.

Weakland, J., and Jackson, D. D. Patient and therapist observations on the circumstances of a schizophrenic episode. *Arch. Neurol. Psychiat., 79,* 554-575, 1958.

Whitaker, C. A. The growing edge in techiques of family therapy. In *Techniques of Family Therapy,* (eds). J. Haley and L. Hoffman. pp, 255-260. New York: Basic Books, 1968.

Williams, F. Family therapy: Its role in adolescent psychiatry. In *Adolescent Psychiatry, Development and Clincial Studies,* (eds.) S. C. Feinstein and P. G. Giovacchini. New York: Basic Books, *2,* 1973.

Winnicott, D. W. Why children play. In *The Child, the Family and the Outside World.* Middlesex, England: Penguin Books, 1964, pp. 143-146.

Winnicott, D. W. *Playing and Reality.* New York: Basic Books, 1971, pp. 1-25.

Winnicott, D. W. *Therapeutic Consultations in Child Psychiatry.* New York: Basic Books, 1971.

Winnicott, D. W. *Through Paediatrics to Psycho-Analysis.* New York: Basic Books, 1975.

Wolff, S. *Children under Stress.* London: Penguin Press, 1969.

Zeligs, R. *Children's Experience with Death.* Springfield, Illinois: Charles C. Thomas, 1974.

Zucker, L. A case of obesity: Projective techniques before and after treatments. *Journal of Projective Technology, 12,* 202-215, 1948.

INDEX

DATE DUE

Demco, Inc. 38-293